Adobe Photoshop Elements 7

Unleash the hidden performance of Elements

Mark Galer

ELSEVIER

AMSTERDAM • BOSTON • HEIDELBERG • LONDON • NEW YORK • OXFORD
PARIS • SAN DIEGO • SAN FRANCISCO • SINGAPORE • SYDNEY • TOKYO
Focal Press is an imprint of Elsevier

Focal Press

Focal Press is an imprint of Elsevier
Linacre House, Jordan Hill, Oxford OX2 8DP, UK
30 Corporate Drive, Suite 400, Burlington, MA 01803, USA

First edition 2009

British Library Cataloguing in Publication Data
A catalogue record for this book is available from the British Library

Library of Congress Control Number: 2008938715

ISBN: 978-0-240-52135-0

For more information on all Focal Press publications
visit our website at: www.focalpress.com

Printed and bound in Canada

09 10 11 12 12   11 10 9 8 7 6 5 4 3 2 1

for Dorothy

Contents - part 1

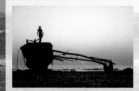
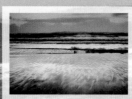
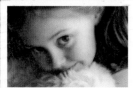
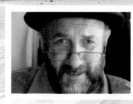
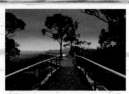
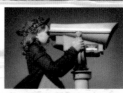
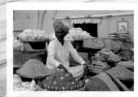
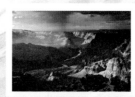

1

optimize

Contents - part 2

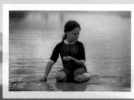
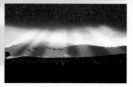
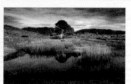
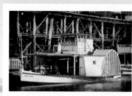
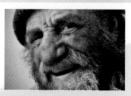
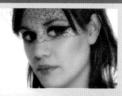
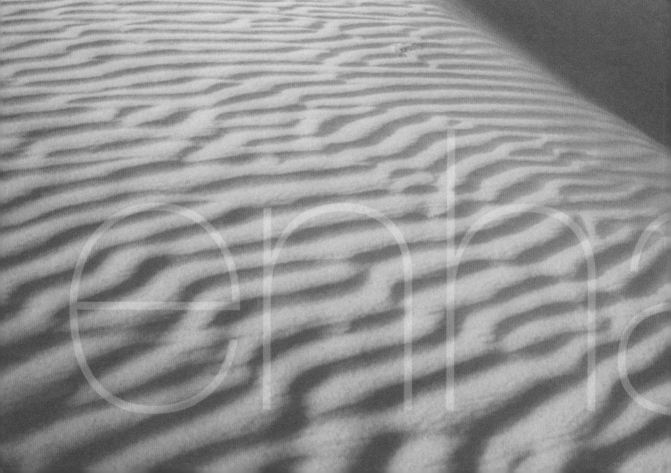

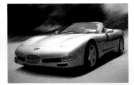
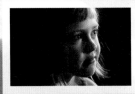
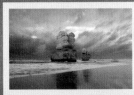
2

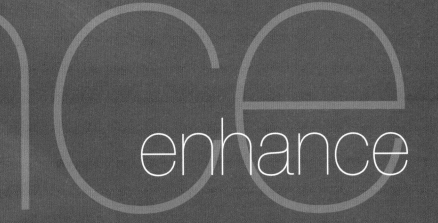

enhance

Contents - part 3

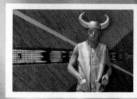
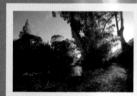
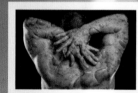
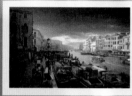
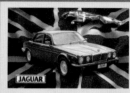
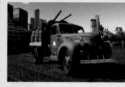
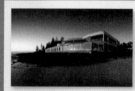
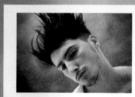

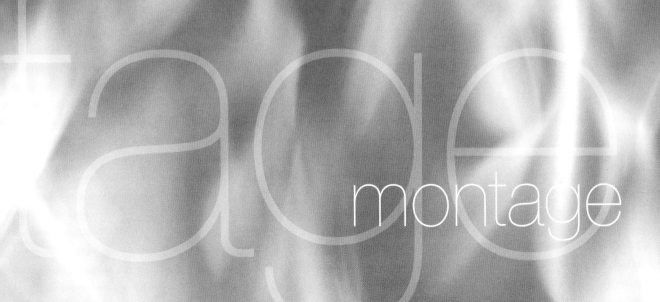

3

tage

montage

Contents - dvd

The DVD is a veritable treasure trove of supporting files for the projects in this book as well as a resource for your own creative projects. Just transfer the supporting files to your Photoshop Elements Organizer (see 'Getting Started - page xiv') for fast access to the images and movies. The movies are an invaluable resource, allowing you to start, stop and rewind so that the skills can be quickly and easily acquired at your own pace. The DVD also contains multilayered image files (PSDs) of the completed projects, uncompressed TIFF files with saved selections, Raw files and high-quality 16 Bits/Channel files. Loadable presets are also available to enhance your software together with a rich stock library of royalty-free images.

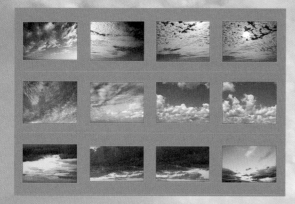

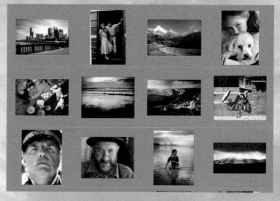

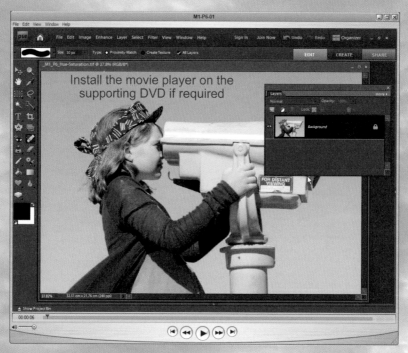

THE DVD PROVIDES EXTENSIVE SUPPORT IN THE FORM OF:

- Over seven hours of movie tutorials to guide you through all of the projects in this book. You may need to install the QuickTime movie player from the supporting DVD to watch the movies from the Organizer within Photoshop Elements 7.

- High-resolution, high-quality JPEG images to support all of the imaging projects.

- Full-resolution TIFF images with 'saved selections' for users interested in completing the projects in the least amount of time whilst achieving maximum quality.

- Camera Raw and 16 Bits/Channel files.

- Multilayered Photoshop documents (PSD files) of completed projects.

- A stock library of 100 high-resolution, royalty-free images for creative montage work.

- Adobe presets (Layer Styles and Gradients) to enhance the performance capabilities of your Adobe Photoshop Elements software.

- Maximum Performance Action files to fast-track your workflows and editing tasks.

- Maximum Performance Smart Brushes to enhance your editing tasks.

- Printable PDF file of keyboard shortcuts to act as a quick and handy reference guide to speed up your image-editing tasks.

- Bonus project on DVD with supporting images and movie tutorial.

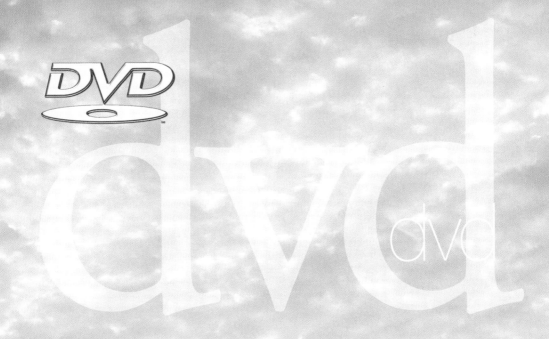

Preface

The creative projects in *Adobe Photoshop Elements 7 Maximum Performance* are designed to provide you with the essential techniques for professional quality editing – without the need to upgrade to the full version of Photoshop. The projects are designed to unleash the hidden potential of the budget software through a series of workarounds, advanced techniques and loadable presets. Each creative project is supported by a QuickTime movie tutorial and high-resolution images – all available on a supporting DVD. The DVD contains full and comprehensive movie support together with a library of royalty-free, high-resolution stock images for self-initiated creative projects. Each project is designed to build the skills required so that any photographer can attain the status of 'imaging guru'. The magic is deconstructed using a series of easy to follow step-by-step projects using large clear screen grabs and jargon-free explanations. Completed multilayered project files are also available on the DVD for those users who like to have access to the completed project for comparison and analysis.

This book will act as your guide to some of Elements' less well-known and more powerful post-production editing techniques. It will enable you to attain the same high-quality images as professionals using the full version of Photoshop. This book makes Elements a viable alternative to the full version of Photoshop for imaging professionals and enthusiasts looking to extract the maximum performance from their software.

This book is primarily concerned with the post-production stage of the creative process and demonstrates how this part of the creative process can optimize and enhance the original capture or create an entirely new image out of several images (the creation of a composite photograph or photomontage). Where appropriate the book will discuss measures that can be taken by the photographer in pre-production or production to enable the highest-quality outcome as a result of the post-production stage. To ensure the best quality image from our sophisticated and professional post-production techniques we should ensure that we access quality Raw materials whenever possible – 'quality in, quality out'. The vast majority of the JPEG images on the supporting DVD were processed from either camera Raw files or high-quality 16 Bits/Channel scans. Many of the images featured in this book were captured using budget digital SLR and fixed lens digital cameras, affordable cameras used to capture information-rich images.

The techniques used in this book promote a non-destructive approach to image editing wherever possible. The term 'non-destructive image editing' refers to the process of editing an image whilst retaining as much of the original information as possible and editing in such a way that any modifications can be usually undone or modified. Editing on the base layer of the image can often mean that modifications to the pixel information cannot be undone easily or at all, e.g. sharpening an image file cannot be undone once the file has been saved and flattened. It is, however, possible to sharpen non-destructively in post-production so that the amount of sharpening can be altered when the file is opened at a later date. This latter approach would be termed 'non-destructive'. When capturing images with a digital camera many users do not realize that if the JPEG file format is used image processing starts in the camera. Color correction, contrast adjustment, saturation levels and sharpening all take place in the camera. If maximum quality is to be realized the Raw format should be chosen in preference to the JPEG format, if possible. The post-production decisions can then be left to the Adobe software, allowing the user many more options.

Photoshop Elements replaced 'Photoshop LE' (limited edition – as in limited function and not availability); both of these software packages share something in common – they offer limited elements of the full version of Photoshop. Adobe strips out some of the features that would be the first port of call for some professional image editors and photographers, but this does not mean that the same level of control cannot be achieved when using the budget software. Professional post-production image editing does NOT have to be compromised by using Photoshop Elements. With editing images there is usually more than a single way to reach the destination or required outcome. With a good roadmap the Elements user can reach the same destination by taking a slightly different course. These roads are often poorly signposted, so are often inaccessible to the casual user of the software. This book will act as your guide to enable you to attain a broad range of sophisticated post-production image-editing skills through a series of creative projects designed to circumnavigate the missing features.

Photoshop Elements IS a viable alternative to the full version of Photoshop for most professional image-editing tasks. Many professionals may disagree with this statement, as a quick glance at the Elements package may result in a long list of the elements that are missing rather than taking a long hard look at the elements that remain (a case of 'the glass is half empty' rather than 'the glass is half full'). After a decade of professional image editing I have learnt that there is more than one way to create an image. There is no 'one way'. In short, it is possible to take a high-quality image file and work non-destructively to create an image which is indistinguishable from one that has been optimized using the full version of Photoshop. This book does not aim to outline every tool in your kit (a paintbrush doesn't really require an owner's manual and some of the automated features are sometimes more trouble than they are worth). It just deals with how to adapt the tools you do have to perform the tasks you didn't think you were able to. It aims to show you that Elements is better equipped than you were led to believe. Photoshop Elements really is the proverbial wolf in sheep's clothes.

mark galer

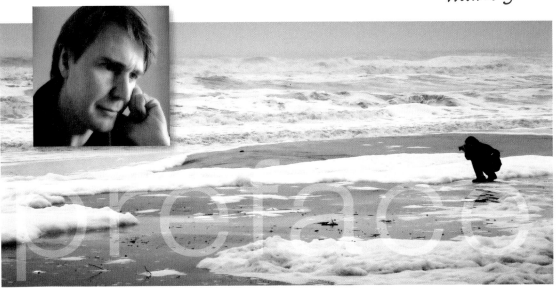

Location Image by Dorothy Connop

Getting Started

Most users of this book will have some experience of digital imaging and Photoshop Elements, but just check the following to make sure all is in order before you start.

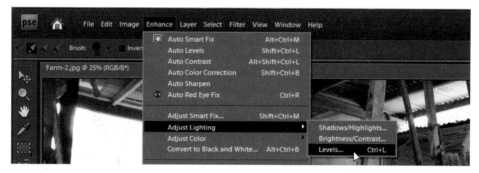

Following orders

The commands in Photoshop Elements allow the user to modify digital files and are accessed via menus and submenus. The commands used in the projects are listed as a hierarchy, with the main menu indicated first and the submenu or command second, e.g. Main menu > Command. For example, the command for applying a Levels adjustment would be indicated as follows: Enhance > Adjust Lighting > Levels. If you get stuck or are unclear, watch the movie on the supporting DVD and follow my mouse cursor to help you find what you are looking for.

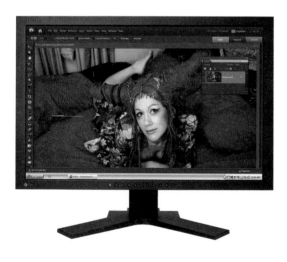 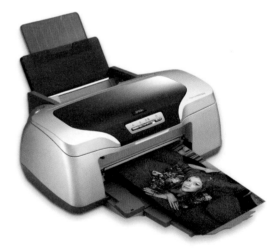

Calibrate your monitor

If your images are going to look good everywhere – not just on your own monitor – it is advised that you calibrate your monitor (set the optimum color, brightness and contrast). I recommend that you use a 'Hardware White Point' or 'Color Temperature' of '6500º K (daylight)' and a Gamma of 2.2.

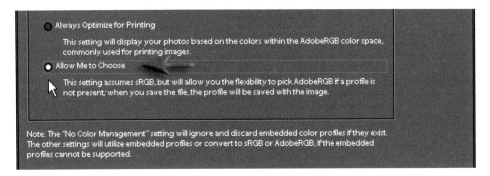

Color Settings

The colors are kept consistent between devices such as cameras, computers and printers through the use of color profiles. If you intend to print your images you would be advised to go to Edit > Color Settings and then click on the radio button that says 'Always Optimize for Printing'. Elements will now use the larger Adobe RGB profile instead of the smaller sRGB profile.

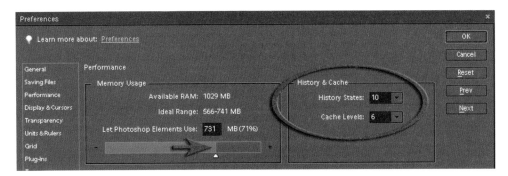

Memory

You will be working on images in excess of 5 megapixels (the supporting DVD provides high-resolution images for ALL of the creative projects in this book). This professional level of image editing can place a strain on a computer's working memory or RAM. It is advised that you install at least 1 GB of RAM (2 gigabyte or more is not considered excessive when editing very large image files) so that the image editing you are about to undertake does not begin to crawl. Shut down any other applications that you are not using so that all of the available memory is made available to Photoshop Elements. Photoshop Elements keeps a memory of your image-editing process, which it calls the 'History States'. The default setting in the General Preferences (Edit > Preferences > General) is 50 History States. Allowing the user to track back 50 commands, or clicks of the mouse, can again place an enormous strain on the working memory. I would recommend that you lower this figure to 20 for most editing work. This can be readjusted without restarting the software should you wish to increase Photoshop's memory for your editing actions. Just remember that the more memory you dedicate to what you have just done, the less you have available for what you are about to do. In Preferences > Performance you will see the Available RAM and the Ideal Range that can be assigned to Photoshop Elements. Adjust the slider so that you are using the top of the suggested range. Photoshop Elements will also be using your 'scratch disk' or 'hard drive' in the image-editing process so be sure to keep plenty of gigabytes of free space available.

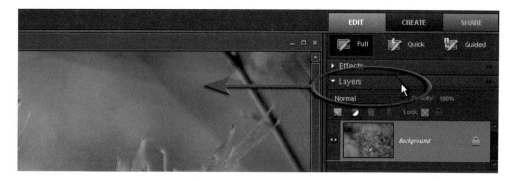

Give yourself some elbow room

I recommend that you keep the 'Photo Bin' and 'Palette Bin' closed until you need them (go to Window > Palette Bin). This will maximize the area on your screen for viewing the image you are editing. Only the Layers palette is used all of the time in advanced image editing. In the default mode it is stacked with the other palettes in the Palette Bin. Locate the Layers palette and drag it out into the working area before closing the Bins. Similarly the Tools palette on the left side of the screen can be dragged to new locations so that it can be close to the action. I prefer to view the image in a window rather than in 'Maximize' mode. This allows me to see the additional information that is displayed in the title bar together with the magnification. I like to view my images at 50% or 100% (actual pixels) to gain a more accurate idea of the image quality. This information is also available in the Navigator palette but, as I use 'keyboard shortcuts' for moving and zooming in and out of images, I usually keep this palette closed as well.

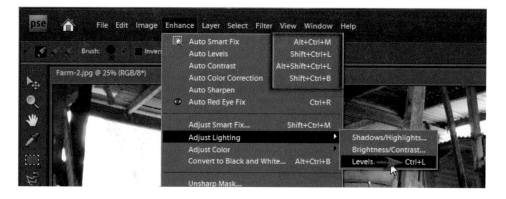

Keyboard shortcuts

Many commands that can be accessed via the menus and submenus can also be accessed via keyboard shortcuts. A shortcut is the action of pressing keys on the keyboard to carry out a command (rather than clicking a command or option in a menu). Shortcuts speed up digital image processing enormously and it is worth learning the examples given in the study guides. If in doubt use the menu (the shortcut will be indicated next to the command) until you become more familiar with the key combinations. See the 'Keyboard shortcuts' section at the end of the book for a list of the most frequently used shortcuts.

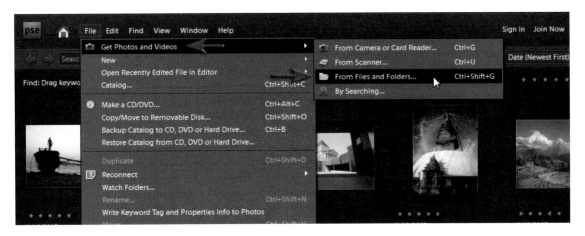

Accessing the support images and movies

Open the Organizer from the Photoshop Elements welcome screen or click on the Organize icon directly above the Options bar in the Edit workspace. Install the DVD and click on the 'Organize and Edit' option if asked. Alternatively, go to the File > Get Photos and Videos in the Organizer workspace (the little camera) and choose the 'From Files and Folders' option. Then locate the DVD (My Computer > MP7-DVD) and the resource folder you want to import. The JPEG files are high quality and will not take up much space on your hard drive. The TIFF files take up a little more room on your hard drive but have the advantage of containing saved selections that can be used to speed up the completion of the projects.

IMPORTANT: Download one folder of images or movies at a time so they are separated in the Organizer space. **You may need to install the QuickTime movie player that is available on the DVD before watching the movies in the Organizer workspace.**

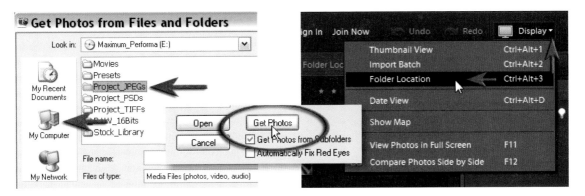

When the Get Photos and Videos dialog box opens make sure the 'Automatically fix Red Eye' option in not checked and then click on the Get Photos button. Your images or movies will be imported and organized. Click on the 'Folder Location' option from the Display menu in the Organizer window (top right-hand corner) to see the images as a collection. Use the keyboard shortcut Ctrl + I to open any image in the Editor workspace. Double-click on any movie icon to watch the movie within the Organizer workspace.

Maximum Performance actions

On the DVD are two folders titled MP7_Photo-Effects and MP7_Action-Player in the MP7_ Auto-Features folder. These folders contain files that may enable you to perform automated editing procedures for fast-tracking some of the skills presented in this book – a few clicks of the mouse that will then instruct Photoshop Elements to conduct an automated series of steps in just a few seconds. These actions may complete the editing task or just fast-track some of the repetitive editing procedures with the minimum of fuss. The actions may be installed using the Max performance installer package (automated installation) on the DVD or manually by adding a series of action files and XML files that will help classify the new content for Elements 7. The actions can then be accessed via the Action Player in the Guided Edit space or from the Effects panel in the Full Edit space of Photoshop Elements.

Note > After installation you must restart Photoshop Elements. Photoshop may take more than 10 minutes to rebuild its database before the new content appears in the Effects palette.

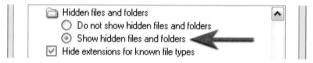

IMPORTANT: Some of the folders you need to find in order to add these files manually are 'hidden'. To find these folders you MUST select 'Show hidden files and folders' in the 'Folder Views' advanced settings of your computer's operating system.

DISCLAIMER: The Maximum Performance actions will only work when using an English language version of Photoshop Elements 7 (they may not work on previous versions of Elements). There is no guarantee that the Maximum Performance actions can be made to work on your computer. Every effort has been made to ensure that these actions can be implemented on standard systems running either Windows XP or Windows Vista, but it is possible that a particular system setup or configuration may prevent these actions from working. Consult your local IT consultant if in doubt about any of these procedures.

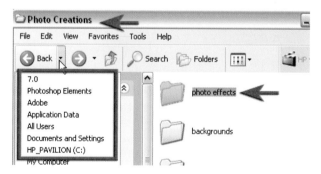

Locating the folders in Windows XP for manual installation

The Action Player folder can be located by going to <windows volume>:\Documents and Settings\All Users\ApplicationData\Adobe\Photoshop Elements\7.0\Locale\<installed locale>\Workflow Panels\ Actions. The Photo Effects folder is located at <windows volume>: (usually C:)\Documents and Settings\All Users\Application Data\Adobe\Photoshop Elements\7.0\Photo Creations\Photo Effects.

Note > Restart Elements after installing new content.

Locating the folders in Windows Vista for manual installation

Like application data on XP, program data resides in a hidden folder, so the user will need to show hidden folders to find these folders. The Action Player files are placed in the Locale file: <windows volume>: (usually C:)\Program Data\Adobe\Photoshop Elements\7.0\<installed locale>\Workflow Panels\Actions. The Photo Creations folder for the MP7_Photo-Effects on Vista is in C:\Program Data\Adobe\Photoshop Elements\7.0\Photo Creations.

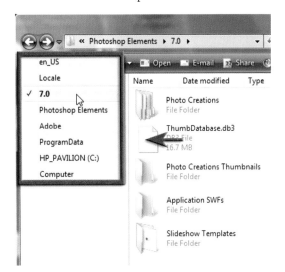
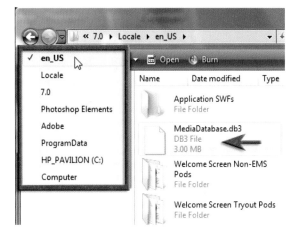

Loading the Maximum Performance actions manually

1. Drag the contents of the MP7_Photo-Effects folder into the Photo Effects folder in the **Photo Creations** folder (do not place the folder - only the contents).
2. Drag the contents of the MP7_Action-Player folder into the Actions folder in the Workflow Panels folder (do not place the folder - only the contents).
3. Delete the MediaDatabase.db3 and ThumbDatabase.db3 files (see illustration above).
4. Launch Photoshop Elements and wait while the Photoshop Elements database rebuilds itself (**this may take more than 10 minutes**).

PROBLEMS: If the MP7_Photo-Effects or Actions do not appear check the correct installation folders were selected. Try deleting the two database files before restarting Photoshop Elements. If you cannot locate the required folders use the search option of your computer, ensuring that you have the 'search for hidden files and folders' option selected.

Deleting content

To delete actions or content such as layer styles you must delete the content and also the 'MediaDatabase' file in the 'Locale/<Installed Locale>' folder and the 'ThumbDatabase' file in the '7.0' folder. When Photoshop Elements is restarted the database will be rebuilt using the remaining content installed. Rebuilding the database may also help to locate any new content that has been installed.

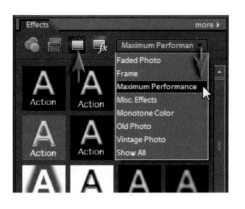

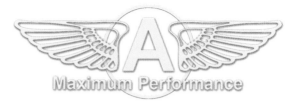

When you see the Maximum Performance Action logo in Part 2 and Part 3 of this book certain steps can be fast-tracked with just a few clicks of your mouse.

Actions from the Photo Effects panel

Actions can be accessed through the Effects palette or via the new Actions Player in Photoshop Elements 7 (see page xxii). Click on the Photo Effects icon in this palette and choose Maximum Performance from the menu. Click on an action and then click the Apply button. Some of the actions may require opacity changes in the layers to fine-tune the effect or some further work as in the case of the Dodge and Burn action. Try combining various actions to create different effects.

Note > The masking actions are intended for the montage projects outlined in Part 3 of this book and will only work when a second layer named Layer 1 is sitting above the background layer.

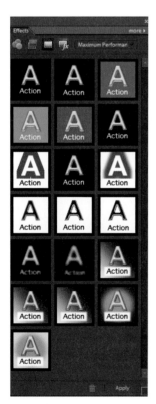

BlackWhite and **BW_Luminosity** - converts color images into a black and white images using non-destructive adjustment layers or blend modes (*see* Module 2, Project 3, and Module 2, Project 8).

Channel_Blue, Channel_Green and Channel_Blue - extracts the red, green or blue channel information from a color image and places it as a gray layer above the background layer (*see* Module 2, Project 9).

Dodge-Burn - places a gray layer in the Overlay blend mode that can be used for non-destructive dodging and burning.

Mask_black and Mask_white - can be used to fast-track extracting a subject from a black or white background (*see* Module 3, Project 8).

Mask_HDR - fast-tracks the montage of two separate exposures to achieve an image with a higher dynamic range (*see* Module 3, Project 3).

Sharp_Print and Sharp_Screen - applies a composite layer and sharpens the image for screen or for print.

Softer_3-6MP and Softer_6-12MP - creates smooth tone images that are either 3 to 6 megapixels or 6 to 12 megapixels (*see* Module 2, Project 6).

Tone _1, Tone_2 and Tone_3 - creates split tone images using a non-destructive adjustment layers and gradient presets (*see* Module 2, Project 4).

Vignette_dark and Vignette_light - darkens or lightens the corners of an image using a non-destructive layer and blend mode.

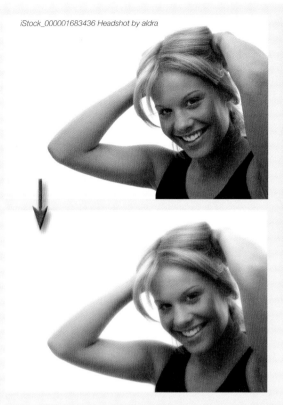

iStock_000001683436 Headshot by aldra

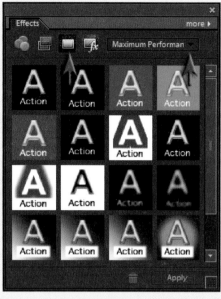

USING THE ACTIONS FROM THE PHOTO EFFECTS PANEL

This stock image (courtesy of www.iStockphoto.com) was created using multiple actions. The soft focus effect was first applied and then followed by the Vignette, Dodge and Burn, Split Tone and Sharpen actions. A Transform command was used on the vignette and a little painting in the Dodge and Burn layer was needed to brighten the teeth and eyes in this 3-minute makeover.

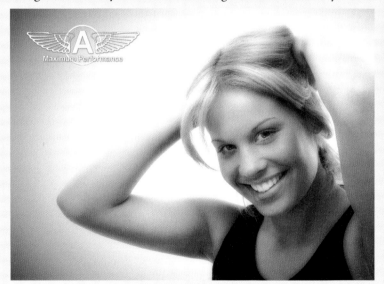

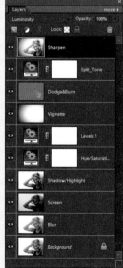

Maximum Performance Actions via the Action Player

In Photoshop Elements 7 users can now play actions via the Guided Edit panel in addition to the Effects panel. The Action Player provides access to the Maximum Performance actions that can be used to fast-track or enhance your imaging projects. The additional actions that can be loaded into the Action player include Black and White conversions, Channel Splitting, Smooth Tone effects, Surface Blur, Tone Mapping, Toning and Vignettes.

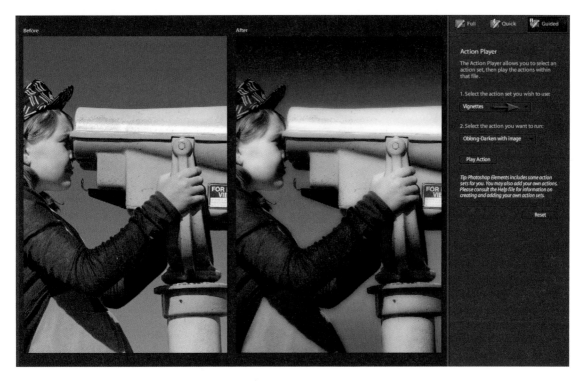

Advantages to using the Action Player

Although the user has to leave the Full Edit workspace to apply the action the Action Player has the added flexibility of being able to preview a before and after view of the effect and allow you to reset the image to the step prior to applying the action using a single click.

Easier installation of actions

Unlike Photo Effects, actions created in the full version of Photoshop can be installed in Photoshop Elements 7 without the need for additional xml files to create listings for the new content. If you are installing actions manually rather than via an installer you can locate the Action Player folder by going to <windows volume>:\Documents and Settings\All Users\ApplicationData\Adobe\Photoshop Elements\7.0\Locale\<installed locale>\Workflow Panels\Actions. Close the software and then delete the MediaDatabase.db3 and ThumbDatabase.db3 files (see page xix).

Note > After installation you must restart Photoshop Elements. Photoshop may take more than 10 minutes to rebuild its database before the new content appears in the Effects palette.

Maximum Performance Smart Brushes (adjustment layers)

In Photoshop Elements 7 it is now possible to paint with adjustment presets using either the new Smart Brush Tool or Detail Smart Brush Tool. The Smart Brush tool creates its own mask as it applies the adjustment by looking for the edges of your subject matter. If the adjustment invades your subject you can hold down the Alt key and then paint to remove the adjustment. Photoshop 7 comes loaded with many 'interesting' presets that can be used to 'enhance' or 'erode' the quality of your photographic images. Most advanced users of Photoshop Elements will probably still prefer to make their own adjustments by applying adjustment layers via the Layers panel and then using the layer masks to hide or reveal their adjustments.

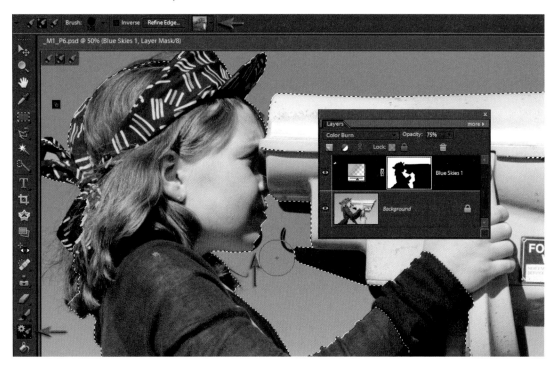

Luminosity brushes

Most of the projects in this book utilize this manual approach to making adjustments. There is one area, however, where adjustments are difficult to make using the limited range of adjustment layers afforded to users of Photoshop Elements. I have therefore decided to include a range of Maximum Performance Luminosity brushes that can be accessed from the MP7 menu in the Options bar (when the Smart Brush Tool or Detail Smart Brush Tool is selected) that will increase the performance of many of your retouching tasks. These Luminosity brushes allow the user to adjust the brightness of color without upsetting the saturation value of the color (something the Lightness slider in the Hue/Saturation adjustment feature is unable to do). See Project 6 in Module 1 for a full step-by-step guide of applying these luminance adjustments using the new Detail Smart Brush in conjunction with the Maximum Performance Luminosity presets (MP7_Photo-Effects).

Note > There are also Smart Brush presets in the Maximum Performance collection to create High Key, Midtone contrast and cross process special effects (MP7-Effects).

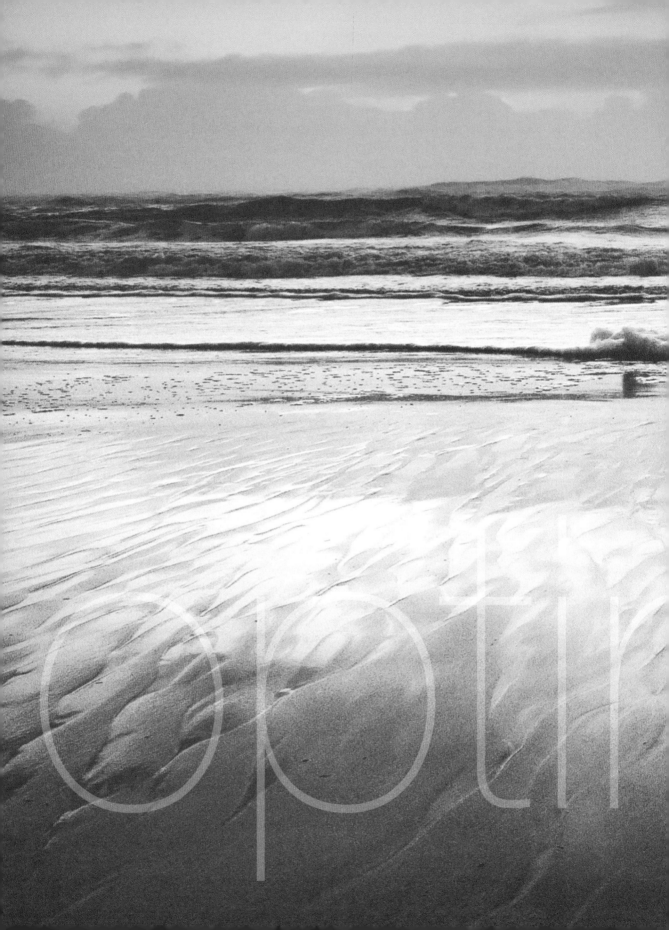

part 1

optimize

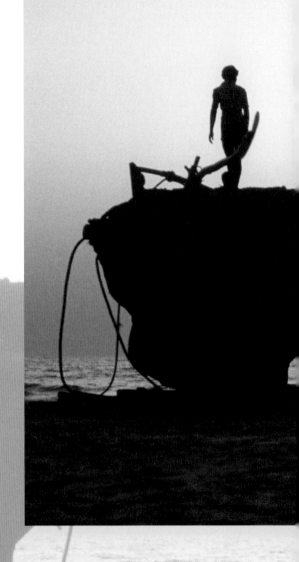

Project 1

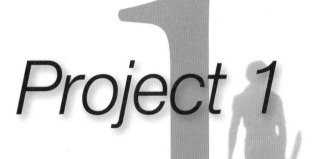

Crop and Correct

This simple project will unmask some of the hidden features of the Straighten and Crop tools, enabling you to optimize your images for print or screen viewing. You will learn that you can straighten, resize and crop your image with just a few clicks, and that the Free Transform command can correct any unnatural perspective resulting from using wide-angle lenses. Quality starts here.

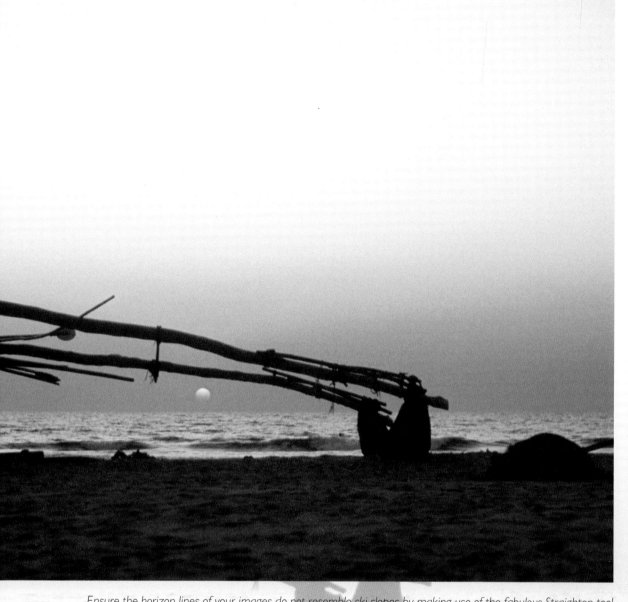

Ensure the horizon lines of your images do not resemble ski slopes by making use of the fabulous Straighten tool

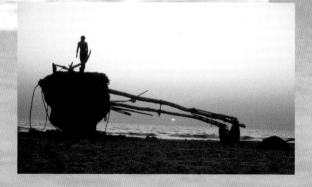

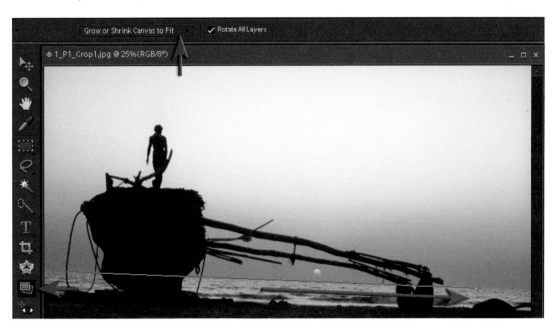

1. Open the image from the supporting DVD in the Full Edit workspace. Click on the 'Straighten tool' in the Tools panel. Select the option 'Grow or Shrink Canvas to Fit' in the Options bar above the image window. Now click on the horizon line and, with the mouse button held down, drag a line along the horizon line of the image. The image will automatically be straightened when you release the mouse.

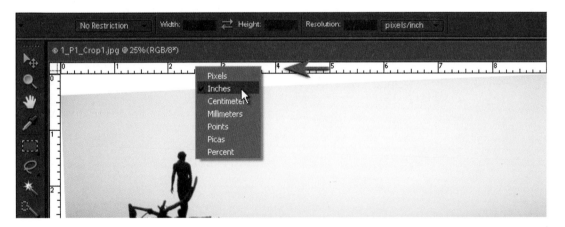

2. Select the Crop tool in the Tools panel and view the options in the Options bar. When we size an image we should select the width and height in pixels for screen or web viewing, and in centimeters or inches for printing. Typing in 'px', 'in' or 'cm' after each measurement will tell Photoshop Elements to crop using these units. If no measurement is entered in the field then Photoshop Elements will choose the default unit measurement entered in the preferences (Preferences > Units & Rulers). The preference can be quickly changed by right-clicking on either ruler (select 'View > Rulers' if they are not currently selected).

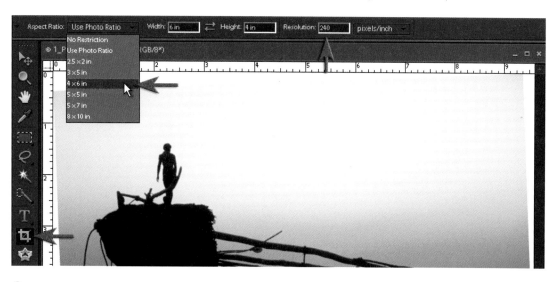

3. The action of entering measurements and a resolution at the time of cropping ensures that the image is sized (pixel dimensions altered) and cropped (shaped) in one action. Entering the size at the time of cropping ensures the aspect ratio or shape of the final image will match the printing paper, photo frame or screen where the image will finally be output.

Note > If an aspect ratio or both width and height measurements are entered into the measurement fields, the proportions of the final crop will be locked. This new aspect ratio may differ from that of the original capture and this in turn may prevent you from selecting either the full width or full height of the image, e.g. if you have entered the same measurement in both the width and height fields the final crop proportions are constrained to a square.

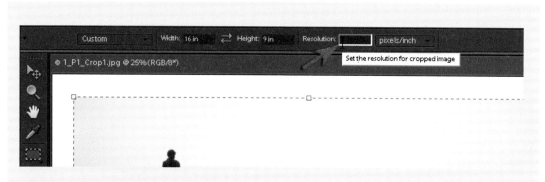

PERFORMANCE TIP

The process of cropping an image to a specific size and resolution will change the total number of pixels in the image file to the optimum number of pixels for the image size and output device, no more, no less. If you need to crop to a specific shape, but are uncertain as to whether it is destined for screen or print, you should leave the 'Resolution field' in the Options bar blank. This will maintain the original number of pixels until you know where this image is going to be presented. You also have the option of choosing an alternate shield color when cropping images by going to 'Edit > Preferences > Display and Cursors > Crop Tool'.

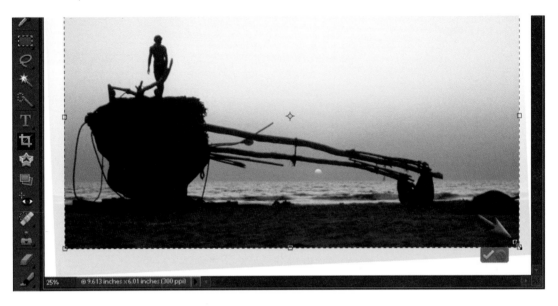

4. Drag the cropping marquee over the image to create the best composition. Drag any of the corner handles, or click and drag inside the crop marquee, to adjust the composition and then commit the crop by clicking on the check mark or double-clicking inside the crop marquee. The image should get smaller on the screen as excess pixels are discarded. If the image grows on screen, Photoshop Elements is upsampling (adding pixels). This is caused by the dimensions in the Crop tool options being larger than the size of your original image, and can reduce the quality. It is important to save this cropped version using a different name to ensure the higher resolution master file is preserved.

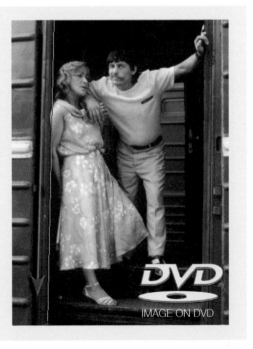

PERFORMANCE TIP

To use the Straighten tool to straighten a vertical rather than a horizontal, hold down the Ctrl key while you drag the line.

You can also straighten an image using only the Crop tool. First create the crop marquee on the edge of a horizontal or vertical line within the image. Move the cursor to a position just outside one of the corner handles of the cropping marquee and when the double-headed curved arrow appears you can rotate the cropping marquee to align it with the horizontal or vertical within the image. Then extend the cropping marquee by dragging one of the corner handles.

Note > **The Straighten tool is disabled for 16 Bits/Channel images.**

IMAGE ON DVD

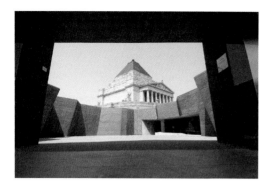 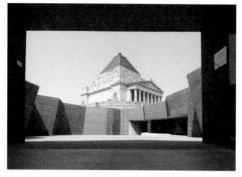

Correct Camera Distortion

When a camera is tilted up or down with a short focal length lens (wide angle) the verticals within the image can lean excessively inwards or outwards (converging verticals). Professional architectural photographers use cameras with movements or special lenses to remove this excessive distortion. To correct perspective use the Correct Camera Distortion filter. The process of correcting the verticals in an image is often referred to as 'keystoning'.

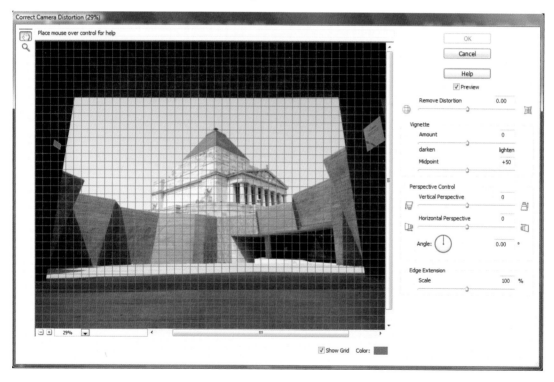

1. Select Filter > Correct Camera Distortion. The grid should be on by default and you can change its color if it's not clear against the subject you are viewing. The top slider in this dialog box corrects either barrel distortion or pincushion distortion, which sometimes results when using the extreme focal lengths of the zoom lens. Both result in curved straight lines which are usually most noticeable with the curvature of a horizon line when using a short focal length lens (wide angle).

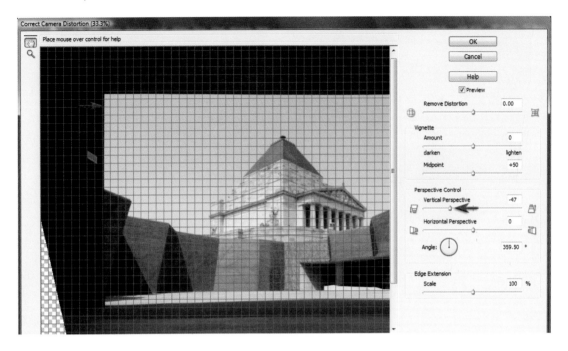

2. To render all the vertical lines in the image used in this illustration parallel, drag the Vertical Perspective slider in the Perspective Control section of the dialog box to the left. Use the grid lines to align the verticals within the image. Use the keyboard shortcuts to access the Zoom tool (Control + Spacebar and Alt + Spacebar) if you need to zoom in on a vertical to check the accuracy of the correction. You may need to alter the angle to ensure absolute accuracy.

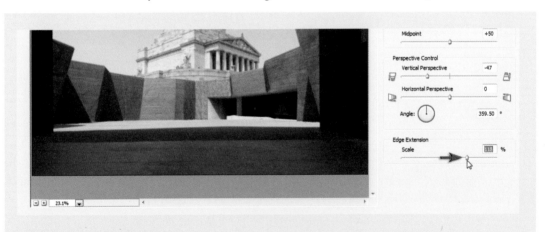

PERFORMANCE TIP

As the corrected image is narrower on one or more edges after using the Remove Distortion or Perspective Correction sliders you can use the Edge Extension slider at the bottom of the dialog box so that the corrected image fills the image window. As this process involves Photoshop adding pixels to grow the image you may want to crop the image instead of scaling the image in this dialog.

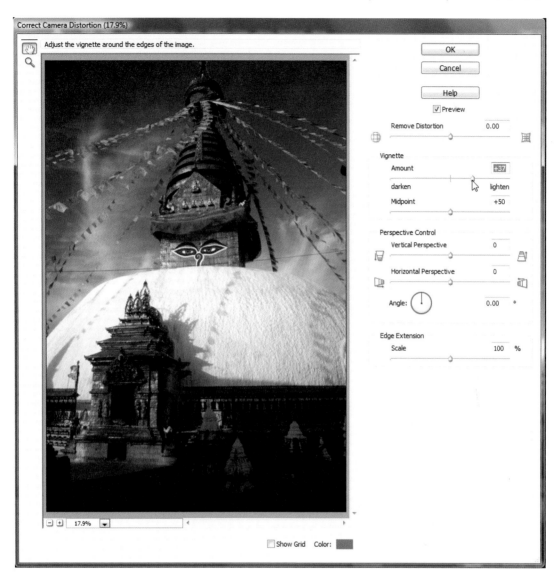

3. The Correct Camera Distortion filter also has control over vignetting (where the tone in the corners of the image appears darker or lighter than the overall tones within the rest of the image). Vignettes are often used for creative reasons to fade an image to black or white at the edges and corners. Some wide-angle lenses vignette when used at very wide apertures and these effects can be reduced or removed using the sliders in the Correct Camera Distortion dialog box. In the example image above a value of +35 is used to remove the darkened corners of the image that resulted from using a wide-angle lens. The Midpoint slider should be used to control the width of the correction, i.e. raising the value of the Midpoint slider will restrict the lightening effect to just the extreme outer regions of the image window whilst lowering the value will broaden the lightening effect. In later projects the Correct Camera Distortion filter can be used to creatively darken the corners of images to increase the sense of drama and mood.

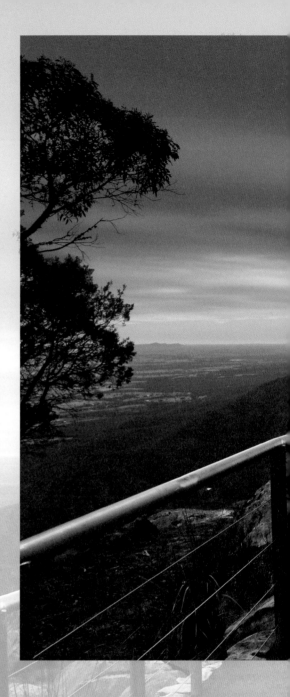

Project 2

Levels

This project will guide the user safely through the tricky mountain passes of this primary and essential technique used to achieve quality digital images. The adjustment feature is called 'Levels', but when you are presented with the virtual mountain range on opening the Levels dialog box, you begin to wonder what the clever people at Adobe were thinking of when they gave this indispensable adjustment feature its wonderful name (I think it's called irony).

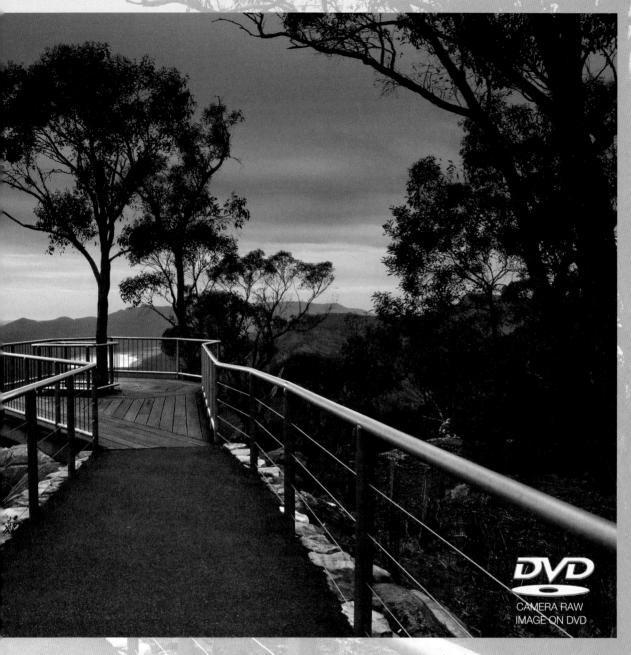

DVD

Levels – optimized quality starts here

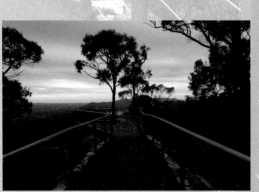

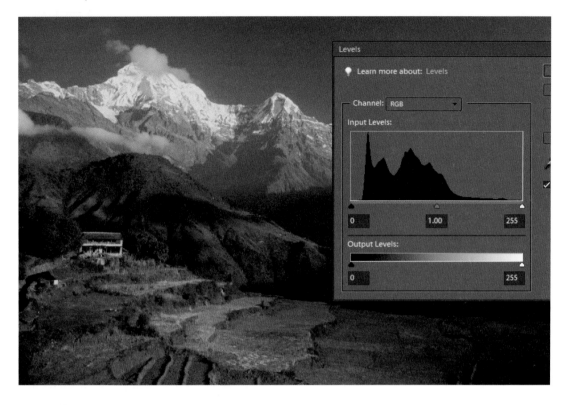

Setting the black and white points

In the illustration above one might be forgiven for thinking that the black peaks in the dialog box are an indication of how high the mountains are in the image, but no, the pixel mountains (called a histogram) are really an indication of how many pixels of each tone are present in the image. If the image is dark then the pixel mountains or histogram in the dialog box will be higher on the left side. If the image is very light, the histogram will be taller on the right side. The first step in nearly all image-editing tasks is the need to optimize the tonality or dynamic range of the image by adjusting the Levels.

> **Finding your levels > To open the Levels dialog, go to the Enhance menu and choose Adjust Lighting > Levels.**

If you are a newcomer to this dialog box you may simply want to click on the Auto button and then click OK. This simple procedure ensures the tonality of the digital image starts with a deep black and finishes with a bright white for optimum contrast and visual impact. If you want to perform the task manually click on the black input slider underneath the mountain range (the triangle on the left) and drag it to where the histogram begins to slope upwards on the left side. If you are now looking for the little triangle at the foot of the photographic mountains instead of the virtual ones, then I suggest you go and lie down for a moment and come back refreshed. Do the same with the white input slider on the right and you are almost finished. Click and drag the gray slider in the middle to make the image brighter or darker (depending on which way you drag the slider). If you want to start impressing the neighbors then you may like to start calling the gray triangle the 'Gamma slider'.

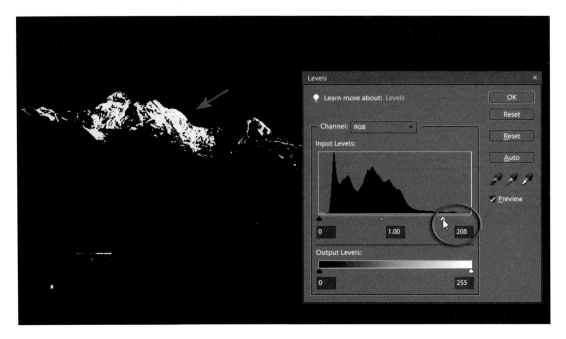

Clipping

If you drag the sliders too far you will lose or clip information from the image file. Shadows will become black and highlights will become white (this is called clipping the shadows or highlights). Your detail will have sunk without a trace into the black holes of our virtual valleys (called level 0) or have been pushed off the top of the virtual peaks (called level 255). If you fear the numbers 0 and 255 (which every self-respecting photographer should) you could try the following tip. Hold down the Alt key and drag the Black or White input sliders towards the mountains (your image will disappear momentarily but fear not). As you move the slider closer to the middle, colors will start to appear in your main image window when information is being lost. Move the sliders back until these colors disappear, but no farther. If colors are still appearing in the image window with the sliders all the way back to the edge of the histogram then your image was either underexposed or overexposed by the camera. If you are really unlucky you will have lost detail both in the shadows and in the highlights as a result of the photographer's worst enemy – excessive contrast. Not even the magic called Photoshop Elements can dig you out of this hole, my friend.

A video tutorial is available on the DVD that takes you through a series of steps used to edit this image. This includes removing a color cast, setting the black and white points and changing the contrast and color of the foreground fields.

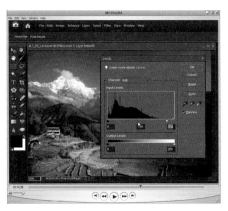

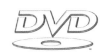

IMAGE AND MOVIE ON DVD

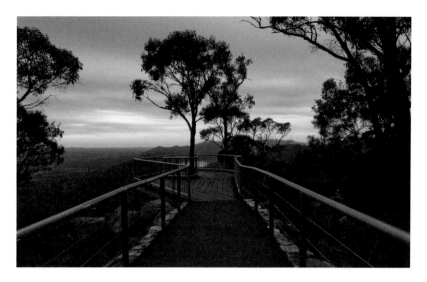

Localized adjustment of levels

1. In the image above the levels have been set so that the image file had both a black point and white point. The foreground still lacks localized contrast however. This is a result of the brightest tone in the foreground being Level 160. It is possible to expand the contrast of the foreground without clipping the lighter tones in the sky using the layer mask on the adjustment layer.

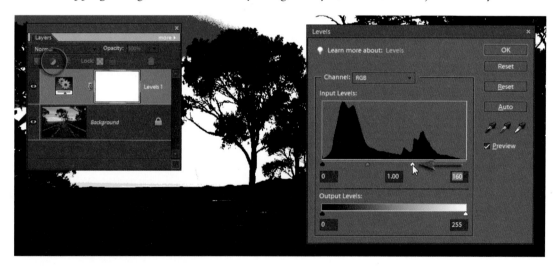

2. In the Layers panel select Levels from the Create Adjustment Layer menu. As you drag the white input slider to the left the sky will clip to white before any of the highlights appear in the foreground. The steel bars and brightest highlights just behind the base of the tree will start to appear first. Move the white input slider back a little until there is minimal clipping. Let go of the Alt key to see the effect this adjustment has had on the foreground contrast. Move the gray (Gamma) slider to the right to darken the image slightly. We have now increased the contrast in the foreground at the expense of the sky (which is now clipped). Sometimes things have to get worse before they can get better so select OK.

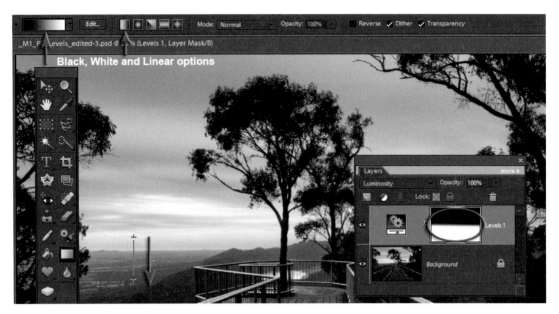

3. Increased contrast brings with it, increased saturation, which in this instance is an unwelcome visitor to the proceedings. We can remove the increase in saturation by simply setting the adjustment layer to Luminosity mode (as long as you don't have one of the painting tools selected, the keyboard shortcut is Alt + Shift + Y). Select the gradient Tool in the Tools panel and in the Options bar choose the Black, White and Linear options from the Options bar. Drag a gradient from a short distance above the horizon line to a short distance below the horizon line. This will effectively shield the sky from the effects of this aggressive adjustment layer and return the tonality of the sky back to 'normal'. Normal does not mean dramatic and seeing as this is an exercise in drama we will rectify this in the next step.

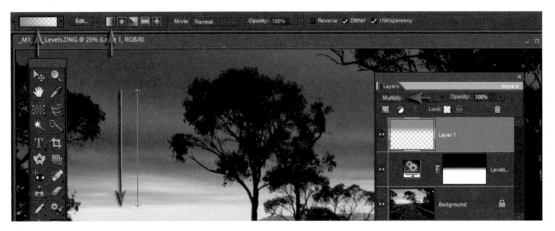

4. In the Layers panel click on the Create a new layer icon. Set the new layer to Multiply mode. Hold down the Alt key and click on a dark area of the sky to sample the color. Select the Foreground to Transparent and linear options in the Options bar and drag a long gradient from the top of the image to the horizon line to darken the sky further which will give further emphasis to the foreground detail.

Project *3*

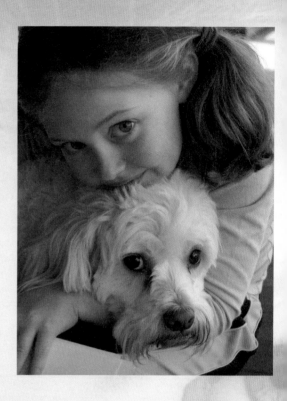

Camera Raw

All digital cameras capture in Raw but only digital SLRs and the medium-to high-end 'prosumer' cameras offer the user the option of saving the images in this Raw format. Selecting the Raw format in the camera instead of JPEG or TIFF stops the camera from processing the color data collected from the sensor. Digital cameras typically process the data collected by the sensor by applying the white balance, sharpening and contrast settings set by the user in the camera's menus. The camera then compresses the bit depth of the color data from 12 to 8 bits per channel before saving the file as a JPEG or TIFF file. Selecting the Raw format prevents this image processing taking place. The Raw data is what the sensor 'saw' before the camera processed the image, and many photographers have started to refer to this file as the 'digital negative'. This digital negative allows you to take control over the conversion process to access maximum quality.

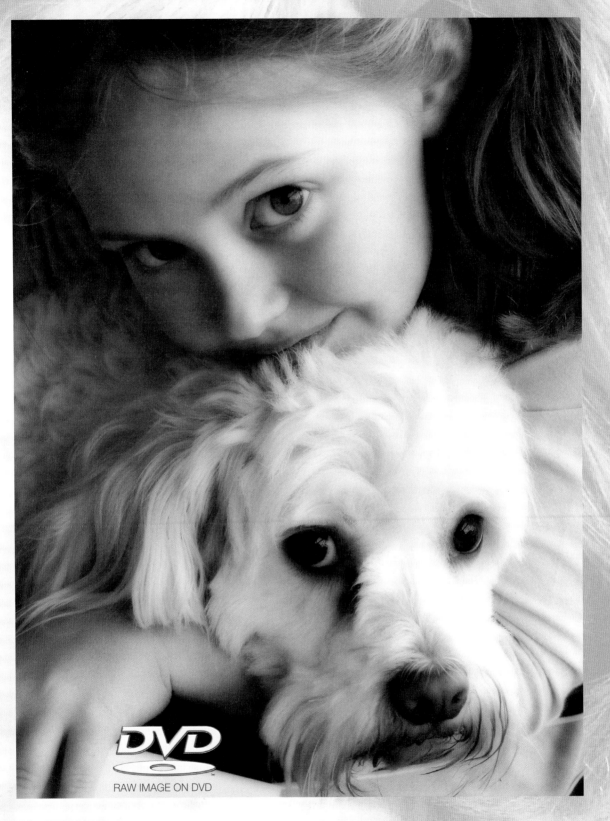

RAW IMAGE ON DVD

For maximum quality choose to save your files using the camera Raw format. This image was further edited in the main editing workspace using techniques from the Hue and Saturation and Glamor Portrait projects

Processing Raw data

White balance, brightness, contrast, saturation and sharpness can all be assigned as part of the conversion process in Adobe Camera Raw rather than in the camera. Performing these image-editing tasks on the full high-bit Raw data enables you to achieve a higher quality end result. After the image has been processed in the Camera Raw dialog box the file is then opened into the image-editing workspace and the Raw file closes and remains in its Raw state, i.e. unaffected by the processing procedure. Although the Camera Raw dialog box appears a little daunting at first sight, it is reasonably intuitive and easy to master.

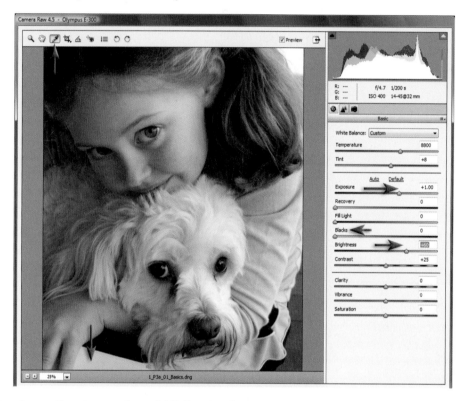

1. Basic adjustments - White balance

Open the Raw file from the supporting DVD. Set the white balance by clicking on the White Balance eyedropper in the small tools panel (top left-hand corner of the dialog box) and then click on any neutral tone you can find in the image. In this image click on the white paper the girl is holding. You can also set the white balance by choosing one of the presets from the drop-down menu or manually adjusting the Temperature and Tint sliders to remove any color cast present. The Temperature slider controls the blue/yellow color balance whilst the Tint slider controls the green/magenta balance. Moving both the sliders in the same direction controls the red/cyan balance.

Note > Although it is a 'White Balance' you actually need to click on a tone that is not so bright that it has become clipped (255). Clicking on any light neutral tone (one without any color) is preferable. A photographer looking to save a little time later may introduce a 'gray card' or 'white balance' reference card in the first frame of a shoot to simplify this task.

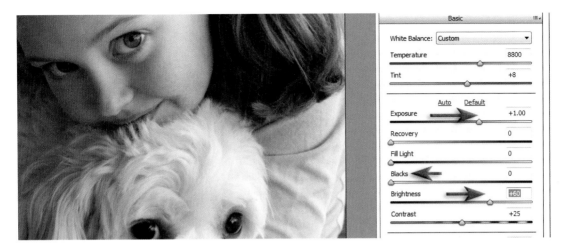

2. Basic adjustments - Tonality

Set the tonal range of the image using the Exposure, Blacks and Brightness sliders. These sliders behave similarly to the input sliders in the Levels dialog box and will set the black and white points within the image. The Brightness slider adjusts the midtone values in a similar way to the Gamma slider when using the Levels dialog. When tall peaks appear at either end of the histogram you will lose shadow, highlight or color detail when you open the file to the main editing software. Careful adjustment of these sliders will allow you to get the best out of the dynamic range of your imaging sensor, thereby creating a tonally rich image with full detail.

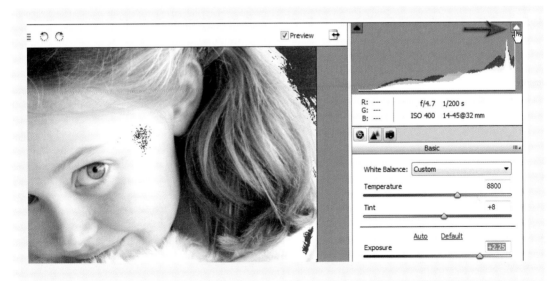

PERFORMANCE TIP

Hold down the Alt key when adjusting either the Exposure or Shadows slider to view the point at which highlight or shadow clipping begins to occur (white or black indicates the point at which pixels lose detail in all channels). Alternatively you can check the Shadows and Highlights boxes above the main image window instead of holding down the Alt key.

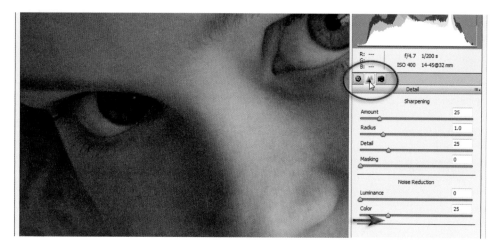

3. Detail

Zoom to 100% and click on the Detail tab to access the Sharpening and Noise Reduction controls. Sharpening controls can be left at their default settings if you intend to implement the advanced sharpening techniques (*see* Project 7) or use the techniques outlined on page 32 if you wish to apply sharpening settings to a batch of images. The Luminance Smoothing and Color Noise Reduction sliders (designed to tackle the camera noise that occurs when the image sensors' ISO is high) should only be raised from 0 if you notice image artifacts such as noise appearing in the image window.

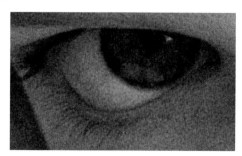 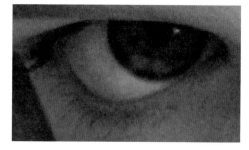

In the project image the sensor was set to 400 ISO on a budget DSLR. Both luminance and color noise are evident when the image is set to 100%. When cameras are set to 100 or 200 ISO it may be possible to leave the Luminance slider at 0 as noise will be low or non-existent. It is recommended that you only perform a gentle amount of sharpening in the Raw dialog box if you intend to selectively sharpen the image in the main image-editing workspace (*see* 'Project 7 - Sharpening' for localized sharpening techniques that are unavailable in the Camera Raw dialog box).

PERFORMANCE TIP
The Luminance Smoothing and Color Noise Reduction sliders can remove subtle detail and color information that may go unnoticed if the photographer does not pay attention to the effects of these sliders. Zoom in to 100% to see the effects of these sliders and unless you can see either little white speckles or color artifacts set these sliders to 0.

4. Depth

Select the 'Depth' in the lower left-hand corner of the dialog box and then click OK. If the user selects the '16 Bits/Channel' option, the 12 bits per channel data from the image sensor is rounded up - each channel is now capable of supporting 32,769 levels instead of 256. Many of the advanced editing features are unavailable in 16 Bits/Channel mode so the user may choose to go for the '8 Bits/ Channel' option now. This is OK as long as the tonality (black and white points) and color have been corrected in the Camera Raw dialog box.

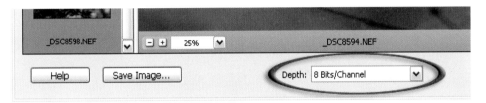

If the color and tonal information is edited significantly in the main editing space, with the files in 8 Bits/Channel mode, the final quality will be compromised. If the digital image has been corrected sufficiently for the requirements of the output device in the Raw dialog box the file can be edited in 8-bit mode with no apparent loss in quality.

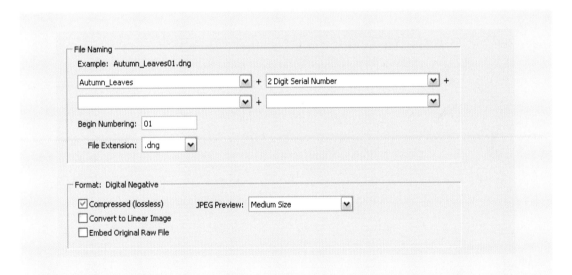

PERFORMANCE TIP

Adobe has created a universal Raw file format called 'DNG' (Digital Negative) in an attempt to ensure that all camera Raw files (whichever camera they originate from) will be accessible in the future. The 'Save' option in the Camera Raw dialog box gives you access to convert your camera's Raw file to the Adobe Digital Negative format with no loss of quality. The conversion will ensure that your files are archived in a format that will be understood in the future. Expect to see future models of many digital cameras using this DNG format as standard. One thing is for sure – Raw files are a valuable source of the rich visual data that many of us value, and so the format will be around for many years to come.

Workflows

Photoshop Elements users who purchased version 5.0 were able to take advantage and enjoy the advances made to the Adobe Camera Raw (ACR) interface over the last 12 months. Things started really improving in ACR after Photoshop Lightroom was released at the start of 2007. The new Camera Raw plug-ins that Adobe made available on their website (Versions 4.0 and higher) shared the much-improved Raw engine that first saw the light of day in Photoshop Lightroom. Since the release of Adobe Camera Raw 4 users can now enjoy not just the increased number of controls and features, but also synchronize the adjustments over an entire shoot or folder of images opened into the ACR space.

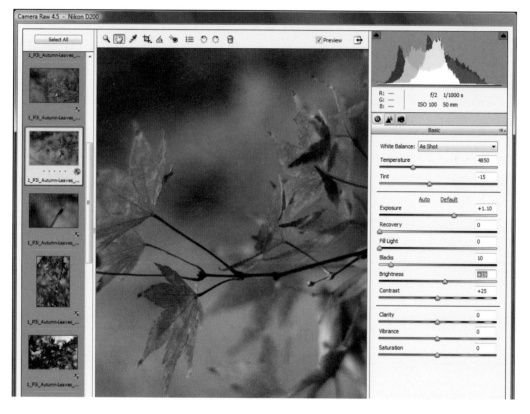

The ability to batch process Raw files was perhaps the most significant new feature of Adobe Camera Raw 4. In Photoshop Elements 6 and 7 we can now optimize, crop and process all of the files ready for print or for web with the minimum of fuss but with an astonishing amount of control.

This tutorial will look at the following new features:
- Straighten and Crop
- Recovery and Fill Light
- Clarity
- Vibrance
- Batch processing
- Sharpening (including the new Radius, Detail and Masking controls)

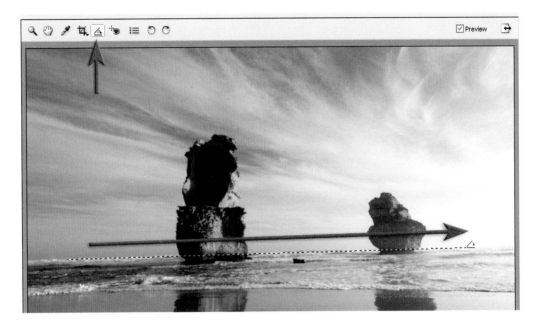

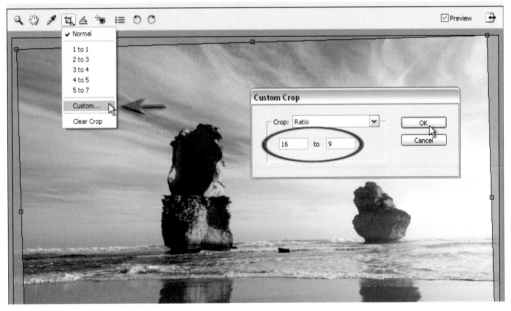

1. Straighten and Crop

It is now possible to straighten and crop images in the Adobe Camera Raw interface; it is important to remember that these adjustments, just like all other adjustments in the Adobe Camera Raw interface, are non-destructive. Pixels are not permanently removed by the cropping process, i.e. all the original pixels are preserved and you can crop to a different format or shape at any time. The Crop menu allows you to select the format (image shape) that you wish to crop to. In the example above I have created a custom Crop setting using the popular widescreen 16:9 format. This format will be added to the Crop presets for future use.

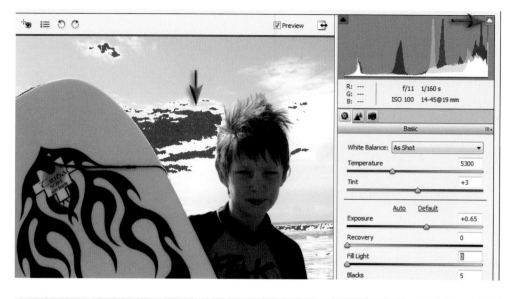

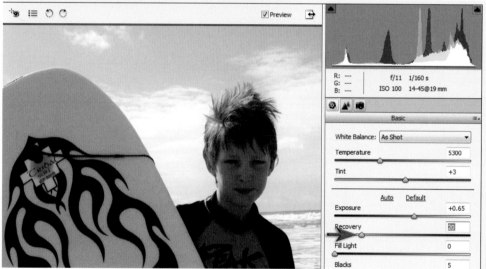

2. Recovery and Fill Light

The Recovery and Fill Light sliders can rescue bright highlights that have become clipped and dark shadows that may otherwise be too dark to print. When the contrast of the scene is very high (bright sunlight) many good quality digital cameras can be set to warn us of overexposure by blinking the overexposed highlights. Sometimes we can lower the contrast by using a reflector or fill flash and sometimes we can rescue the highlights in Adobe Camera Raw. In the illustration above the highlight warning has been switched on by clicking on the triangle in the top right-hand corner of the histogram window. The red color indicates overexposure (pixels that would be rendered 255 if left unadjusted). Dragging the Recovery slider to the right brings these overexposed tones back under 255 and will allow them to print with texture and detail.

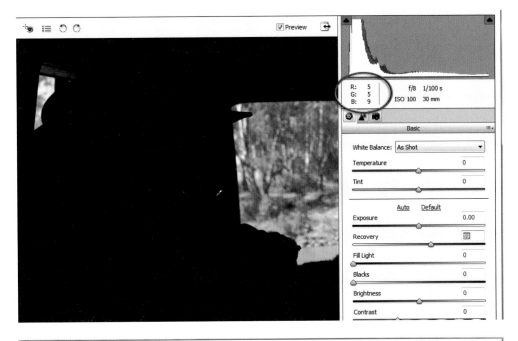

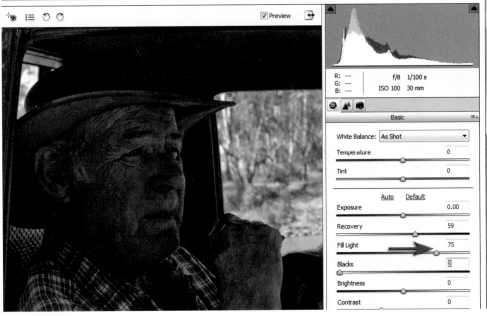

Great care needs to be taken when using the Fill Light slider to rescue dark shadow tones. In this example an extreme adjustment is being made to rescue the shadow tones that have been accidentally underexposed due to the bright tones in the center of the viewfinder. Be careful with raising the Fill Light value too high, especially with photos taken with a high ISO, as Fill Light will also brighten noise in the photo and make it more apparent. Photos taken at a lower ISO, like ISO 100, will be more forgiving to the Fill Light slider and not expose problems like noise and tonal banding so readily.

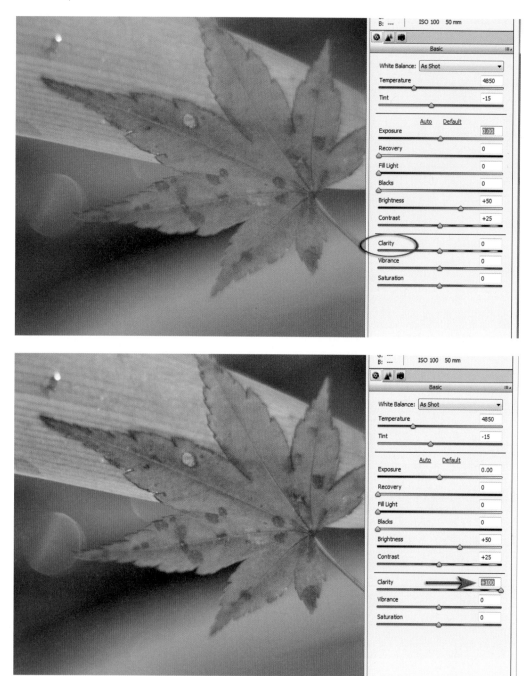

3. Clarity

The Clarity slider can be used to effectively increase localized contrast and make images appear to have more depth (and sometimes a little sharper). Notice how contrast is raised both in the areas of fine detail and the broader areas of continuous tone. Unlike the Recovery and Fill Light sliders that have to be used in moderation, this slider is slow to introduce unpleasant artifacts – especially in images where the light quality was soft and even.

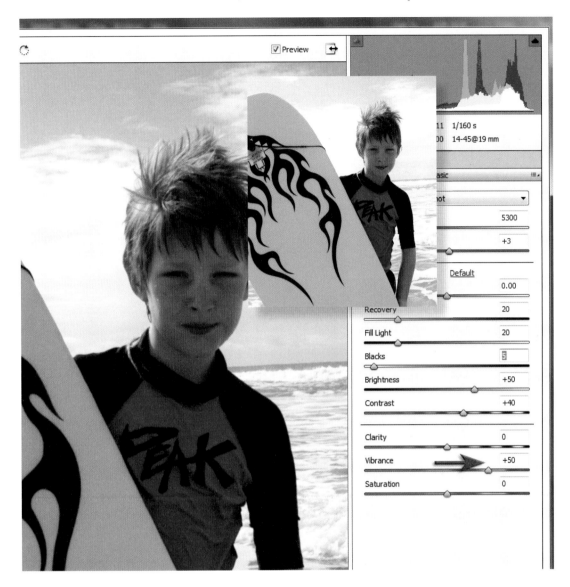

4. Vibrance

Increasing saturation in Adobe Camera Raw can lead to clipping in the color channels. Clipping saturated colors can lead to a loss of fine detail and texture. The Vibrance slider applies a non-linear increase in saturation (primarily targeting pixels of lower saturation more than colors that are already vibrant). The adjustment feature has also been designed to protect skin tones from becoming oversaturated and unnatural. The Vibrance adjustment feature should lead to fewer problems when compared to the Saturation control and should be used for most situations where increased color saturation is required.

Note > Choosing Adobe RGB in the Color Settings dialog box in the main editing space (Edit > Color Settings) will enable a working space with a larger color gamut than sRGB. This will allow saturation or vibrance to be increased to a greater degree before clipping occurs.

5. Correcting the White Balance across a batch of images

As we have seen with editing the previous image, it is sometimes quick to use the White Balance tool in the Adobe Camera Raw interface to quickly color-correct an image by simply clicking on a neutral tone within the image to quickly set the correct color temperature and tint.

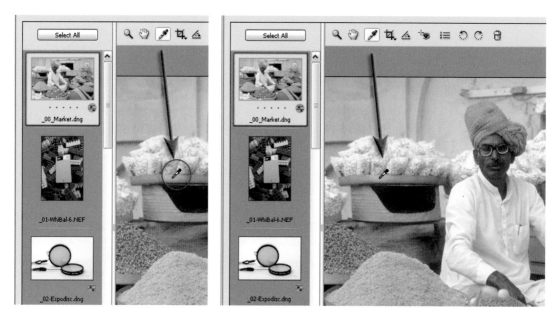

If the subject you wish to capture does not have an obvious neutral tone then you can introduce a neutral tone as reference point in the first image of the shoot. This will enable you to measure the precise temperature and tint required to color-correct all the other images that share the same lighting conditions.

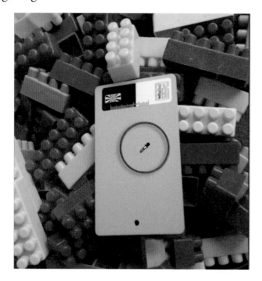
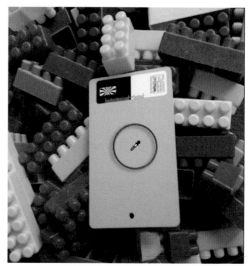

In this image a white balance card (a 'WhiBal' is used in the image above) has been introduced into the image and then the White Balance tool is used to set accurate temperature and tint settings.

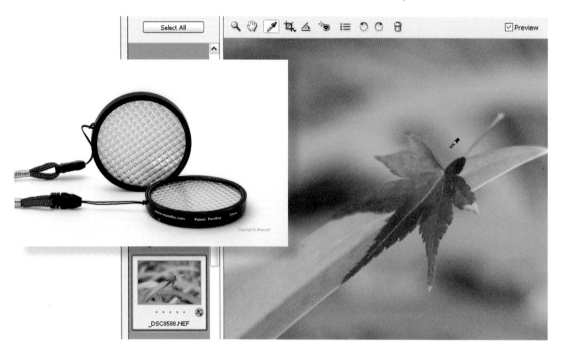

In some scenes there may be no neutral tones to click on and no opportunity to include a white balance reference card into the scene. In these instances it is important to either create a custom white balance setting in the camera at the time of capture, or capture a reference image using a product such as the 'Expodisc'. The Expodisc is placed in front of the lens and an image captured by pointing the camera back towards the light source (with the camera set to manual focus). The resulting image provides the photographer with a reference image that can be used to assign the correct white balance to all of the images captured in those lighting conditions.

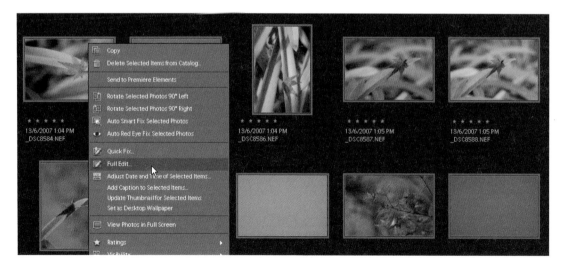

When you want to assign the correct white balance across a group of images, select multiple Raw files in the Organizer space and then open them in the Adobe Camera Raw interface.

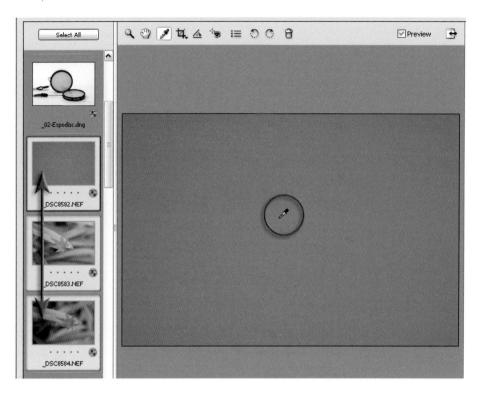

Click on the reference image thumbnail on the left-hand side of the Adobe Camera Raw interface. Then hold down the Shift key and click on the last thumbnail in the group of images that share the same lighting conditions. Select the White Balance tool and click on the main reference image preview to assign the correct white balance to all of the images.

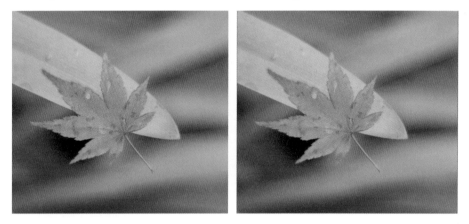

This is before and after and clearly demonstrates how the Auto White Balance setting in the camera has misjudged the correct white balance for these images of Autumn leaves.

Note > The Expodisc can also be used create custom white balance settings in the camera, take accurate incident light meter readings and also help locate any dust on the camera's sensor (go to www.expodisc.com for more details about this useful product).

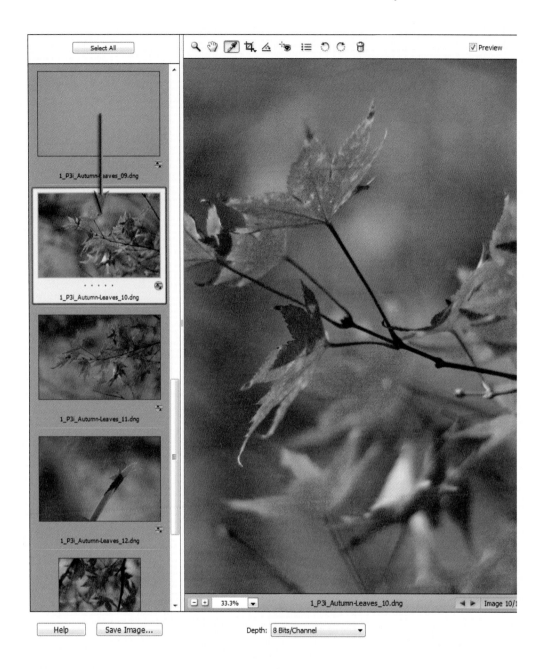

PERFORMANCE TIP

As long as the photographer takes frequent reference images as the lighting conditions change, e.g. cloudy, sunny, time of day, etc., color accuracy is assured with just a few clicks. Remember this color accuracy can only be fully appreciated if both the computer monitor and printer are calibrated to display accurate color (*see* Project 8 - Printing).

6. Sharpening

Just as a white balance setting can be applied across multiple images open in Adobe Camera Raw, the same batch processing can be achieved when sharpening images. Although the sharpening controls have vastly improved in the Adobe Camera Raw interface it is still recommended that you sharpen in the main editing space to achieve maximum performance when sharpening (*see* Project 7 - Sharpening).

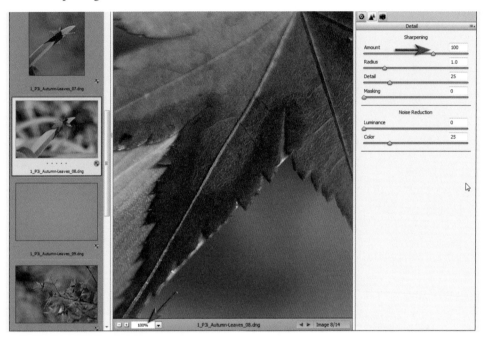

Set the magnification of the image to 100% before sharpening any image in Adobe Camera Raw as the results are not visible at smaller magnifications. Start by increasing the Amount slider until the edges that have the most contrast are suitably sharp. Amounts up to 100% are considered normal. Generally it is recommended to leave the Radius slider at its default setting of 1.0.

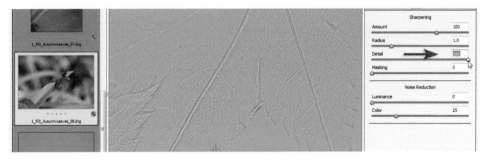

Hold down the Alt key and drag the Detail slider to left or right to observe the amount of detail that will be targeted for sharpening. Drag to the right to increase detail in the areas of continuous tone and to the left to decrease apparent detail. Let go of the Alt key to observe the effect on the image.

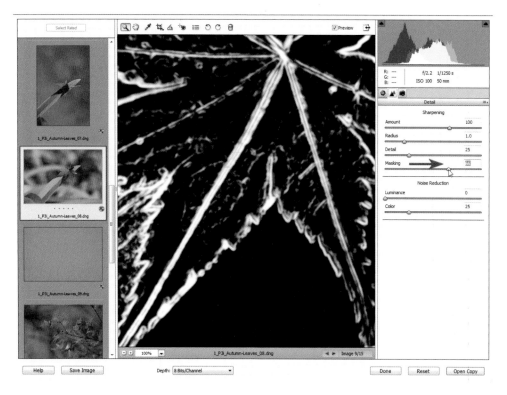

To eliminate the sharpening process from areas of continuous tone we can drag the Masking slider to the right. Hold down the Alt key as you drag this slider to observe the areas of the image that will not be sharpened (as indicated by the black mask).

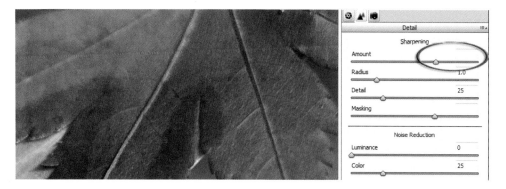

To apply these setting to the other images in the shoot simply choose the Select All option above the thumbnails on the left side of the Adobe Camera Raw interface. The numbers for each slider will be blank if the settings are not the same for all of the selected images. Click on each slider in turn to sync the sharpening settings for all images. Click on Done to apply all of these changes and close the Adobe Camera Raw dialog box, 'Save' to process files using these Raw settings or select one or more images to open into the main editing space of Elements.

Note > Sharpening and other corrections applied over a batch of images may not always be desirable for every image. Check each image in turn to see if specific adjustments are required.

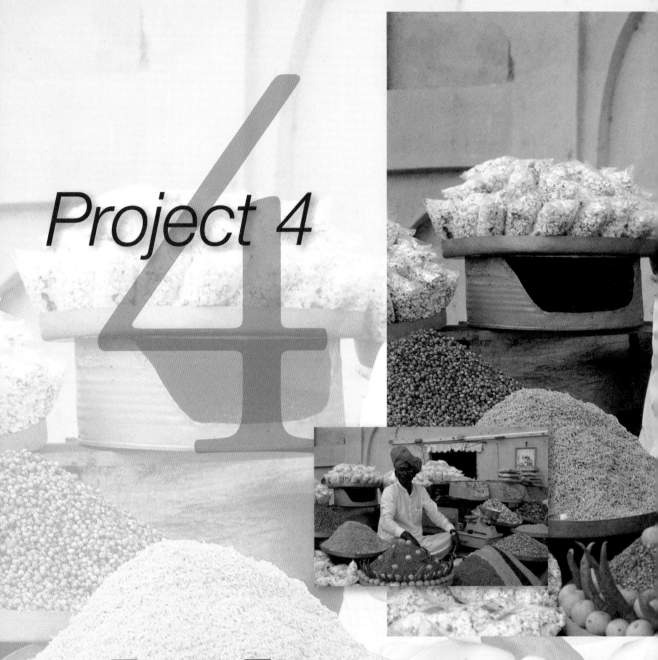

Project 4

Target Tones

Setting the levels in a digital image is only the first step to achieving optimized images. It is also necessary to optimize the image for the intended output device. To achieve optimum tonal quality in your digital images it is important to target both the highlight and shadow tones within each image. When using Elements the Eyedropper tool is a key to unlocking the quality that lies dormant in any one of your images which has been correctly exposed.

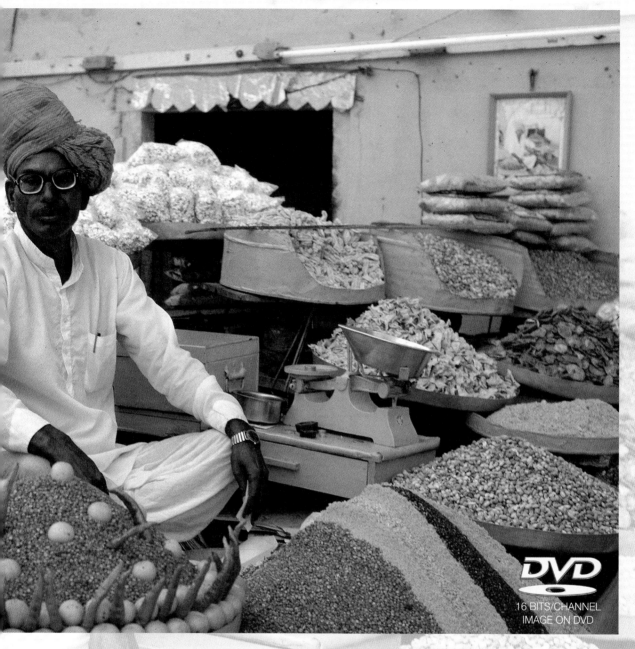

DVD
16 BITS/CHANNEL
IMAGE ON DVD

What you see is not what you always get – target your levels to your output device for predictable results

To achieve maximum quality set the target levels in images that are in 16 Bits/Channel mode (accessed through the camera Raw format or via scans from film that have been requested as 48-bit output scans). If you are optimizing your files in 8 Bits/Channel mode (via JPEG files) be sure to use an adjustment layer rather than an adjustment from the Enhance menu.

Ansel Adams was responsible for creating the famous/infamous 'Zone System' in order to precisely control the tonal range of each of his masterpieces. If you look carefully at one of his beautiful landscape photographs you will notice that only the light source (or its reflection - something termed a 'specular highlight') appears as paper white. All the rest of the bright highlights reveal tone or texture. Likewise, the shadows may appear very dark, but they are not devoid of detail. Ansel was careful only to render holes as black (the absence of a surface). Any surface, even those in shadow, would render glorious amounts of subtle detail.

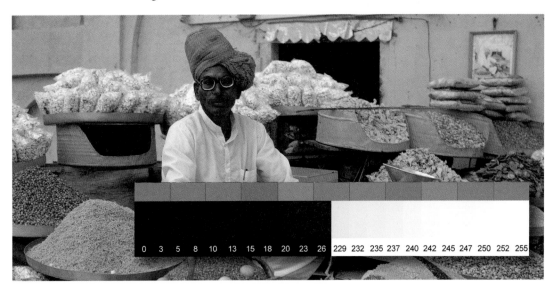

Even though you have set your levels (as guided in Project 2 or 3) it is no guarantee that your highlight or shadow tones will be visible in the final print. To make sure the highlight detail does not 'blow out' (become white) and the shadow detail is not lost in a sea of black ink it is possible to target the highlights and shadows in your image to the brightest and darkest tones that the printer can reproduce. The default settings of the eyedroppers to be found in the Levels dialog box are set to 0 (black) and 255 (white). These settings are only useful for targeting the white overexposed areas or black underexposed areas. These tools can, however, be recalibrated to something much more useful, i.e. tones with detail. A typical photo quality inkjet printer printing on premium grade photo paper will usually render detail between the levels 15 and 250. Precise values can be gained by printing a 'step wedge' of specific tones to evaluate the darkest tone that is not black and the brightest tone that is not paper white (*see* 'Project 8 - Printing' for more guidance on this subject).

PERFORMANCE TIP
The precise target values for images destined for the commercial printing industry are dependent on the inks, papers and processes in use. Images are sometimes optimized for press by skilled operatives during the conversion to CMYK. Sometimes they are not. If in doubt you should check with the publication to get an idea of what you are expected to do and what you should be aiming for if the responsibility is yours.

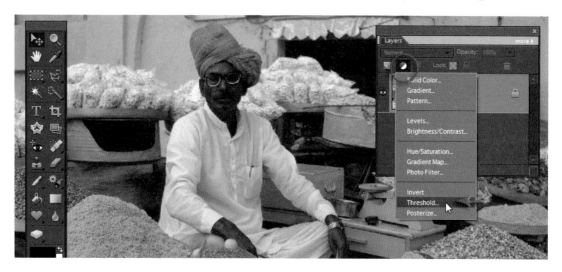

1. For maximum quality you would be wise to optimize your histogram in camera Raw or in 16 Bits/Channel mode. If the file is in 16 Bits/Channel mode you will need to access a levels adjustment from the Enhance > Adjust Lighting submenu. If the file is in 8 Bits/Channel mode (due to being captured using the JPEG file format) you are advised to create a Levels adjustment layer by clicking on the Create New Fill or Adjustment Layer icon in the Layers panel. A tall peak at either level 0 or level 255 is a strong indicator that detail has already been lost either by excessive subject contrast or inappropriate exposure during the capture stage. If this is the case your shadow or highlight detail is already irrecoverable.

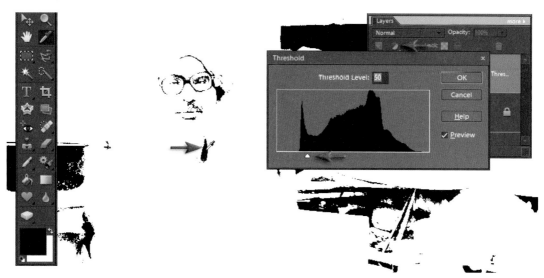

2. In this step we will locate the darkest area of the image that has shadow detail and the lightest area of the image that has highlight detail. From the Create adjustment layer menu in the Layers panel choose a Threshold adjustment layer. Move the slider under the histogram until just the darkest areas of the image are visible as black islands in a sea of white pixels. Select OK in the Threshold dialog to close it.

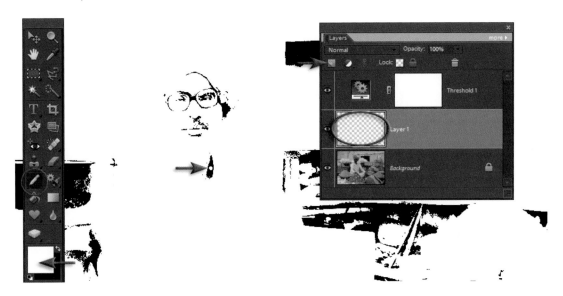

3. Click on the Background layer to make it the active layer in the Layers panel and then click on the Create a new layer icon in the Layers panel to create an empty new layer above the background layer and below the Threshold adjustment layer. Select the Pencil Tool in the Tools panel that lives behind the Brush Tool (press the N key on the keyboard to select it without having to click on it). Set the Foreground color to white (press the D key followed by the X key) and set the size to 10px in the Options bar. Click to paint a white spot on the shadow tone that you isolated in the previous step.

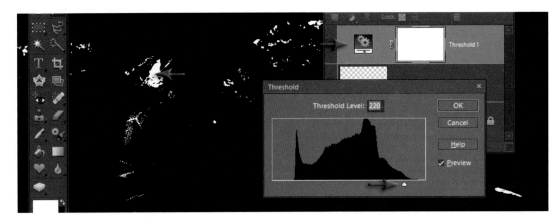

4. Double-click on the Threshold layer thumbnail to open the Threshold dialog. Move the slider under the histogram to the right until just the brightest tones appear as islands surrounded by black. Select OK to close the dialog. Click on Layer 1 (below the Threshold layer) to make it the active layer. With the Pencil tool selected set the foreground color to Black (press the X key) and then paint a black spot in one of the bright white islands of tone. Do not select a specular highlight such as a light source or a reflection of the light source that should be 255. Switch off the visibility of the Threshold layer by clicking on the small eye icon next to the Threshold layer thumbnail.

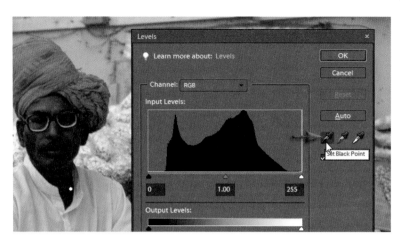
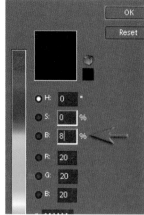

5. With the shadows and highlights accurately targeted and the effects of Threshold adjustment layer hidden from view we can now optimize these tones for our printer. Click on the Background layer to make it the active layer in the Layers panel. From the Create adjustment layer menu in the Layers panel choose a Levels adjustment layer. Double-click the Set Black Point eyedropper in the Levels dialog to display the Color Picker. Enter a value of 7 or 8 in the 'Brightness' field (part of the hue, saturation and brightness or HSB controls) and select OK. The precise value is dependent on your printer, paper and ink choice. You can experiment with alternative values later when you have completed the printing project.

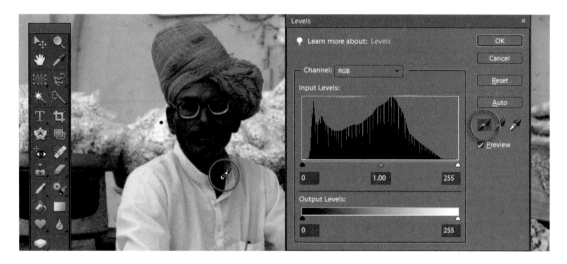

6. Move your mouse cursor into the image window and click on the white pencil spot that you created in step 3 (the darkest shadow tone that requires visible detail). This action will set your shadow tone.

Note > Layer 1 (the layer with the black and white pencil spots in it) MUST be above this adjustment layer for this step to work. If it is not, hit the Escape key and select the Background layer before creating a Levels adjustment layer.

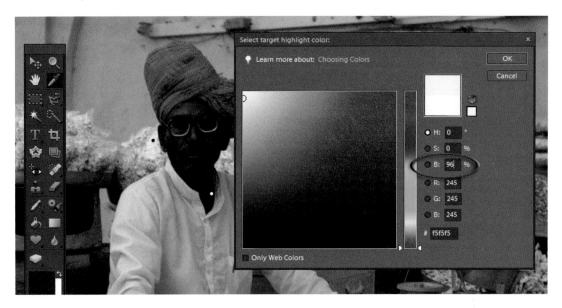

7. Double-click the Set White Point eyedropper to display the Color Picker again. This time enter a value of 96 in the 'Brightness' field and select OK.

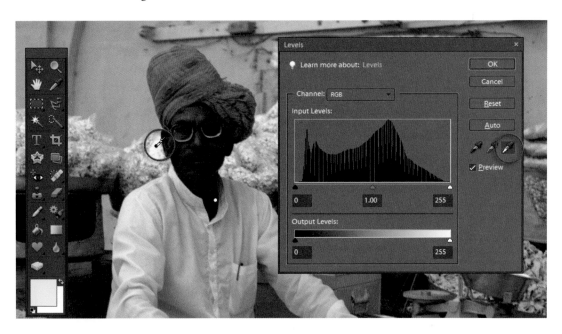

8. With the Set White Point eyedropper still selected move into the image window and click on the target highlight to set this as the brightest highlight tone within your image.

Note > When targeting highlights and shadows of a color image a color cast may be introduced into the image if the tones to be targeted are not neutral or desaturated. This can be rectified using the Set Gray Point eyedropper to correct any cast introduced.

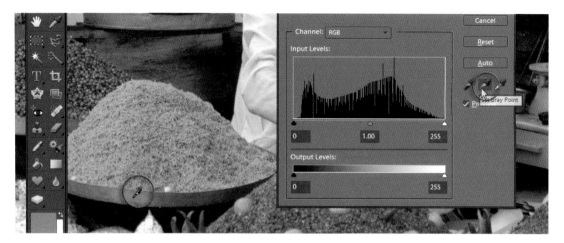

9. Select the Set Gray Point eyedropper (between the black and white eyedroppers). Click on a suitable tone you wish to desaturate in an attempt to remove the color cast present in the image (try clicking on the metal trays holding the produce). The neutral tone selected to be the 'Gray Point' can be a dark or light tone within the image. If the tone selected is not representative of a neutral tone the color cast cannot be rectified effectively.

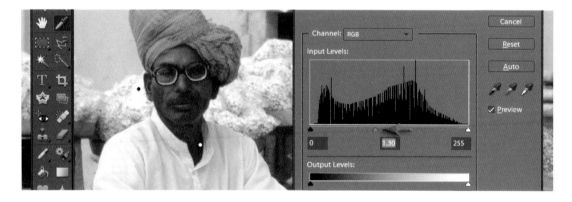

10. Move the Gamma slider to fine-tune the overall brightness of the midtones. Excessive movement of the Gamma slider, however, will upset the targeted tones set previously.

11. Click OK to apply the tonality changes to the image. When presented with the dialog box that reads 'Save the new target colors as defaults?' you can select 'Yes'. This will ensure that when you use the eyedroppers on your next image all you need do is click once with each of the three eyedroppers. Delete Layer 1 and the Threshold adjustment layer by dragging them to the small trash can in the Layers panel to complete the project.

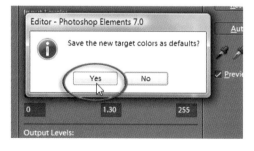

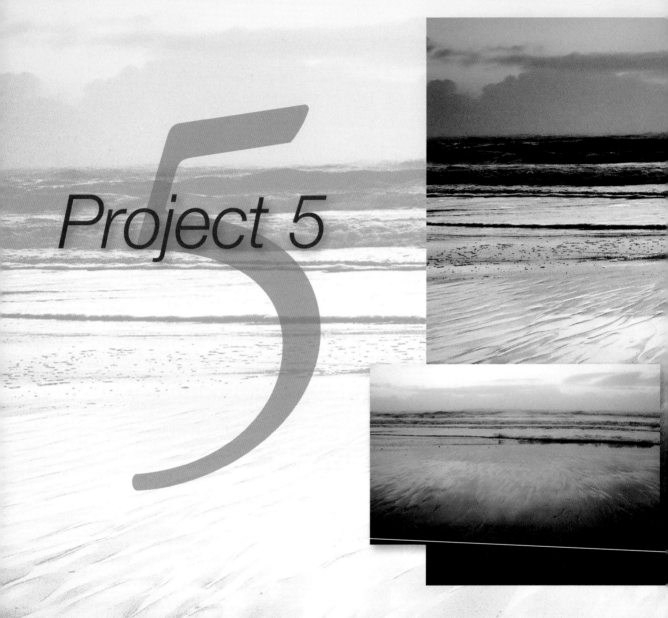

Project 5

Contrast

One of the most important image adjustment features in a professional photographer's workflow is Curves (a sort of Levels command on steroids). Adobe in their wisdom decided to include this feature in Photoshop Elements 5.0. Color Curves now made a welcome appearance in the Enhance menu but it is still not available as an adjustment layer. This project shows you several ways to control contrast using adjustment layers to increase your post-production editing power to maximum performance.

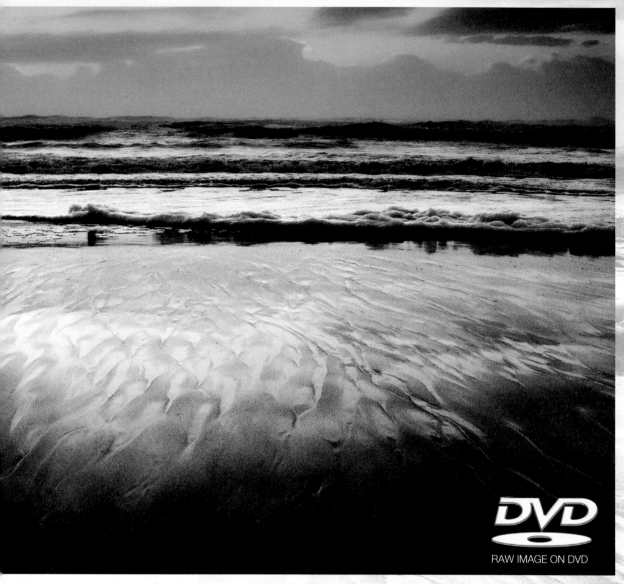

Create dramatic images by building in some non-destructive contrast

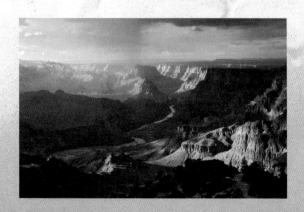

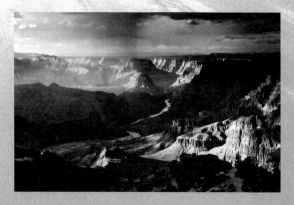

The revised Brightness/Contrast adjustment feature

If you have been image editing for some time you will know that 'Levels' has always been a superior option to enhance the brightness and contrast of your image rather than the Brightness/Contrast feature. Adjusting the brightness or contrast of an image using the Brightness/Contrast adjustment used to be very destructive, e.g. if you wanted to make the shadows brighter and elected to use the Brightness/Contrast control, all of the pixels in the image were made brighter (not just the shadows) - causing the pixels that were already bright to fall off the end of the histogram and lose their detail or become white (level 255). The Brightness/Contrast adjustment feature has now been fully revised so that its behavior falls in line with the non-destructive nature of the Brightness and Contrast sliders in Adobe Camera Raw.

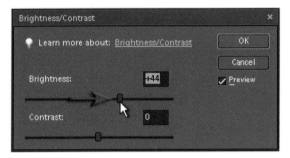

Using the Brightness slider is now like moving the center (Gamma) slider in the Levels adjustment feature, i.e. the image is made brighter whilst preserving the black and white points within the image. The Contrast slider, on the other hand, makes the shadows darker and the highlights brighter but not at the expense of the black and white points of the image. The only problem with new Brightness/Contrast adjustment feature is that it cannot focus its attention on a limited range of tones, e.g. make the shadows darker or lighter but leave the midtones and highlights as they were.

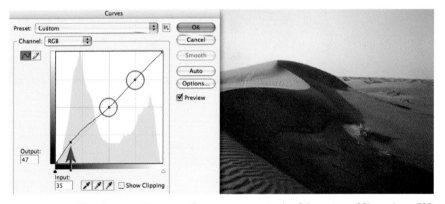

The Curves adjustment feature as seen in the full version of Photoshop CS3

The Curves adjustment feature allows the user to target tones within the image and move them independently, e.g. the user can decide to make only the darker tones lighter whilst preserving the value of both the midtones and the highlights. It is also possible to move the shadows in one direction and the highlights in another. In this way the midtone contrast of the image can be increased with a great deal more control than the new Brightness/Contrast adjustment feature.

Resolving the problem

Now there are four ways to enable you to harness the power of curves in Adobe Elements 7. The first way is 'Adjust Color Curves' (Enhance > Adjust Color > Adjust Color Curves) and is a user-friendly version of the Curves adjustment feature found in the full version of Photoshop.

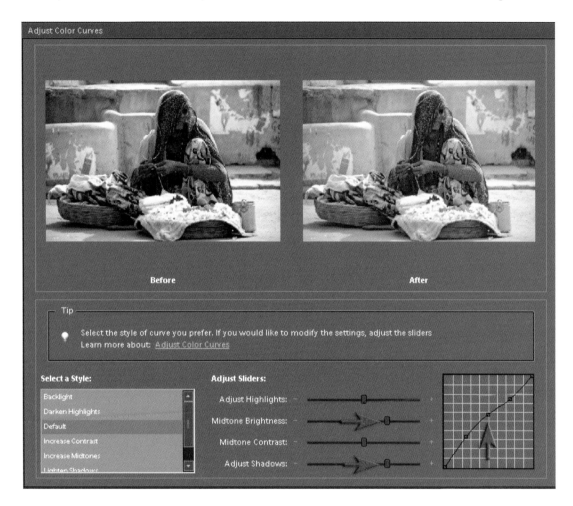

Method 1 - Color Curves

'Adjust Color Curves' can be accessed from the Enhance menu (Enhance > Adjust Color > Adjust Color Curves). The user should first set the levels of the image file by using the techniques outlined in Project 2. Unfortunately 'Adjust Color Curves' is not available as an adjustment layer so it would be advisable to first duplicate the background layer and apply the changes to this duplicate layer. Start by clicking on the thumbnail of your choice and then click on the advanced options to access the sliders that are required to fine-tune the tonality of your image. It may be necessary to add a Hue/Saturation adjustment layer to modify any changes in the color saturation that may have occurred as a result of the Color Curves adjustment.

Accessing curves as an adjustment layer

The second way of using curves, but this time as an adjustment layer, is a bit cheeky and is available if you have access to a multilayered file created in the full version of Photoshop (check out the supporting DVD to download the file used in the example below).

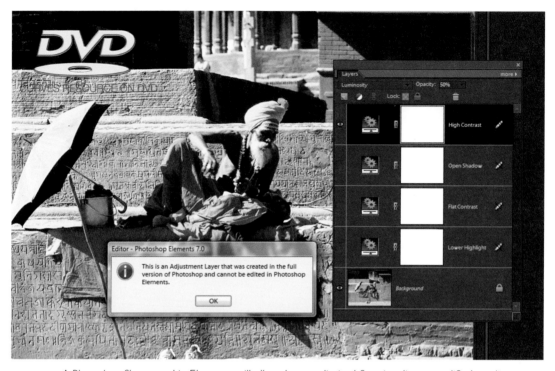

A Photoshop file opened in Elements will allow the user limited functionality to modify the adjustments

Method 2 - Grand theft

One of the great mysteries of life is that although you can't 'create' a Curves adjustment layer in Photoshop Elements you can 'open' an image that already has one. Photoshop Elements allows you to see the effects of the Curves adjustment layer (that was created in the full version of Photoshop), switch it off and on, and lower the opacity of the Curves adjustment layer (enabling you to lower the effect of the adjustment layer gradually). You can also drag this Curves adjustment layer into any other image file that is open in Elements (just click on the adjustment layer thumbnail in the Layers panel and drag it into another image window). Theoretically this means that if you had a single file that was created in Photoshop with a wide range of Curves adjustment layers to suit your everyday image-editing tasks you could use this as a 'Curves resource' – just drag, drop and adjust the opacity to suit the needs of each image you are editing. The sort of adjustment layers that would be particularly useful would be those that enabled the Photoshop Elements user to increase and decrease image contrast, raise or lower shadow brightness independently, and raise or lower highlight brightness independently. If the adjustment layers contain generous adjustments they can be simply tailored to suit each new image-editing task by just lowering or increasing the layer opacity. The adjustment layers are resolution independent, which is another way of saying that they will fit any image, big or small – naughty but very nice!

Method 3 - Gradients

The third version is for users of Elements who want a little more control, have a guilty conscience or prefer to explore the advanced features of the package they have purchased rather than the one they have not. This third method allows you to access the ultimate tonal control that Curves has to offer using a different adjustment feature not really designed for the job but which, when push comes to shove, can be adapted to fit the needs of the cash-strapped image editor seeking quality and control.

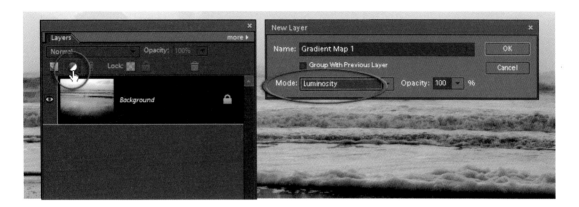

1. The first step is to hold down the Alt key and mouse button whilst selecting the Gradient Map adjustment layer from the Create adjustment layer menu in the Layers panel. This will open the New Layer dialog box. Select 'Luminosity' from the Mode menu and select OK.

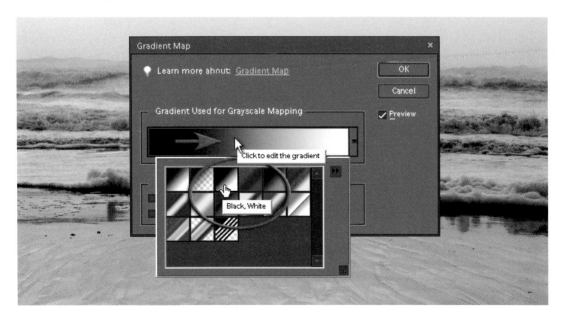

2. Click on the third gradient swatch in the presets menu (Black, White). Click on the gradient in the dialog box to open the Gradient Editor.

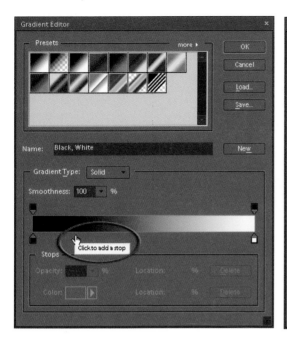
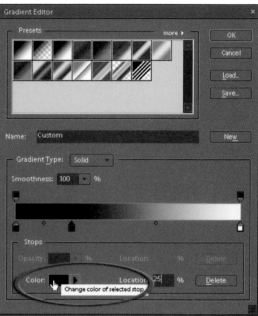

3. Move the cursor to just below the gray ramp and click to add a 'stop' slightly left of center. Type in 25% as the location and double-click on the color swatch to open the Color Picker.

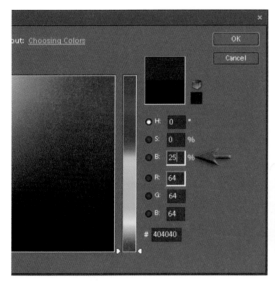
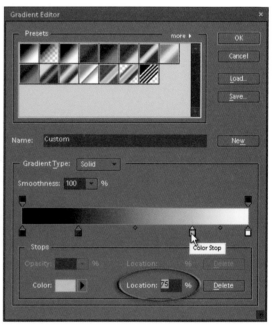

4. Choose a brightness value of 25% and click OK (ensure a value of 0 is entered in the other two fields of the HSB radio buttons). Add another stop right of center (at a location of approximately 75%) and again click on the color swatch to open the Color Picker. This time choose a brightness value of 75% and again click OK.

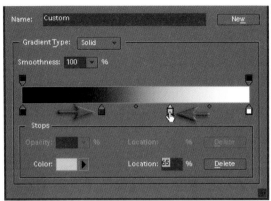
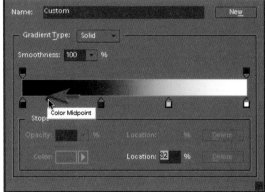

5. The 'Black/White' Gradient Map in Luminosity mode will leave the existing tonal values of your image the same as before. The magic starts when you start to drag the stops you created to new positions on the gray ramp. Moving the two sliders further apart will lower the contrast whilst dragging them closer together will increase contrast. A 'Color Midpoint' also appears between the two stops that you are adjusting to allow you to fine-tune your adjustment. In this project drag the two sliders together to increase the contrast but move the color midpoint to the left so that deep shadows do not become too dark. Be amazed – you are exercising absolute control over the brightness values of your image! This technique allows all of the versatility of a Curves adjustment layer when editing the luminosity of your image.

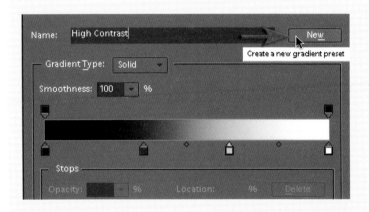
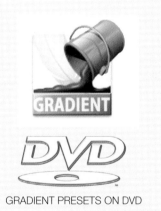

GRADIENT PRESETS ON DVD

PERFORMANCE TIP

When you have created a modified gradient map you can name and add the map to the list of presets for future use. Download the Gradient presets file (Tonal_Gradients.grd) from the supporting DVD and use either your 'Preset Manager' from the Edit menu to add them to your gradient library or load them directly using the Gradient Editor by clicking on the Load button.

Note > Moving stops too close together can create steps or bands in the tonality of your image, creating an effect that is posterized and unnatural. It is important to realize there are limits to how much tonal manipulation an image is capable of handling before the quality suffers.

The Gradient Map adjustment layer set to Luminosity mode acts like a 'hot-wired' Levels adjustment layer. Its advantage is that you can set as many stops or 'sliders' as you like, giving the user total control. Any localized areas that require further attention can simply be masked on the adjacent layer mask and tackled separately on a second Gradient Map layer.

Note > If you have a selection active when you choose the Gradient Map adjustment layer it automatically translates the selection into a layer mask, restricting any adjustments to the selected area.

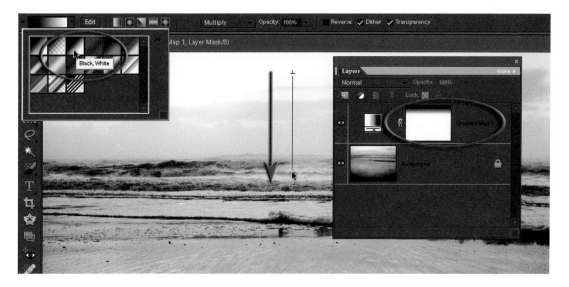

6. If you are looking to achieve a simple global contrast adjustment the project is complete. If, however, you want to enhance the image further using more gradients try the following techniques. Select the Gradient Map adjustment layer, choose the 'Gradient tool' from the Tools panel (or type the letter G on the keyboard). Choose the 'Black/White' and 'Linear' options and then drag a gradient from the top of the image window to just below the horizon line. This will shield the sky from the contrast adjustment applied by the Gradient Map adjustment layer.

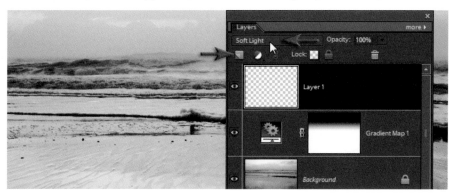

7. We will now balance the tonality in the image by darkening the sky. Click on the Create a New Layer icon in the Layers panel and set the blending mode of this new layer to 'Soft Light'.

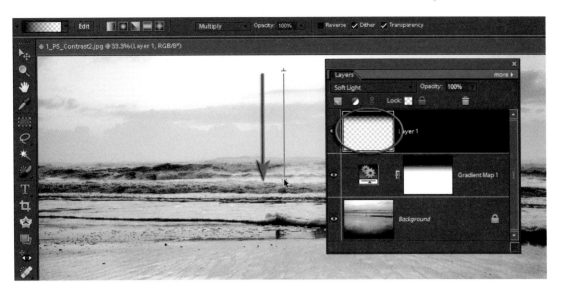

8. Ensure that black is the foreground default color (type the letter D on the keyboard) and then choose the 'Foreground to Transparent' gradient. Drag a gradient from the top of the image to a position just below the horizon line. Holding down the Shift key as you drag a gradient will 'constrain' the gradient to ensure that it is absolutely straight. Try changing the blend mode of this gradient layer to 'Overlay' and 'Multiply' to see the variations of tonality that can be achieved.

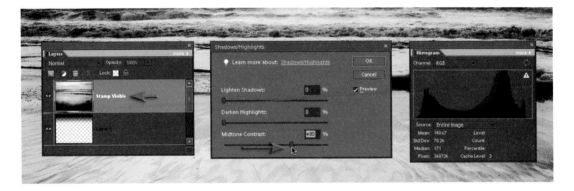

9. Yet another way of targeting tones for adjustment is using the Shadows/Highlights adjustment feature. This very useful adjustment feature is not available as an adjustment layer so you will need to create a 'composite' layer of the work carried out so far before you can apply it. This action of creating a composite layer (merging the visible elements from all of the other layers) is called 'Stamp Visible' by professional image editors (Adobe does not list this command in their menus). Select the top layer in the Layers panel and then hold down the Shift + Alt + Ctrl keys whilst you type the letter E on the keyboard. The new layer should appear on top of the layers stack. Double-click the name of the layer to rename it 'Stamp Visible'. Now choose 'Shadows/Highlights' from the Enhance > Adjust Lighting submenu. Set the Lighten Shadows and Darken Highlights sliders to 0 and raise the Midtone Contrast to +30. You can watch the effects of raising this slider by clicking on the Preview box and by viewing the histogram in the Histogram panel.

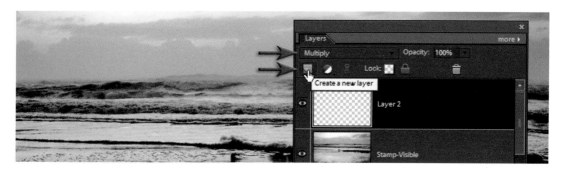

10. Create another new layer and this time set the blend mode to 'Multiply'. As with the previous gradient you can experiment with alternative blend modes after you have finished creating this second gradient.

Note > You can also set the blend mode for a new layer in the New Layer dialog box.

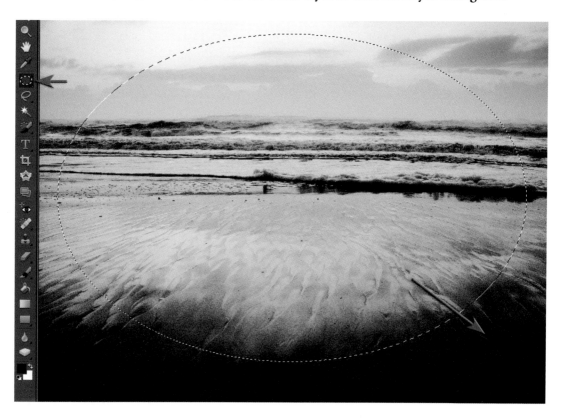

11. Choose the 'Elliptical Marquee tool' from the Tools panel and choose a large amount of feather (increase the amount of feather as the resolution of the file gets bigger). Draw an elliptical selection in the image window.

Note > You can check how soft this edge is by choosing the 'Selection Brush tool'. Choose Mask from the Mode drop-down menu in the Options bar.

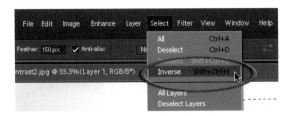

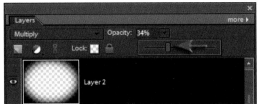

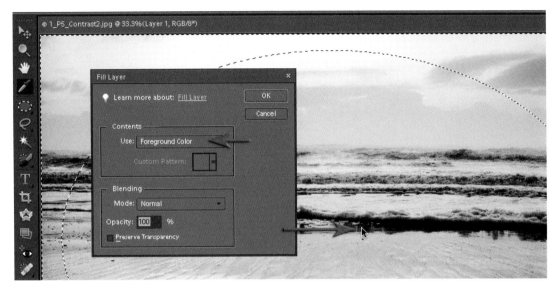

12. From the Select menu choose 'Inverse' (Shift + Ctrl + I) and then from the Edit menu choose the command 'Fill Selection'. From the Contents section of the dialog box choose 'Foreground Color'. Move the mouse cursor into the image and choose a deep blue color from the image window and then click OK. Lower the opacity of the layer until the vignette is subtle.

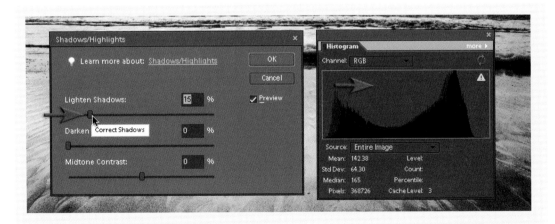

PERFORMANCE TIP
Use the Shadows/Highlights adjustment feature on the Stamp Visible layer if the darkening of the shadows becomes excessive as a result of the vignette.

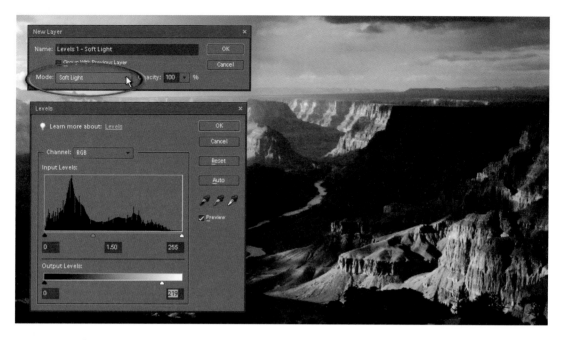

Method 4 - Blend modes

Blend modes are one of the most useful, but least understood, editing features to be found in Elements. One of the groups of layer blend modes that can be applied to layers leads to an increase in contrast of the resulting image. These blend modes can be assigned to any adjustment layer.

1. Open the canyon image from the supporting DVD and hold down the Alt key and the mouse button as you select a Levels adjustment layer. In the New Layer dialog box that opens select 'Soft Light' as the mode. What you now see (if you have the preview box checked in the dialog box) is instant contrast. This contrast is adjustable by moving any of the sliders beneath the histogram. You are able to target shadows, midtones or highlights using these sliders. Select OK to apply the changes.

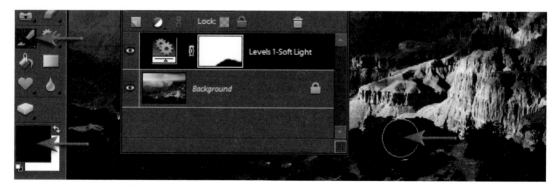

2. Select 'Black' as the foreground color and with a soft-edged brush at a reduced opacity paint out any localized contrast that is not beneficial to the final image. You should see the effects of the painting in the image and in the layer mask of the adjustment layer.

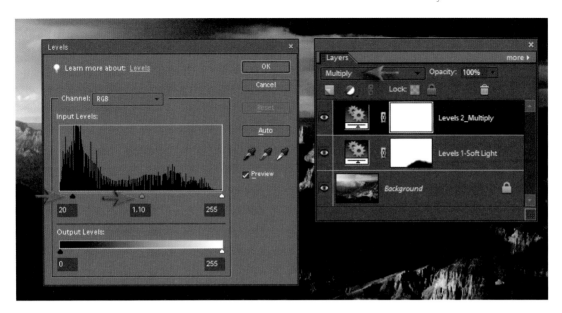

3. Create another new Levels adjustment layer and this time set the blend mode of the layer to 'Multiply'. This blend mode will darken the entire image but we will mask the lower portion of the image later. Focus your attention on just the sky and when you have increased the drama a little, select OK. Although we are focusing our attention primarily on the tonality it is still possible to change the color using the individual color channels in the Levels dialog box.

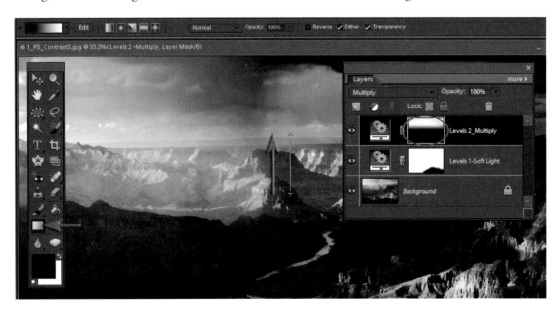

4. Select the 'Gradient tool' from the Tools panel. Select the 'Black, White' option and drag a short gradient from the center of the image up to the horizon line. The resulting mask will release the lower portion of the image from the grip of the Multiply mode but leave the drama and depth in the sky and distant landscape.

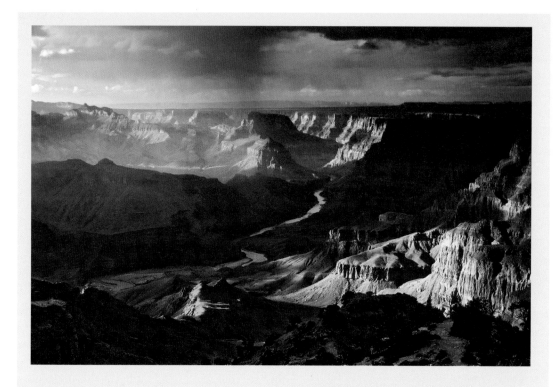

PERFORMANCE TIP

For even more drama and depth duplicate the 'Soft Light' levels adjustment layer (Ctrl + J). Lower the opacity of this layer until you achieve the contrast you are looking for. As with the previous method it is worth keeping the Histogram panel open when making these contrast adjustments so you will notice when the deepest shadows are possibly getting so dark that they will be difficult to print (below level 15). Use the Shadows/Highlights adjustment feature if this becomes the case – either on the background layer or on a new Stamp Visible layer.

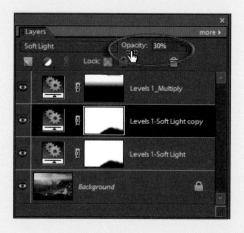

Summary

The Gradient Map adjustment layer in Luminosity mode, a Levels adjustment in Soft Light mode and the targeted adjustments offered by the Shadows/Highlights adjustment feature make the need for a Curves adjustment feature redundant. Absolute tonal and color control is just a blend mode away.

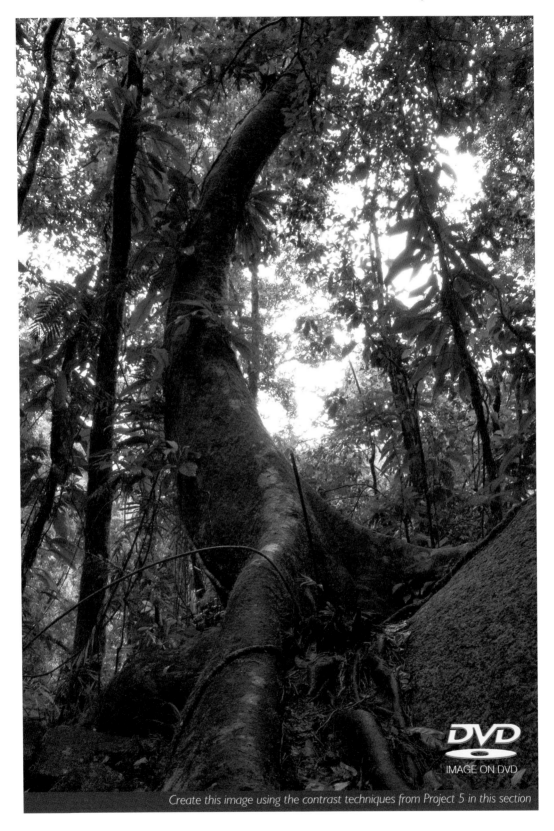

IMAGE ON DVD

Create this image using the contrast techniques from Project 5 in this section

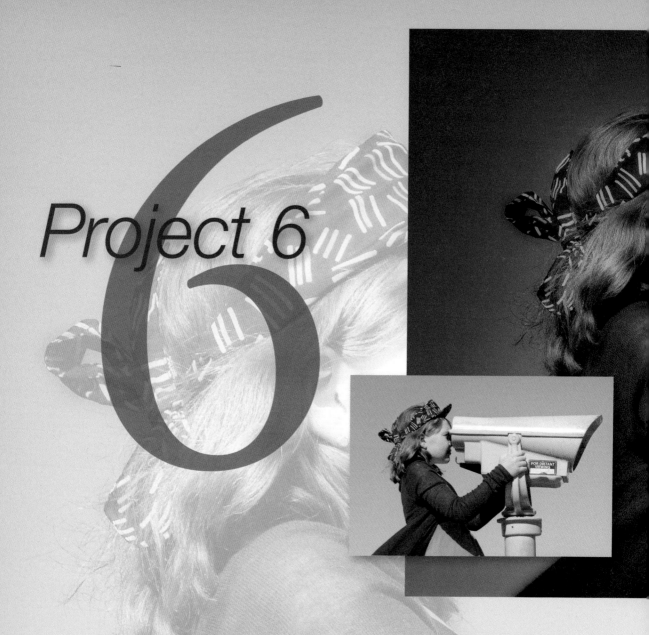

Project 6

Hue/Saturation & Luminance

Levels is a powerful adjustment feature for controlling tonality and overall color balance. It cannot, however, target and control the hue of specific color values or the saturation of color in general. For this final level of control we need to master the powerful Hue/Saturation adjustment feature. In this project we will target specific colors and then change the hue and saturation of these targeted colors to creatively enhance an image.

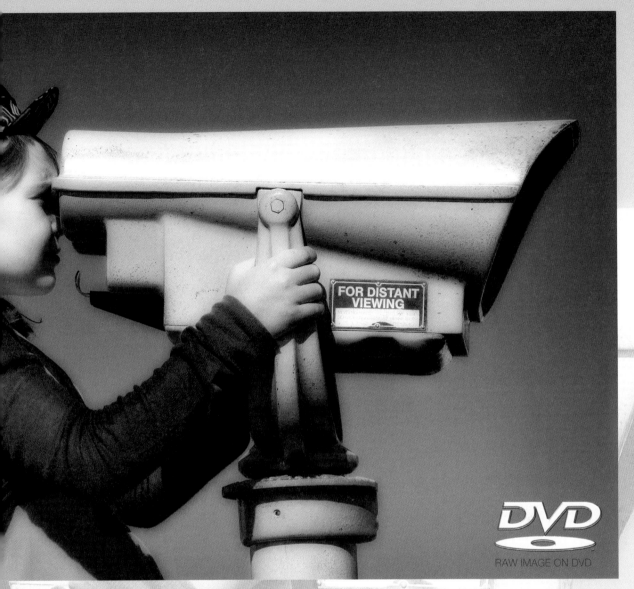

FOR DISTANT VIEWING

DVD

RAW IMAGE ON DVD

Target and adjust the hue, saturation and luminance of selected colors within the image - the blues are made darker and the magentas are moved towards blue. The image is then completed using two of the Maximum Performance actions

The third slider in the Hue/Saturation dialog is the Lightness slider and this is so useful (not), that Adobe decided to leave its name off the name of the adjustment layer. It doesn't matter whether you decide to make the selected color lighter or darker the slider always desaturates the target color. In this project we will explore how to adjust how bright the color appears without desaturating it. This is all made possible with the new Smart Brushes that come with the DVD and some very clever Maximum Performance know-how.

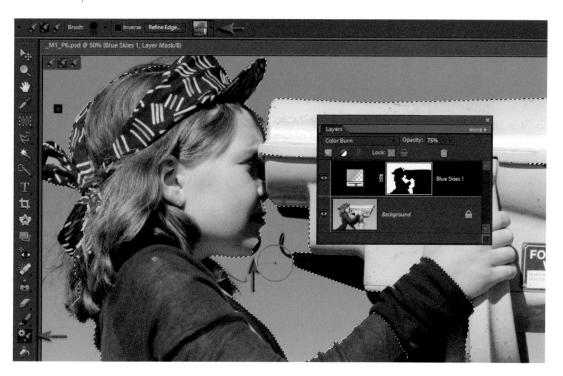

1. In Photoshop Elements 7 it is possible to paint with adjustment presets using either the new Smart Brush Tool or Detail Smart Brush Tool. The Smart Brush tool creates its own mask as it paints the adjustment by looking for the edges of your subject matter. In the example above the Smart Brush Tool is used in conjunction with the Blue Skies preset to increase the vibrancy of the existing sky. If the adjustment invades your subject you can hold down the Alt key and then paint to remove the adjustment in this area. In areas where there is low edge contrast this preset can be difficult to apply. A Hue/Saturation adjustment can also be used to target colors and adjust them without upsetting other colors in the image.

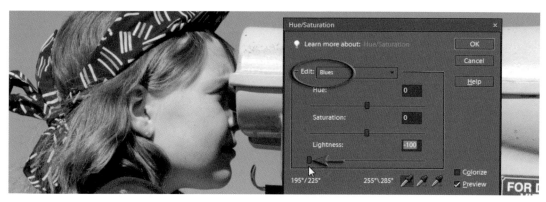

2. Although a Hue/Saturation adjustment layer can be used to effectively adjust the hue or saturation of a selected color (Blues have been selected in the image above) it is less than effective for controlling the brightness of the target color. Note how the blue appears desaturated when the Lightness slider is moved to –100.

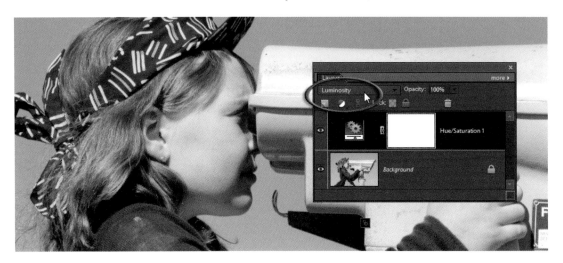

3. Switching the mode of the Hue/Saturation layer to Luminosity will help to restore the saturation levels of the adjusted color but the darkening of lightening effects are limited when using this technique and any Hue or Saturation adjustments that have been made using this adjustment layer are also removed. A better way to adjust the brightness of a target color is to use emulate the powerful and superior Luminance sliders that can be found in Photoshop Lightroom. If you have installed the Maximum Performance actions and presets from the supporting DVD you will be able to create a much darker sky by adjusting the existing colors using the power of my MP7 Luminance presets.

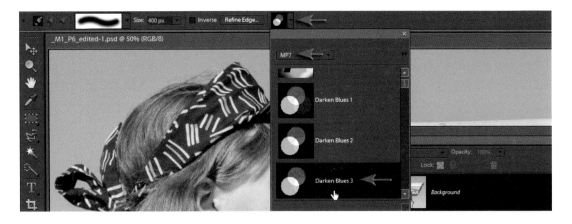

4. The MP7 Luminance presets (designed to make a target color lighter or darker) can be selected from the Options bar after first selecting the Smart Brush Tool or Detail Smart Brush Tool. The Detail Smart Brush Tool does not have the edge detection capability of the Smart Brush Tool but is quicker to use when there is no need for edge detection, i.e. the neighboring colors surrounding the area you want to adjust are a different hue. Select the Darker Blues 3 preset in the Options bar and then paint over the sky with large soft brush (the presets come in 3 strengths, mild, medium and extra strong – 3 being the strongest adjustment).

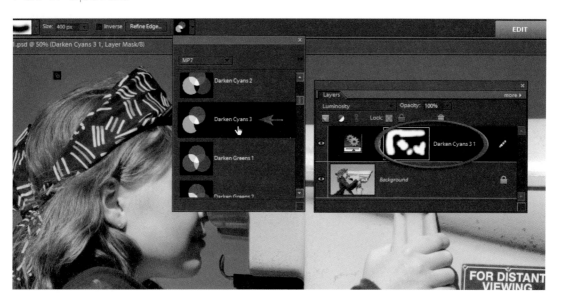

5. In the Layers panel you will see that an adjustment layer has been created. You cannot edit this preset by double-clicking on the Layer thumbnail but you can lower the opacity or click on an alternative color in the Preset options. In the illustration above I have clicked on the Darker Cyans 3 preset to more effectively target the sky in this image (the hue of the sky is closer to Cyan than Blue).

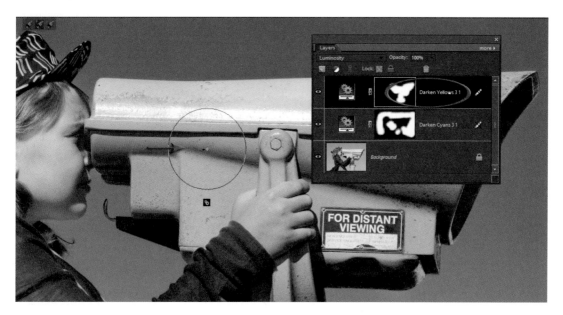

6. To adjust another color you must first click on the Background layer so that when you click on a new preset it does no change the first adjustment. In the illustration above I have selected the Darker yellows 3 preset and then painted over the bright yellow tones in the image to lower their luminance value.

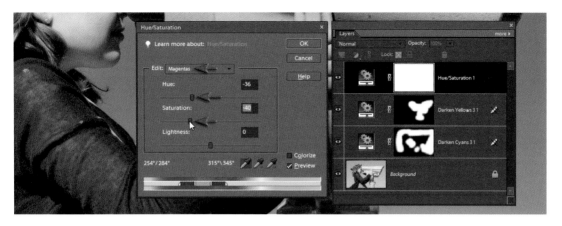

7. The third color adjustment in this project does not need to use the luminance presets. Select a Hue/Saturation adjustment from the Create new adjustment menu in the Layers panel and select Magentas from the Edit pull-down menu. Move the Hue and Saturation sliders to the left to adjust the magenta to a desaturated blue color. Select OK to apply the changes.

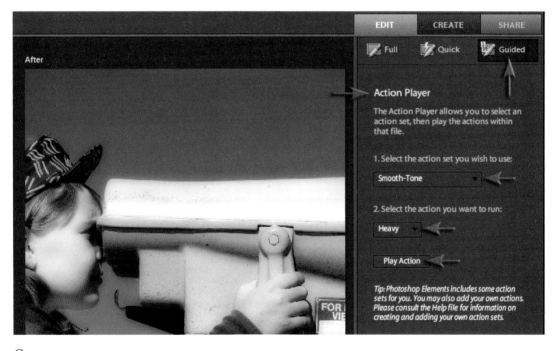

8. To complete this project we will use two of the Maximum Performance actions that come with the supporting DVD. First you will need to Flatten the image (Layer > Flatten Image) or stamp the visible elements of all four layers in the Layers panel into a single new layer (hold down the Shift + Ctrl + Alt keys and press the E key). To access these actions open the right panel and click on the Guided edit option and select the new Action Player from the Automated Actions section. Select the Smooth-Tone action set (you will need to scroll down to find it) and then select the Heavy option. Click on the Play Action button to run the action and give the image smoother tones.

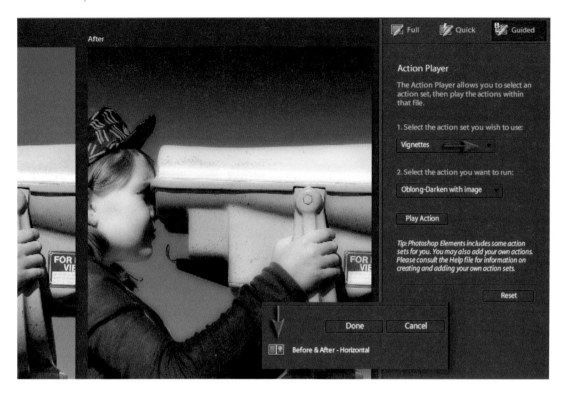

9. We can use the Action Player to apply a Maximum Performance vignette to the image. The Oblong-Darken with image vignette has been optimized to darken the edges of the image without excessively darkening any highlight details at the edge of the frame. In the Bottom-right hand corner of the panel you can access a before and after button. Click on the Full button at the top of the panel to return to the main editing space.

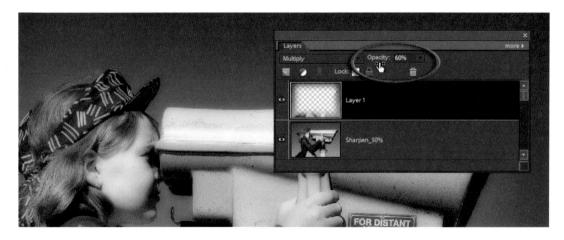

10. In the Layers panel you can observe all of the layers that have been used to create these two effects. If you want to decrease the strength of the vignette simply lower the opacity of the layer in the Layers panel until the appropriate level of darkening is achieved.

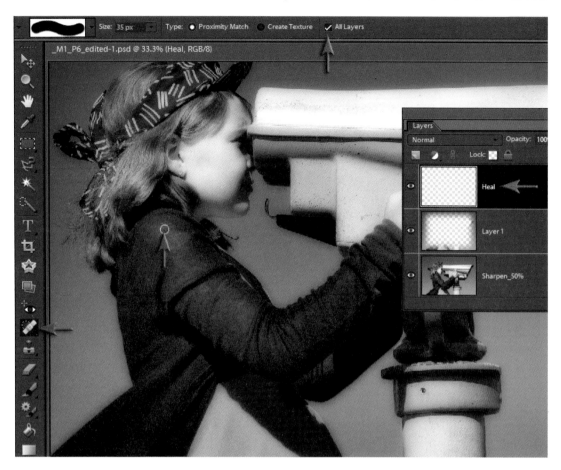

11. To complete the project we can digitally darn a couple of annoying holes in the top the girl is wearing. Click on the Create a new layer icon in the Layers panel and then select the Spot Healing Brush Tool in the Tools panel. Select the All Layers option in the Options bar. Adjust the size of the brush in the Options bar until the brush cursor is slightly larger than the hole in the fabric at the top of the arm. Click once to heal this area (replacing the offending pixels with color and texture from the surrounding area).

Note > The Maximum Performance DVD comes with dozens of useful actions that will help you create visually stunning images and enhance your editing workflows. They turn lengthy, and often complex, editing procedures into simple-to-apply effects that are non-destructive to your background image. Ally layers used to create the effect are left so that you can adjust the technique to fit your own imaging needs.

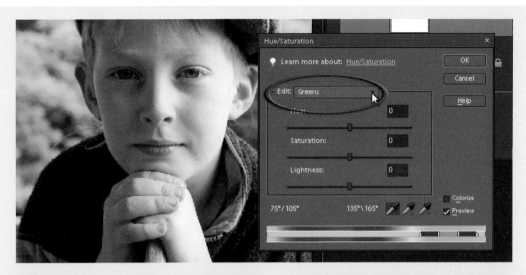

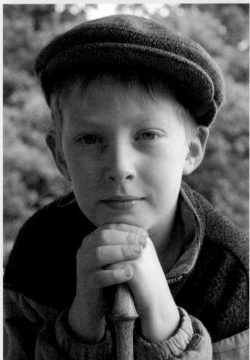

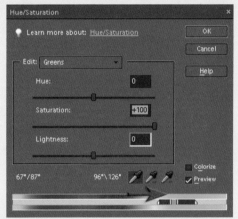

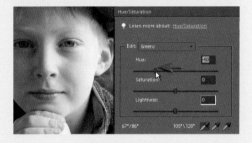

The Hue/Saturation technique has many applications – from changing one odd bloom in a bouquet of flowers to color coordinating a background color with your subject. If you can't capture your subject against the perfect color backdrop it is usually an option to capture it against a color that has nothing in common with the general skin tones and hair color of your subject, e.g. blue sky or green foliage – just remember to mask the blue or green eyes.

Note > It is possible to increase or restrict the range of colors that are targeted by adjusting the sliders on the color ramp at the base of the dialog.

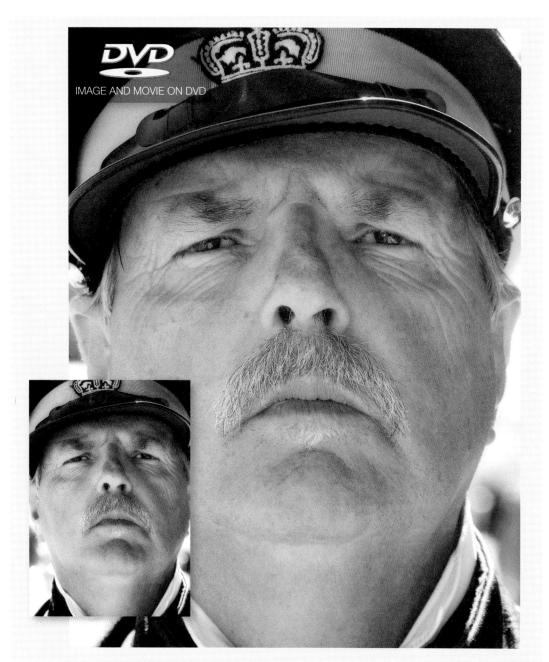

A Hue/Saturation adjustment layer can be used to accurately target an extremely narrow range of colors. In the example above the sunburnt colors on the man's face have been targeted and then adjusted to match the surrounding skin colors. The movie and image used to demonstrate this advanced technique are available on the supporting DVD.

Note > This technique is not recommended as an alternative to an effective sunscreen or a good broad-rimmed hat!

Project 7

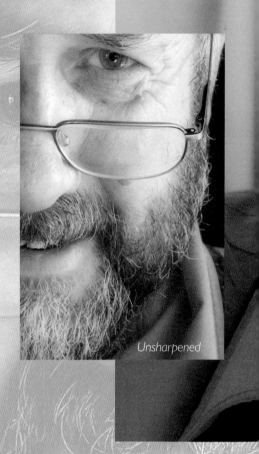

Unsharpened

Sharpening

All digital images require sharpening – even if shot on a state-of-the-art digital SLR in focus. Most cameras can sharpen in-camera but the highest quality sharpening is achieved in post-production. Elements will allow you to select the amount and the areas that require sharpening most. For images destined for print, the monitor preview is just that – a preview. The actual amount of sharpening required for optimum image quality is usually a little more than looks comfortable on screen – especially when using an LCD/TFT monitor (flat panel).

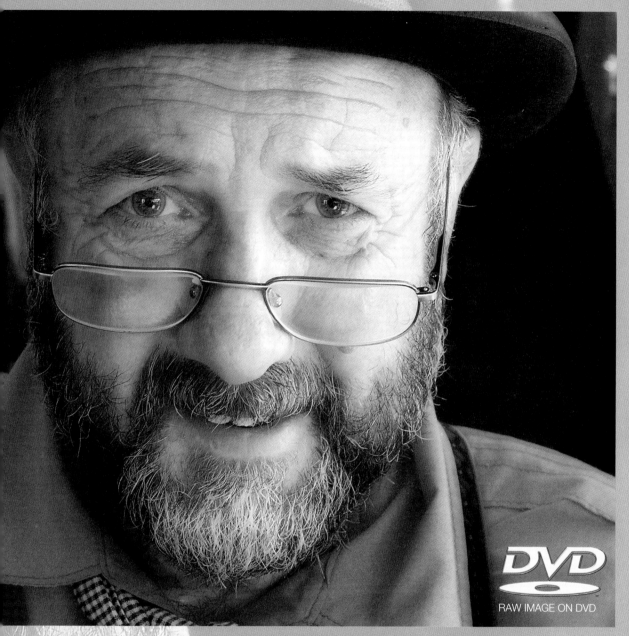

RAW IMAGE ON DVD

Advanced sharpening – targeted sharpening for maximum impact

The basic concept of sharpening is to send the Unsharp Mask filter on a 'seek and manipulate' mission. The filter is programmed to make the pixels on the lighter side of any edge it finds lighter still, and the pixels on the darker side of the edge darker. Think of it as a localized contrast control. Too much and people in your images start to look radioactive (they glow), not enough and the viewers of your images start reaching for the reading glasses they don't own.

The art of advanced sharpening

The best sharpening techniques are those that prioritize the important areas for sharpening and leave the smoother areas of the image well alone, e.g. sharpening the eyes of a portrait but avoiding the skin texture. These advanced techniques are essential when sharpening images that have been scanned from film or have excessive noise, neither of which needs accentuating by the Unsharp Mask. So let the project begin.

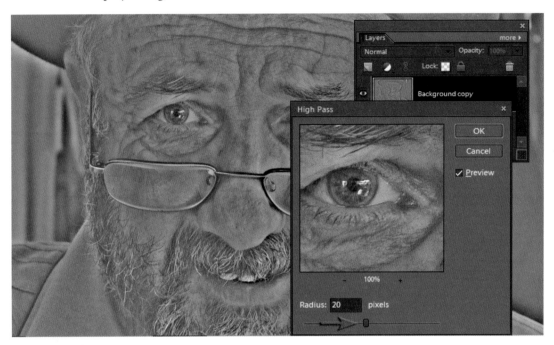

1. Duplicate the background layer by dragging it to the New Layer icon in the Layers panel. Go to 'Filter > Other > High Pass'. Increase the pixel Radius to around 20 to 30 pixels for a 6 to 12 megapixel image. Select OK. Apply the Despeckle filter (Filter > Noise > Despeckle) and also the Dust and Scratches filter (Filter > Noise > Dust and Scratches) using a Radius value of 1 pixel and the Threshold slider set to 0 Levels.

Note > The High Pass filter is sometimes used as an alternative to the Unsharp Mask if the duplicate layer is set to 'Overlay' or 'Soft Light' mode. In this project, however, we are using the High Pass filter to locate the edges within the image only.

PERFORMANCE TIP

If you have any sharpening options in your camera or scanner it is important to switch them off or set them to minimum or low. The sharpening features found in most capture devices are often very crude when compared to the following technique. It is also not advisable to sharpen images that have been saved as JPEG files using high-compression/low-quality settings. The sharpening process that follows should also come at the end of the editing process, i.e. adjust the color and tonality of the image before starting this advanced sharpening technique.

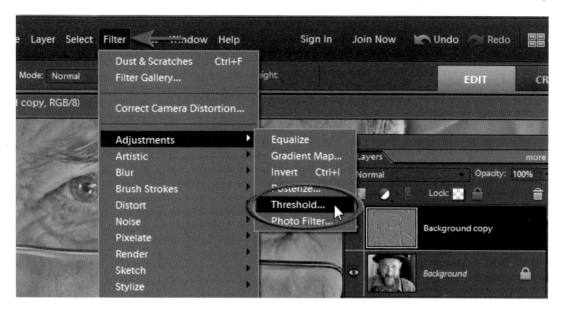

2. Apply a Threshold filter to the High Pass layer from the Filter > Adjustments submenu. The threshold will reduce this layer to two levels – black and white – depending on the brightness value.

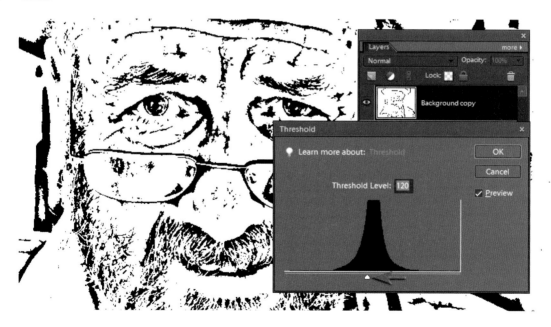

3. Drag the slider just below the histogram to isolate the edges that require sharpening. The aim of moving these sliders is to render all of those areas you do not want to sharpen white (or nearly white). Select OK when you are done. You are half way to creating a sharpening mask. The mask will restrict the sharpening process to the edges only (the edges that you have just defined). Increasing or decreasing the radius in the High Pass filter will render the lines thicker or thinner.

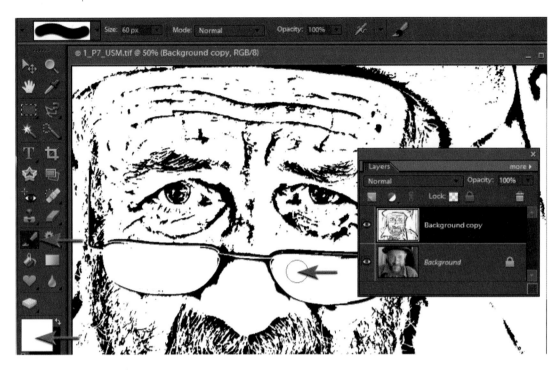

4. Paint out any areas that were not rendered white by the Threshold adjustment that you do not want to be sharpened, e.g. in the portrait used in this example any pixels remaining in the skin away from the eyes, mouth, nose and background were painted over using the Brush tool with 'White' selected as the foreground color.

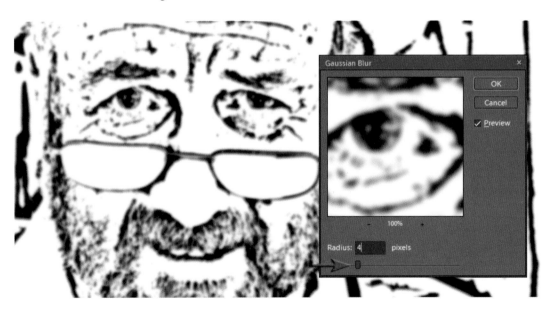

5. Go to 'Filter > Blur > Gaussian Blur' and apply a 4-pixel Radius to blur this layer. This step will ensure that the sharpening process will fade in slowly rather than have an abrupt edge.

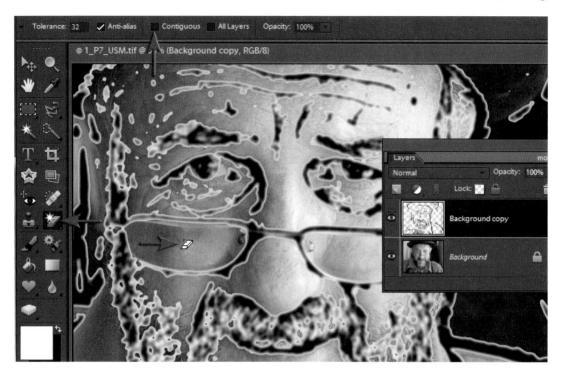

6. Select the 'Magic Eraser tool' in the Tools panel (behind the Eraser tool). Deselect the 'Contiguous' option in the Options bar and then click on any white area within the image. You should be left with only the edge detail on this layer and none of the white areas. The image will appear a little strange until we complete the next couple of steps.

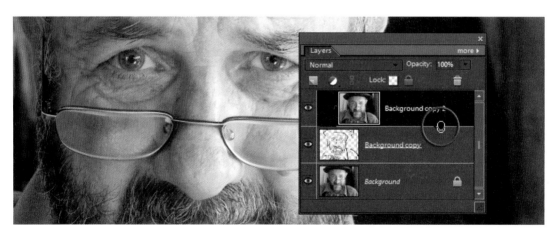

7. Duplicate the background layer and drag this duplicate layer to the top of the layers stack. Ensure the image is zoomed in to 100% for a small image or 50% for a larger print resolution image. From the Layer menu select 'Group with Previous' or position the mouse cursor between the two layers in the Layers panel, hold down the Alt key, and then click when the Group with Previous icon appears. The transparent areas on the Threshold layer will act as a mask so only the important areas of the image will appear sharpened.

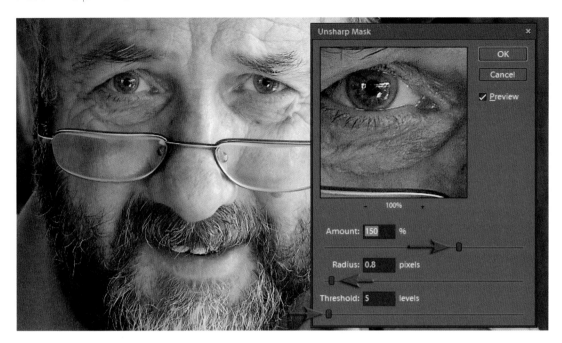

8. Go to 'Enhance > Unsharp Mask'. Adjust the Amount slider to between 80 and 150%. This controls how much darker or lighter the pixels at the edges are rendered. Choose an amount slightly more than what looks comfortable on screen if the image is destined for print rather than screen. The Radius slider should be set to 0.5 for screen images and between 0.8 and 1.5 pixels for print resolution images. The Radius slider controls the width of the edge that is affected by the Amount slider. Raising the Threshold slider to 5 will prevent the Unsharp Mask from sharpening the noise within this image. If the Threshold slider is raised too high the Unsharp Mask will not sharpen the lower contrast edges.

Note > For low noise images (DSLR images where the ISO setting is low) you may get a superior result by using the Adjust Sharpness rather than the Unsharp Mask.

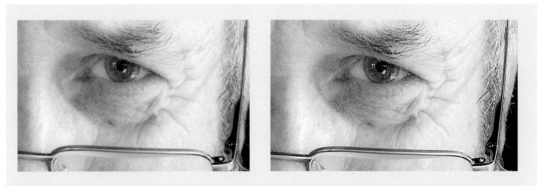

PERFORMANCE TIP
If you are sharpening an excessively 'noisy' or 'grainy' image the Threshold slider is moved progressively higher to avoid sharpening non-image data. The exact Threshold setting is not so critical for this advanced technique.

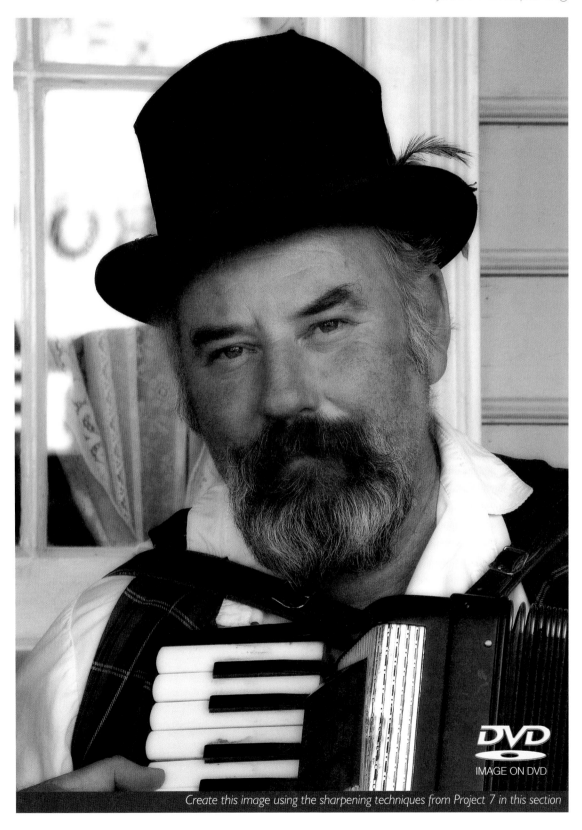

Create this image using the sharpening techniques from Project 7 in this section

Project 8

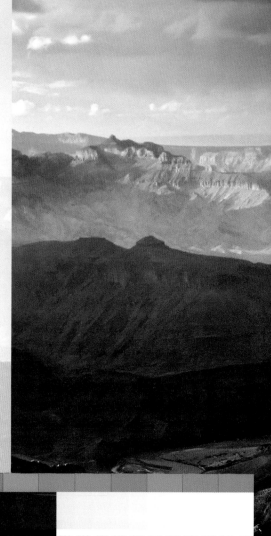

| 0 | 3 | 5 | 8 | 10 | 13 | 15 | 18 | 20 | 23 | 26 | 229 | 232 | 235 | 237 | 240 | 242 | 245 | 247 | 250 | 252 | 255 |

Printing

The secret to successful printing is to adopt a professional print workflow that takes the frustration out of seeing the colors shift as your image moves from camera to monitor, and from monitor to print. Color consistency has never been more easy and affordable to implement for the keen amateur and professional photographer. This project guides you along the path to ultimate print satisfaction, so that you will never say those often heard words ever again – 'why do the colors of my print look different to my monitor?'

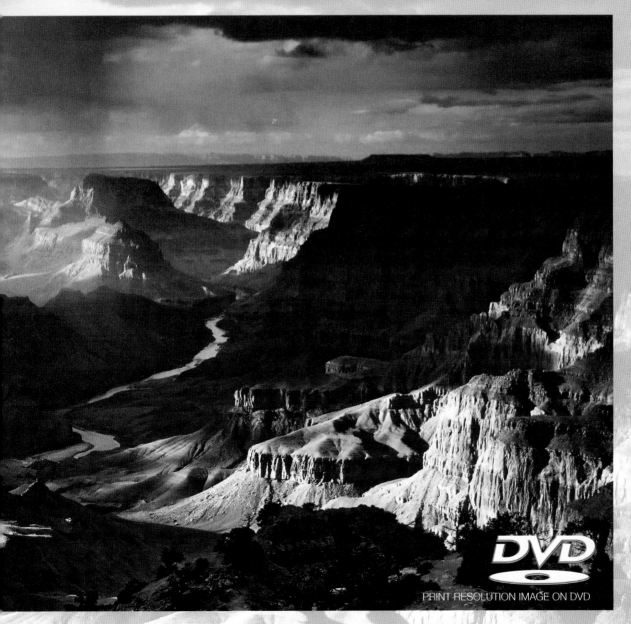

PRINT RESOLUTION IMAGE ON DVD

Adopt a color management workflow that delivers predictable prints every time

The reward for your effort (a small capital outlay and a little button pushing) is perfect pixels – color consistency from camera to screen to print. Once the initial work has been carried out predictable color is a real 'no-brainer', as all of the settings can be saved as presets. As soon as you start printing using your new color-managed workflow you will not only enjoy superior and predictable prints, but you will also quickly recover the money you outlaid to implement this workflow (no more second and third attempts).

The problem and the solution

Have you ever walked into a TV shop or the cabin of an aircraft and noticed that all the TVs are all showing the exactly the same TV program but no two pictures are the same color? All of the TVs are receiving exactly the same signal but each TV has its own unique way of displaying color (its own unique 'color characteristics'). Different settings on each TV for brightness, contrast and color only make the problem worse.

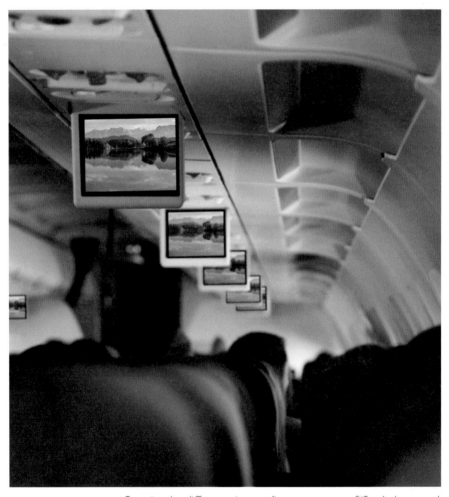

One signal – different pictures (image courtesy of iStockphoto.com)

In the perfect world there would be a way of making sure that all of the TVs could synchronize their settings for brightness, contrast and color, and the unique color characteristics of each TV could be measured and taken into account when displaying a picture. If this could be achieved we could then send 10 different TVs the same picture so that the image appeared nearly identical on all TVs, irrespective of make, model or age. In the world of digital photography, Adobe has made the illusive goal of color consistency possible by implementing a concept and workflow called Color Management. Color Management, at first glance, can seem like an incredibly complex science for the keen amateur to get their head around, but if just a few simple steps are observed and implemented then color consistency can be yours.

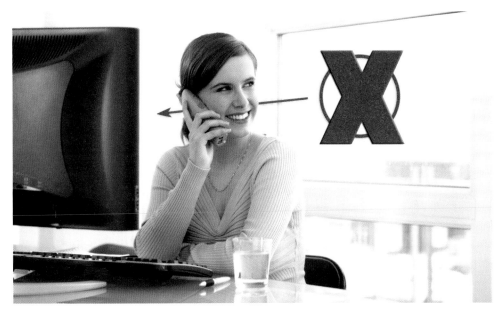

Don't position your monitor so that it faces a window and lower the room lighting so that your monitor is the brightest thing in your field of vision (image courtesy of iStockphoto.com)

Step 1 - Preparing your print workshop

The first step is to optimize the room where your monitor lives. Ideally, the monitor should be brighter than the daylight used to light the room and positioned so the monitor does not reflect any windows or lights in the room (the biggest problems will all be behind you and over your shoulders as you sit at the monitor). Professionals often build hoods around their monitors to prevent stray light falling on the surface of the monitor but if you carefully position the monitor in the room you should be able to avoid this slightly 'geeky' step. Stray light that falls on your monitor will lower the apparent contrast of the image being displayed and could lead you to add more contrast when it is not required. The color of light in the room (warm or cool) is also a critical factor in your judgement of color on the screen. It is advisable to light the room using daylight but this should not be allowed to reflect off brightly colored surfaces in the room, e.g. brightly painted walls or even the brightly colored top you may be wearing when you are sitting in front of your monitor. If the room is your own personal space, or your partner supports your passion/obsession/addiction for digital imaging, then you could go that bit further and paint your walls a neutral gray. The lighting in the room should be entirely daylight – without the possibility of warm sunlight streaming into the room at certain times of the day. The brightness of the daylight in the room can be controlled with blinds or you can introduce artificial daylight by purchasing color corrected lights, e.g. Solux halogen globes or daylight fluorescent lights. If the above recommendations are difficult to achieve, lower the level of the room lighting significantly.

Overview of step 1 > Position your computer monitor so that it does not reflect any windows, lights or brightly colored walls in the room (when you sit at the monitor a neutral colored wall, without a window, should be behind you). Use daylight or daylight globes to light the room and make sure the room lighting is not as bright as the monitor (the monitor should be the brightest thing in your field of view).

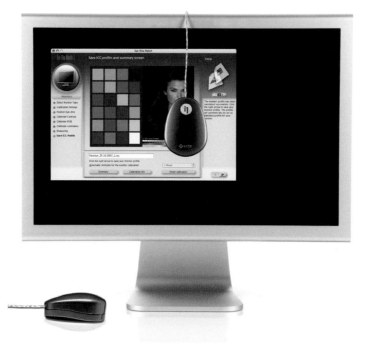

Step 2 - Preparing the monitor

Purchase a monitor calibration device (available for as little as US$100 from X-Rite, ColorVision or Pantone) and follow the step-by-step instructions. The calibration process only takes a few minutes once you have read through the instructions and adjusted a few settings on your monitor. It is now widely accepted that photographers should choose a D65 whitepoint (how cool or warm tones appear on your monitor) and a Gamma of 2.2 (this controls how bright your midtones are on your monitor). The next time you use your calibrated and profiled monitor, Photoshop Elements will pick up the new profile to ensure you are seeing the real color of the image file rather than a version that has been distorted by the monitor's idiosyncrasies and inappropriate default settings.

MONITOR CALIBRATOR RECOMMENDATIONS

If you are on a budget I recommend the ColorVision Spyder 2 Express or the Pantone Huey. If you have a little more money and are looking for a really professional tool, then the Eye One Display 2 is my personal favorite, although it costs a little more. If you decide on the Spyder 2 Express I found the only hiccup in an otherwise easy-to-follow guide was the instruction on how to decide whether your LCD monitor had a 'brightness' or 'backlight' control. As the vast majority of LCD monitors use a 'backlight' to control brightness I think this information is a possible source of confusion. The tiny Pantone Huey is really easy to use, completes the process in just a few minutes, and has an option to measure the brightness of the room and then adjust the brightness of the monitor accordingly. I would recommend that you lower the brightness of the LCD monitor to a setting of between 50 and 75% before calibrating an LCD screen with the Huey. The automatic brightness adjustment of the monitor is only useful if you can't maintain a standard level of illumination in your room. If you think small is cute, then the Huey will do an admirable job and you can put it in your shirtpocket when you're done.

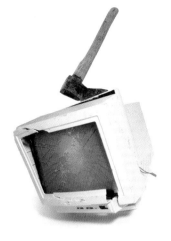

If you are working on a tired and old CRT monitor (one of the ones that look like an old TV) and would like to pursue color consistency, now might be the time to treat yourself to that sleek new LCD monitor you have been promising yourself for ages (the useful life expectancy for a CRT for color critical work is no more than three years). If you currently use a laptop screen I would recommend that you purchase a separate desktop monitor for your color-critical editing work

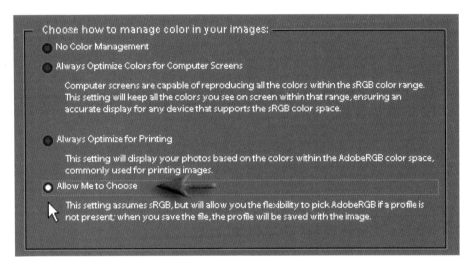

Step 3 - Preparing Photoshop Elements' 'Color Settings'

Photoshop Elements can work with the range of colors (called a color gamut) that can be displayed on a monitor and also those that can be printed using inks and dyes. To work with these additional colors that are out of the range of most monitors, Adobe implemented the concept of using a 'working space' instead of a monitor space for editing digital images. Photoshop Elements has a choice of two working spaces, sRGB and Adobe RGB. When creating images for screen or web viewing use the sRGB working space and when preparing images for print use the Adobe RGB working space. The Adobe RGB color space makes use of a larger color gamut than sRGB – a range of colors that can typically be reproduced by inkjet printers. Go to your Edit menu in Photoshop and open the 'Color Settings' dialog box. Select the 'Allow Me to Choose' option.

PERFORMANCE TIP
When preparing the same images for both print and the web use the Adobe RGB profile. After optimizing the images for print you can then duplicate the images and convert the color profile of the images destined for the web to sRGB (Image > Convert Color Profile > Apply sRGB Profile).

Step 4 - Preparing to print to your own inkjet printer

Just as the color characteristics of the monitor had to be measured and profiled in order to achieve accurate color between camera and monitor, a profile also has to be created that describes the color characteristics of the printer. This ensures color accuracy is maintained between the monitor and the final print. When an accurate profile of the printer has been created Photoshop Elements, rather than the printer, can then be instructed to manage the colors to maintain color consistency. Photoshop Elements can only achieve this remarkable task because it knows (courtesy of the custom profile) how the printer skews color.

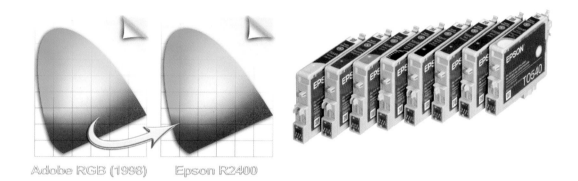

Adobe RGB (1998)   Epson R2400

If you hope to achieve optimum print quality at home it is recommended that you use a photo-quality printer (one with six or more inks), one that will let Photoshop Elements manage the colors for the best results. A custom profile is only accurate so long as you stick to the same ink and paper. Additional profiles will need to be created for every paper surface you would like to use. Printers come shipped with profiles, but these are of the 'one size fits all' variety, affectionately known as 'canned profiles'. For optimum quality, custom printer profiles need to be made for the unique characteristics of every printer (even if they are of the same brand and model number).

PERFORMANCE TIP

In an attempt to make the first time not too memorable, for all the wrong reasons, check that your ink cartridges are not about to run out of ink and that you have a plentiful supply of good quality paper (same surface and same make). Refilling your ink cartridges with a no-name brand and using cheap paper is not recommended if you want to achieve absolute quality and consistency. I would recommend that you stick with the same brand of inks that came shipped with your printer and use the same manufacturer's paper until you have achieved your first successful workflow.

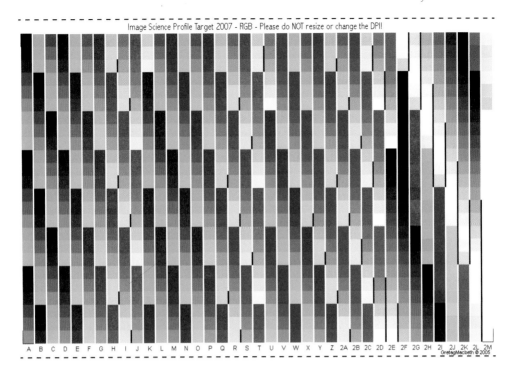

Step 5 - Download a profile target

You can profile your printer, but the equipment is expensive. You can, however, print out a sample pattern and mail it to a company that has the equipment and will make the profile for you. Download a profile target from the website of the company who will create your custom printer profile. The target print can be mailed back to the company and your profile can be emailed back to you once it has been created by analyzing the test print you created.

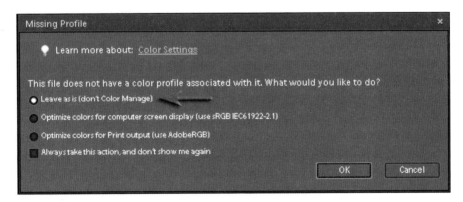

Step 6 - Open the profile target file in Photoshop Elements

Open the target print you have downloaded from your profile service provider and select 'Leave as is' in the 'Missing Profile' dialog box. If the file opens and no dialog box appears then close the file and check that you have changed the Color Settings as outlined in step 3. The color swatches on the target print must remain unchanged by the color management mechanisms for this process to be effective.

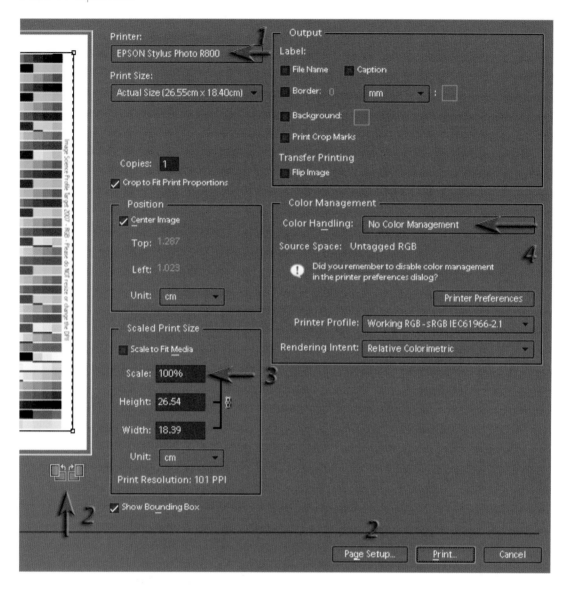

Step 7 - Print settings in Photoshop Elements

When the target image is open in Photoshop Elements proceed to 'File > Print'.

1. Select your printer from the 'Printer' menu.
2. Click on the 'Page Setup' to choose the size of your printing paper (large enough to print the target image at 100%). **Note >** You can also rotate the image or rotate the paper orientation within the Page Setup dialog box.
3. Make sure that the scale is set to 100%.
4. In the 'Color Management' section of the dialog box choose 'No Color Management' for the Color Handling option. The Source Space should read 'Untagged RGB' and there will be a reminder to switch off the color management in the Printer Preferences dialog which we will do in the next step.

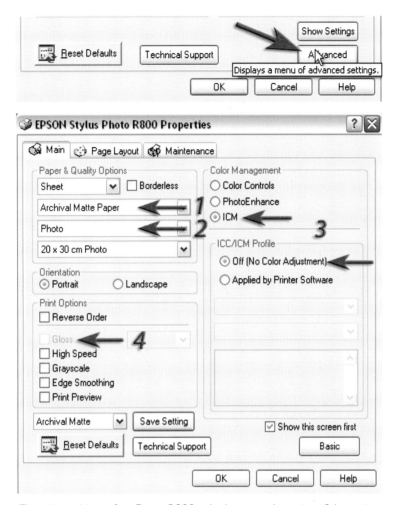

The printer driver of an Epson R800 - the layout and naming of the various options will vary between different makes and models of printers

Step 8 - Printer Preferences

Click on Printer Preferences in Photoshop's printer dialog box (in the Color Management section) and then choose the 'Advanced' options in your printer driver if available. In the printer driver dialog box choose the paper or media type (1), photo print quality (2) and switch off the color management (3), any Auto settings, a 'Gloss' option (4) if available and, for owners of Canon printers, make sure the 'Print Type' is set to 'NONE'. The precise wording for switching off the color management in the printer driver will vary depending on the make of the printer and the operating system your are using. When using an Epson or Canon printer you may see that color management is referred to as ICM or ICC. Other manufacturers may refer to letting the software (Photoshop Elements) manage the color. When you print this target print, the colors are effectively printed in their raw state. In this way the lab that creates your profile can measure how the colors vary from one printer to another and they can then create a unique profile that best describes what your printer does with standard 'unmanaged' color.

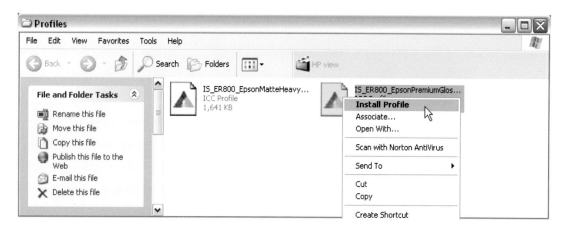

Step 9 - Install your custom profile

Send the target print to the profiling company so that it can be measured using the sophisticated and expensive profiling hardware and software that is best left to the experts. They will email you the profiles after just a few days as an attachment. Right-click the profile and choose Install, and Windows will install it in the correct location.

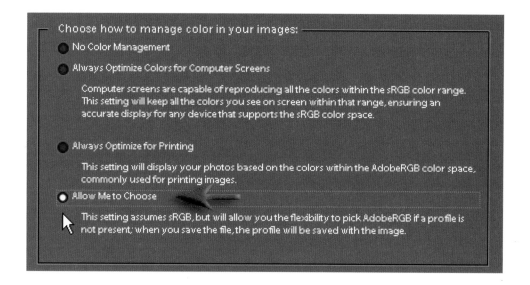

Step 10 - Tag your images with the Adobe RGB profile

When you have installed your custom printer profile make sure that most of your images destined for print are tagged with the Adobe RGB profile. Select the Adobe RGB profile in the camera if possible (digital SLR cameras and many prosumer fixed-lens digicams allow the photographer to choose this setting). Change the Color Settings in Photoshop Elements (Edit > Color Settings) to 'Always Optimize for Printing'. Changing the 'Color Settings' to Always Optimize for Printing in Photoshop Elements will ensure any files being opened from Adobe Camera Raw will automatically be tagged with the Adobe RGB profile rather than the sRGB profile.

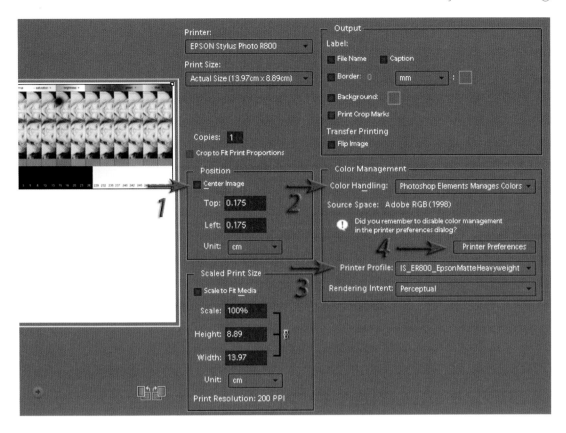

Step 11 - Select Photoshop Elements Manages Colors

It is recommended that the first print you make using your custom profile is a test image – one that has a broad range of colors and tones. A test image with skin tones can be very useful for testing the accuracy of your new print workflow. A small test image is provided on the supporting DVD. When you next open the 'Print' dialog box make sure you change the previous setting used to print the profile target from 'Printer Manages Colors' to 'Photoshop Elements Manages Colors'. Then select your new custom profile from the Printer Profile menu.

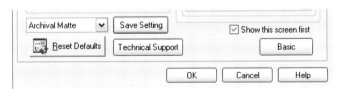

Step 12 - Making printer presets for quick and easy printing

From the Printer Preferences menu select the same settings that were used to print the profile target (don't forget to ensure the color management is turned 'OFF'). Save a 'Preset' or 'Setting' for all of the printing options so that you only choose this one setting each time your revisit this dialog box. View your first print using bright daylight and you will discover, if you have followed these directions to the letter, that you have almost certainly found a solution to one of the mysteries of digital color photography – the search for predictable color.

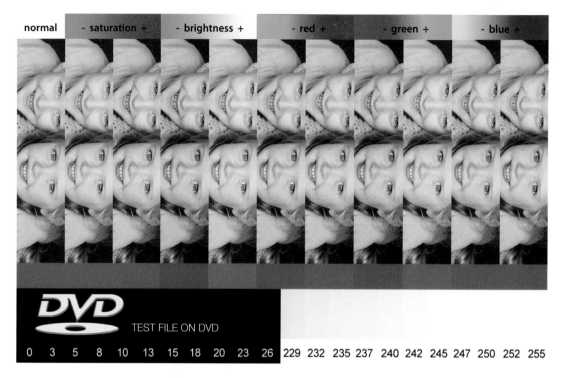

normal	- saturation +	- brightness +	- red +	- green +	- blue +

TEST FILE ON DVD

0 3 5 8 10 13 15 18 20 23 26 **229 232 235 237 240 242 245 247 250 252 255**

Use the test file to help you target the perfect color balance quickly and efficiently

Step 13 - Assessing the test print for accuracy

View the print using daylight (not direct sunlight) when the print is dry, and look for differences between the print and the screen image in terms of hue (color), saturation and brightness.

1. Check that the color swatches at the top of the image are saturated and printing without tracking marks or banding (there should be a gradual transition of color). If there is a problem with missing colors, tracking lines or saturation, clean the printer heads using the Maintenance setting in the Printer Driver.
2. View the skin tones to assess the appropriate level of saturation.
3. View the gray tones directly beneath the images of the children to determine if there is a color cast present in the image. The five tones on the extreme left are gray in the image file. If these print as gray then no further color correction is required.

PERFORMANCE TIP

Any differences between the monitor and the print will usually now be restricted to the differences in color gamuts between RGB monitors and CMYK printers. The vast majority of colors are shared by both output devices but some of the very saturated primary colors on your monitor (red, green and blue) may appear slightly less saturated in print. Choose a printer with an inkset that uses additional primary inks if you want to achieve the maximum gamut from a printer.

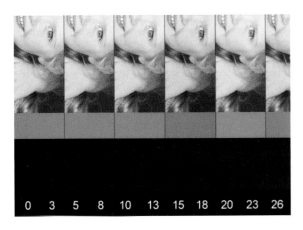

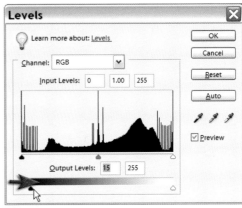

Step 14 - Maximizing shadow and highlight detail

Examine the base of the test strip to establish the optimum highlight and shadow levels that can be printed with the media you have chosen to use. If the shadow tones between level 15 and level 20 are visible on screen but are printing as black then you could either try choosing an alternative media type in the printer driver or establish a Levels adjustment layer to resolve the problem in your Photoshop Elements. The bottom left-hand slider in the Levels dialog box should be moved to the right to reduce the level of black ink being printed (raise it to a value of no higher than 10 if you wish to preserve your black point). This should allow dark shadow detail to be visible in the second print.

Note > It is important to apply these Output level adjustments to an adjustment layer only as these specific adjustments apply only to the output device and media you are currently testing.

PERFORMANCE TIP

Materials
Start by using the printer manufacturer's recommended ink and paper.
Use premium grade 'photo paper' for maximum quality.

Monitor
Position your monitor so that it is clear of reflections.
Let your monitor warm up for a while before judging image quality.
Calibrate your monitor using a calibration device.

Adobe
Set the Color Settings of the Adobe software to allow you to use the Adobe RGB profile.
Select 'Photoshop Elements Manages Color'.
Use a six-ink (or more) inkjet printer or better for maximum quality.
Select the 'Media Type' in the Printer Software dialog box.
Select a high dpi setting (1440 dpi or greater) or 'Photo' quality setting.
Use a custom printer profile.

Proofing
Allow print to dry and use daylight to assess color accuracy of print.

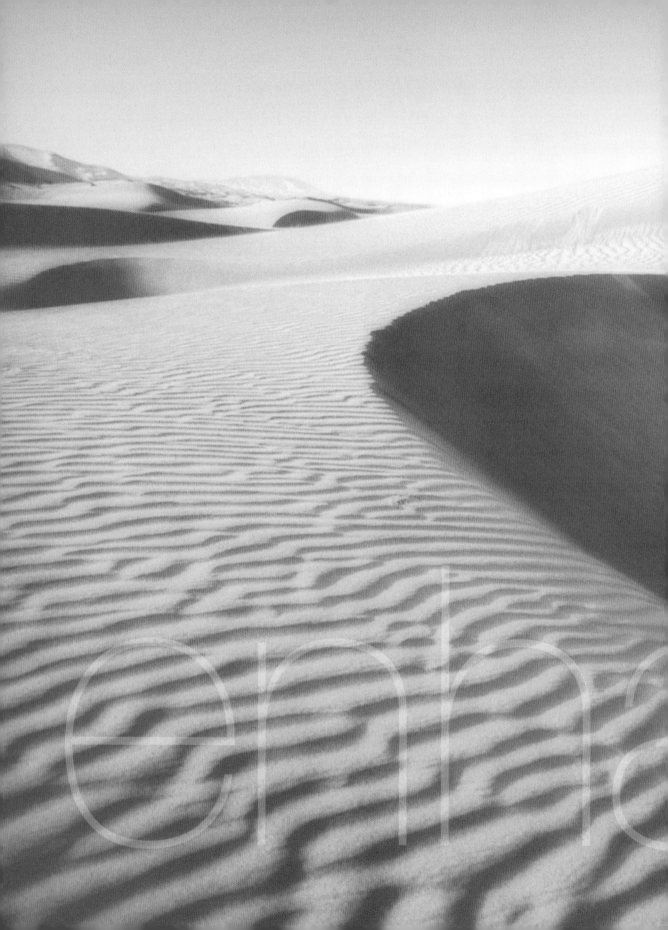

part 2

enhance

Project 1

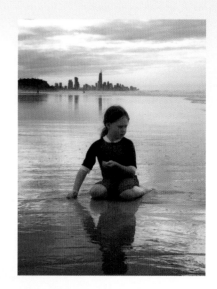

Depth of Field

The Gaussian Blur filter can be used creatively to blur distracting backgrounds. Most digital cameras achieve greater depth of field (more in focus) at the same aperture when compared to their 35 mm film cousins, due to their comparatively small sensor size. This is great in some instances but introduces unwelcome detail and distractions when the attention needs to be firmly fixed on the subject.

There is often a lot to think about during the capture of an image, and the time required to consider the appropriate aperture and shutter speed combination for the desired visual outcome often gets the elbow. Photoshop Elements can, however, come to the rescue and drop a distracting background into a murky sea of out-of-focus oblivion. Problems arise when the resulting image, all too often, looks manipulated rather than realistic. A straight application of the Gaussian Blur filter will have a tendency to 'bleed' strong tonal differences and saturated colors into the background fog, making the background in the image look more like a watercolor painting than a photograph. The Gaussian Blur filter will usually require some additional work if the post-production technique is not to become too obvious.

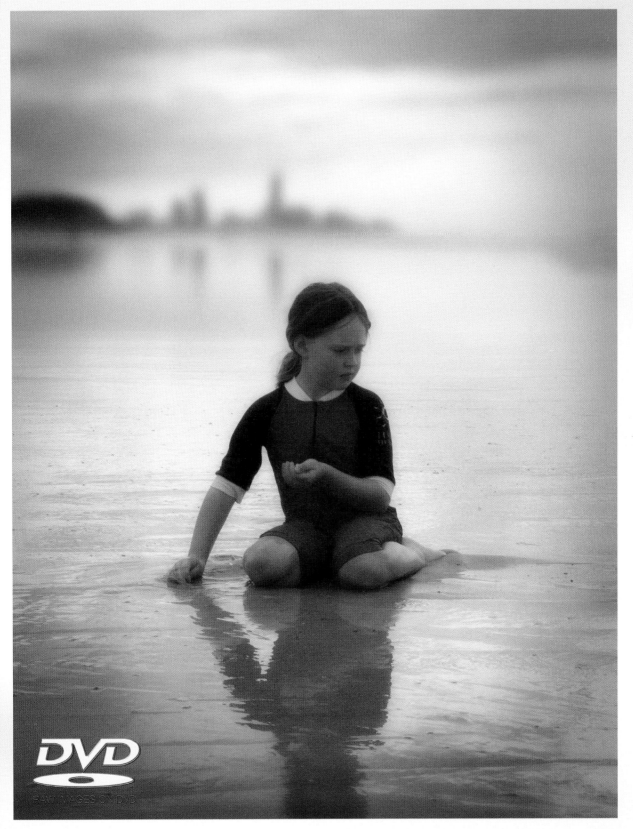

Decrease the depth of field to emphasize your subject

DVD
RAW IMAGES ON DVD

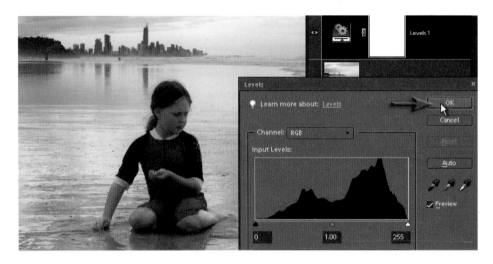

1. Not all subjects lend themselves to automated extraction processes. Professionals using the full version of Photoshop often make use of 'Channels' to start the process of creating a mask where there is not sufficient contrast between the subject and its background. As channels are off limits for Photoshop Elements users (Photoshop Elements uses them but you are not allowed to see them) we need to use a workaround. We can borrow or hijack a layer mask from an adjustment layer for our purposes in this project.

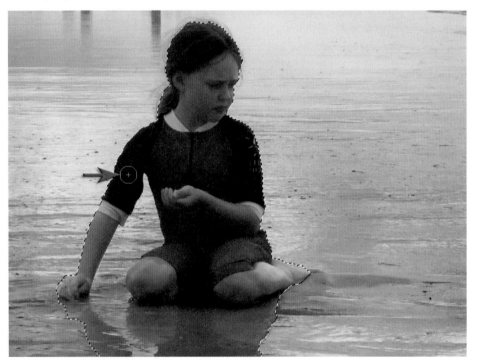

Choose the Quick Selection tool from the Tools panel and drag the tool over the girl and her reflection in the water. The Quick Selection tool will probably include the water underneath the girl's arm as part of the initial selection.

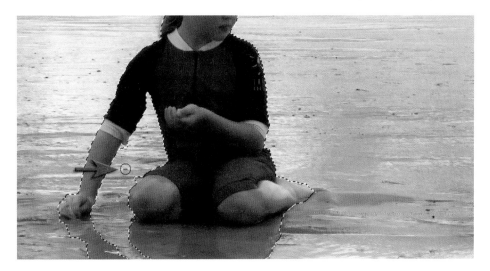

2. Reduce the diameter of the brush size by clicking on the Brush picker icon in the Options bar. Hold down the Alt key and then paint over any areas of water that need to be excluded from the selection.

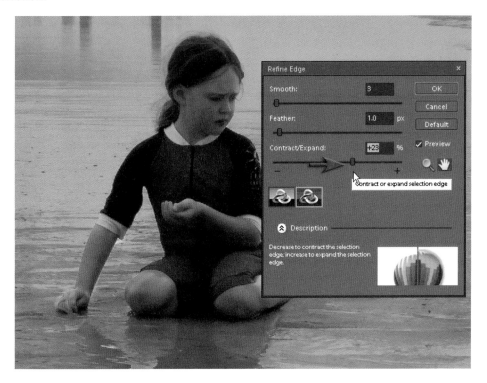

3. Click on the Refine Edge button in the Options bar and choose to view the selection with a mask by selecting the Custom Overlay Color option. Set the Smooth to a value of 3 and enter a 1-pixel feather to soften the edge of the selection. Drag the Contract/Expand slider to the right so that the edge of the mask color sits directly over the edge of the girl. Select OK to apply these adjustments to the selection.

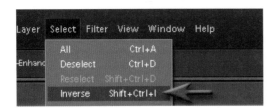 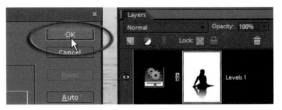

4. From the Select menu choose Inverse. In the Layers panel select Levels from the Create adjustment layer pull-down menu. The selection will create a layer mask and this will become the area of sharp focus. Make no adjustment in the Levels dialog box – just select OK. Hold down the Alt key and click on the layer mask to view the contents of the mask.

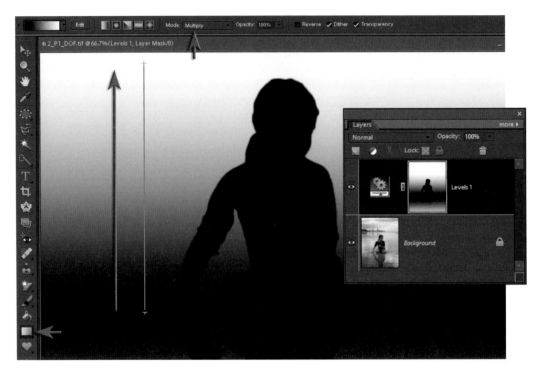

5. Focus is not a brick wall, i.e. it does not start and end suddenly - it gradually fades in and out. Think Gradient tool when you are thinking of fading between masked and unmasked (sharp and unsharp). Choose the 'Gradient tool' in the Tools panel. Choose the 'Black/White' and 'Reflected gradient' options in the Options bar and set the mode to Multiply. Drag a gradient from the base of the girl to somewhere around the horizon line in the distance (holding down the Shift key as you drag will constrain the gradient so that it is not crooked). Drag the gradient a second time to darken the mask further. The resulting gradient will extend the focus in front and behind the girl. This will become our plane of focus.

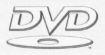 **Note > The TIFF file for this project has a saved selection (Selection > Load Selection > DOF). Creating a layer mask with this active selection will automatically create the layer mask in step 5.**

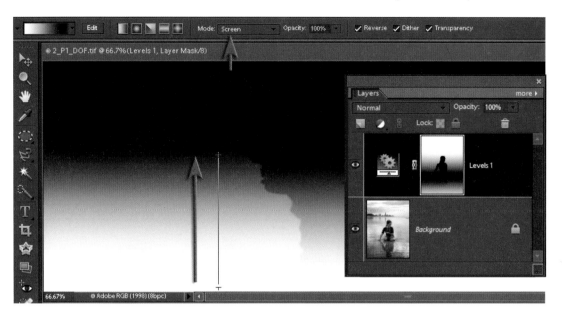

6. Switch to the Linear option in the Options bar, set the mode to Screen and select the Reverse Option. Drag a gradient from the base of the image to the point just below where the girl is in contact with the sand. This will help to reduce focus in the reflection slightly.

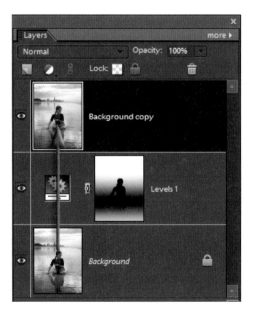
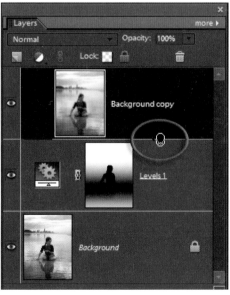

7. Drag the background layer to the New Layer icon and then drag it to the top of the layers stack (shortcuts - Ctrl + J to duplicate background layer, then Ctrl + Shift +] to move this duplicate layer to the top of the layers stack). Group this background copy layer with the adjustment layer below (Layer > Group or Ctrl + G or by holding down the Alt key and clicking on the dividing line between the two layers).

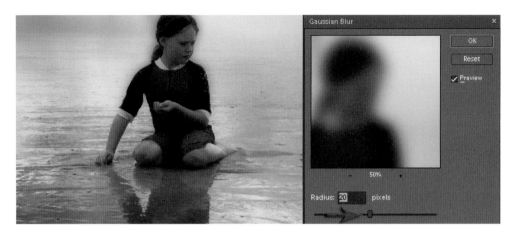

8. Go to Filter > Blur > Gaussian Blur and apply a generous amount of blur (20 pixels in this project). How much you drop the focus is pretty much a subjective step. Very shallow depth of field is achieved with larger apertures, a close vantage point and larger format cameras. If you are generous with the pixel radius in the Gaussian Blur filter the image will appear as though it was created with a large format film camera – something that is impossible to achieve with a digital compact unless you are shooting an insect or flower in macro mode. The power of this effect is to remove distracting background clutter from the image, isolate the subject and keep the focus entirely on the focal point of the image. Unfortunately the effect at this stage has a few shortcomings. The effect of blurring the background has bled some of the darker and more saturated tones into the lighter more desaturated background. A tell-tale halo is forming that indicates this effect has been achieved in post-production rather than in-camera.

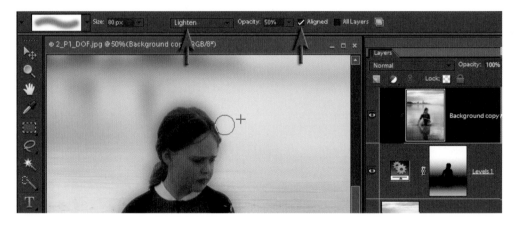

9. The problem is resolved by careful application of the Clone Stamp tool. Select the background copy layer, then pick the Clone Stamp tool. In the Options bar, check the Aligned option and set the Mode to Lighten, and hold down the Alt key as you select some pixels further away from the edge, where the bleed has not extended to, and paint these pixels back into the affected border regions. Switch from Lighten to Darken modes if you encounter brighter tones bleeding into a darker background.

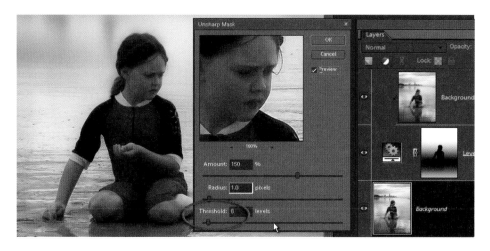

10. Adjustment to the sharpness of the image can be made to the background layer as this is the only portion of the image that remains in focus. There is some noise present in this image so sharpening is best achieved using the Unsharp Mask (Enhance > Unsharp Mask) with the Threshold slider raised to 7 or 8.

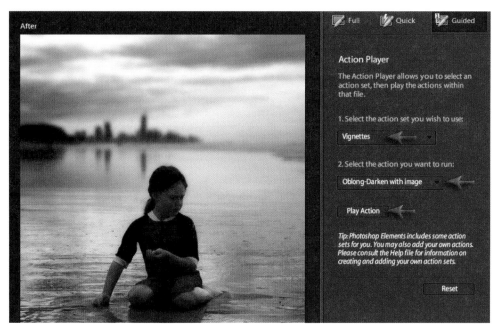

11. The viewer's attention can be further restricted to the central subject by adding a subtle vignette so that the image progressively gets brighter towards the center (we are visually drawn to the light). Click on the Guded button in the right panel and select the Action Player. Select Vignettes and the 'Oblong-Darker with image' option before clicking the Play Action button. This vignette option protects the bright highlights in the sky from excessive darkening.

Note > This action is part of the Maximum Performance actions from the DVD.

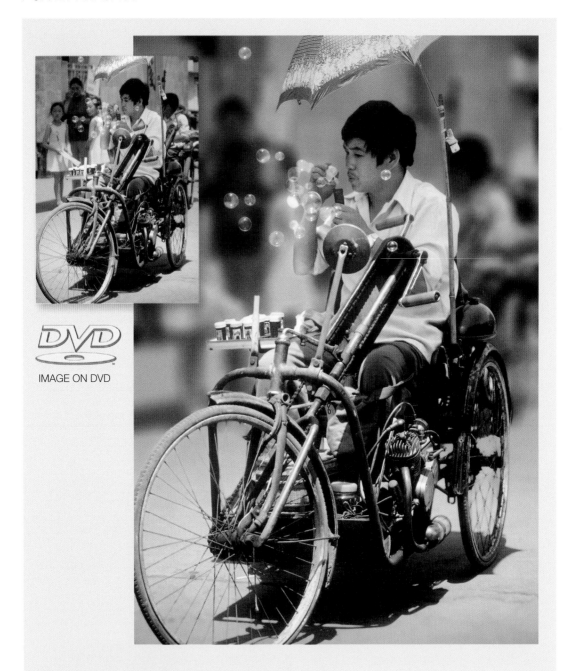

IMAGE ON DVD

FUTURE DEVELOPMENTS SHIFTING FOCUS

If digital cameras are eventually able to record distance information at the time of capture this could be used in the creation of an automatic depth map (the Lens Blur filter in the full version of Photoshop can already use channels or layer masks to create automated depth of field effects, but the channel must still be created manually using the techniques outlined in this project). Choosing the most appropriate depth of field could be relegated to post-production image editing in a similar way to how the white balance is set in camera Raw.

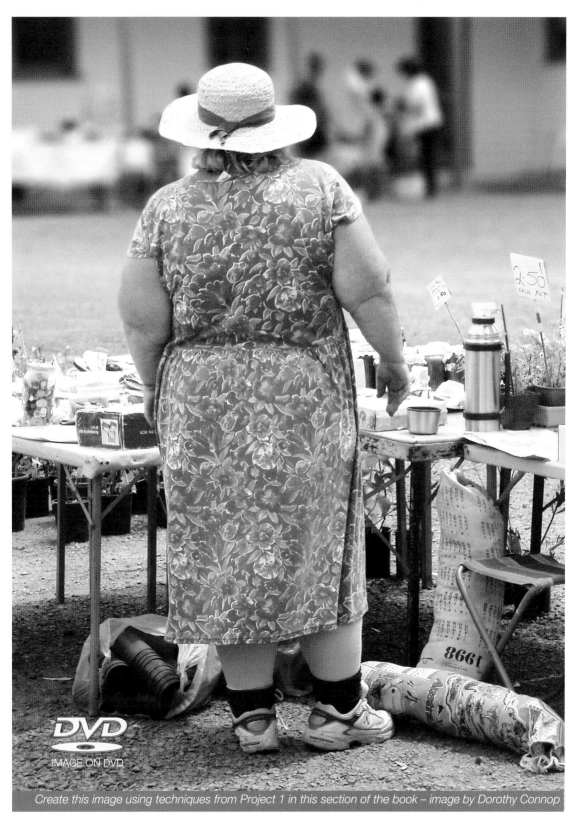

IMAGE ON DVD

Create this image using techniques from Project 1 in this section of the book – image by Dorothy Connop

Project 2

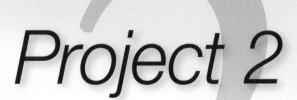

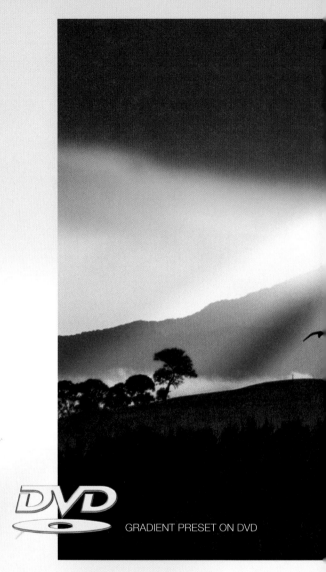

GRADIENT PRESET ON DVD

Shafts of Light

Here we explore the science of making good photographs even more memorable. Discover how to add drama to your landscape images using the 'Fingers of God' tool (a.k.a. the Gradient tool with customized settings). Creating effective landscape images is not exactly rocket science. Choose a beautiful landscape just after dawn, or just before sunset, and add dramatic natural lighting to create emotive and memorable landscape images.

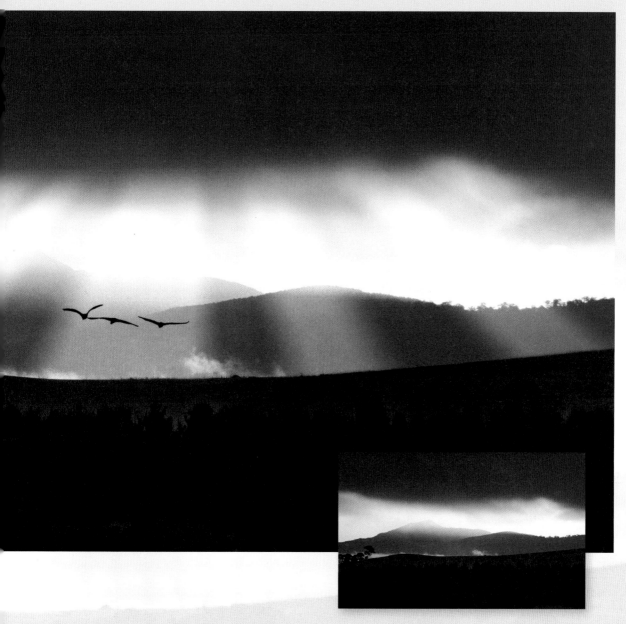

Let there be light – create dramatic lighting effects to enhance the drama of your images

Clear blue skies are great for holidays on the beach but the best natural lighting for photography is provided by broken or filtered sunlight through partial cloud cover. The most memorable of all lighting is when shafts of light break through the clouds. Finding partial cloud cover when the sun is low is relatively easy; being present when shafts of light flood your selected vista, however, can be an elusive and rare event. This final and quintessential ingredient requires patience, persistence and good fortune – or a good helping of post-production editing courtesy of Photoshop Elements.

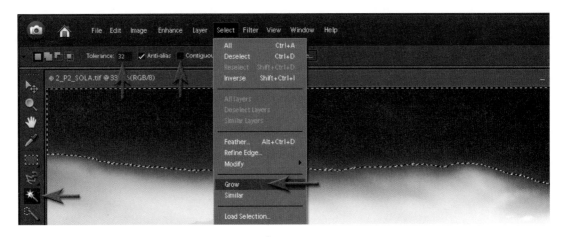

1. Choose the 'Magic Wand' in the Tools panel and deselect the 'Contiguous' option in the Options bar. Click on the dark blue sky at the top of the image to make a selection that excludes the yellow sky (this region will play host to the shafts of light). Hold down the Shift key and keep selecting areas/colors with the Magic Wand until everything except the yellow sky is selected. Selecting the Grow command from the Select menu to expand the selection may also help.

Note > Deselecting the 'Contiguous' option will allow the Magic Wand to select all similar pixels, even if they are not adjoining the area clicked on.

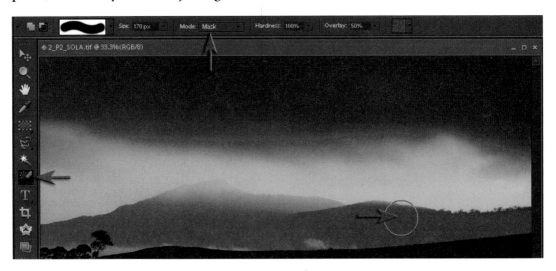

2. Choose the 'Selection Brush tool' from the Tools panel and choose the 'Mask' option from the Options bar. The 'Mask' option enables you to see your selection as a painted mask so you can easily see what areas are selected. Choose an appropriate brush size and paint to add areas of the sky missed by the Magic Wand. Hold down the Alt key as you paint to add areas of the mask (and resulting selection) that are not required.

Note > You can choose an alternative color for the overlay mask and adjust the opacity in the Options bar to make the selection process easier.

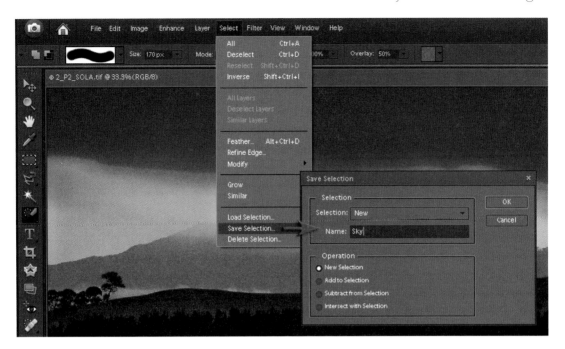

3. Go to the Select menu and choose 'Save Selection'. You can give your selection a name to help you locate this for a later stage in the editing process. Choose 'Deselect' from the Select menu.

Note > Saved selections in Photoshop are stored as additional channels called 'Alpha channels'.

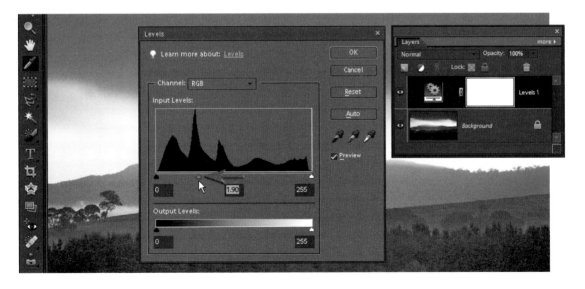

4. From the top of the Layers panel click on the Create New Fill or Adjustment Layer icon and choose 'Levels' from the menu. Drag the central Gamma slider in the dialog box to the left to substantially brighten the image. The tonality for the majority of the image will be returned to normal by creating a sophisticated layer mask for this adjustment layer in the next stages of the tutorial.

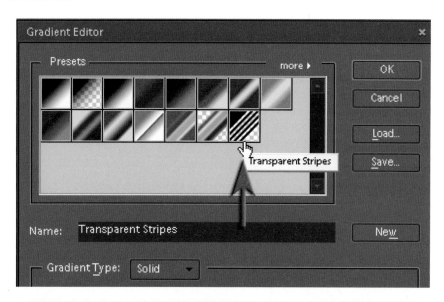

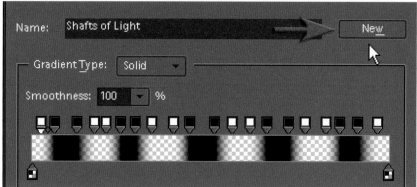

5. Select black as the Foreground color and the 'Gradient tool' in the Tools panel and then click on the Edit button in the Options bar to open the Gradient Editor. Click on the 'Transparent Stripes' gradient. Edit the gradient using the following pointers. The aim of editing the gradient is to make the stripes irregular widths with softer edges to emulate the irregular and softer nature of shafts of light. The white stops on the top of the editing ramp indicate full transparency whilst the black stops indicate full opacity of the foreground color. Click and drag the stops into groups of four. A white stop should be on either end of a grouping of four with two black stops next to each other in the middle. Moving the black stops further apart will broaden the stripe. Moving the white stop further away from the central black stops will broaden the area of transition between full opacity and full transparency. To add a stop hold down the Alt key and drag an existing stop a short distance. To remove a stop drag the stop away from the gradient ramp. To add this modified gradient to the Presets click on the New button and give your shafts of light a suitable name (don't worry that the shafts are colored black for the moment). This gradient can be loaded from the Preset that is available on the DVD.

Note > A black stop can be changed to a white stop or vice versa by clicking on the stop and then adjusting the Opacity slider in the bottom Stops section of the Gradient Editor.

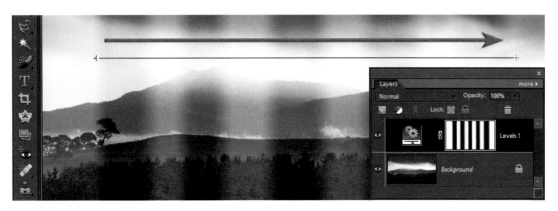

6. Make sure the 'Linear' gradient option is selected in the Options bar and set the opacity to 100% and the mode to 'Normal'. The foreground color should still be set to black. Click on the left side of the image window and drag your mouse cursor to the right side of the image window. The length of the line you draw will be the initial width of the shafts, although this can be modified using the Transform command outlined in the following step.

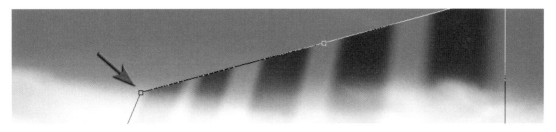

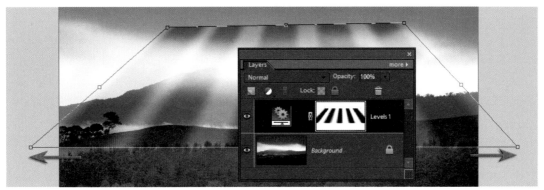

7. From the Image menu select 'Distort' from the Transform submenu. Click on each of the corner handles and drag them to fan the shafts of light. Move the cursor into the Transform bounding box, and click and drag the bounding box to reposition the shafts of light. When you're satisfied with the shape, double-click inside the distorted bounding box to accept the transformation.

Note > You may need to extend the image window so that you can drag the corner handles to the required angle.

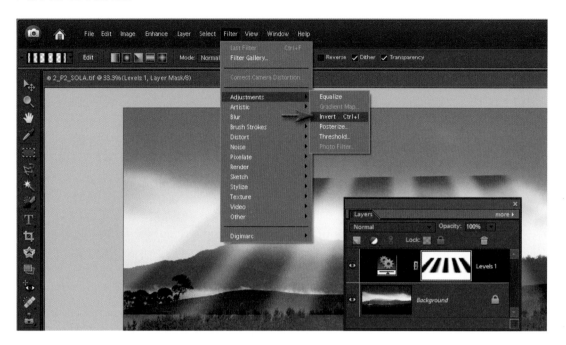

8. Go to the Filter menu and select 'Invert' from the Adjustments submenu. This will turn the black stripes to white and return the brightness level of the rest of the image to normal. The next step will aim to limit the shafts of light to the selection made at the start of the tutorial.

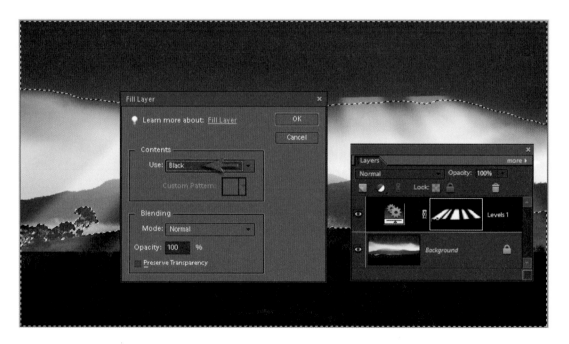

9. From the Select menu choose 'Load Selection' and load the selection saved at the start of the tutorial. From the Edit menu choose the 'Fill Selection' command and select 'Black' as the fill color and then select OK. This will further limit the shafts of light to the desired location.

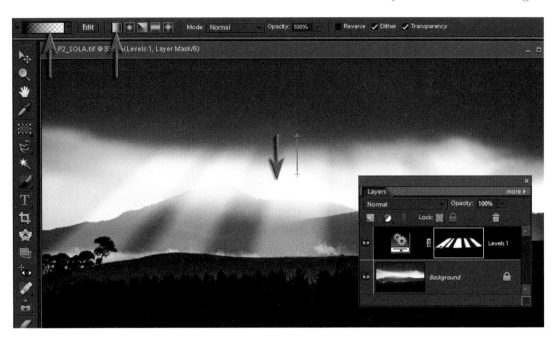

10. Select the Gradient tool and choose the 'Foreground to Transparent' gradient. Drag a short gradient from the start of the shafts of light to conceal their hard edges.

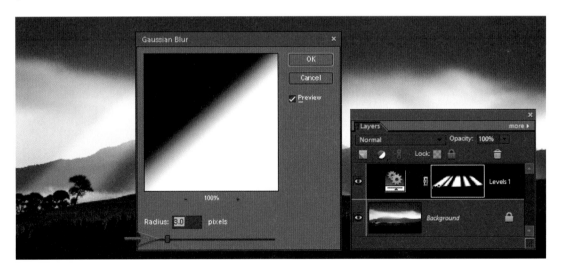

11. To soften the mask further choose Filter > Blur > Gaussian Blur. Select a pixel Radius that will soften the edges of the mask so the cut-off of the lighting behind the distant hill is subtle. The only problem with this technique is that it is almost too effective and therefore tempting to sneak it into too many images in your personal portfolio. When this happens the cat will be well and truly out of the bag.

Note > It is possible to increase the intensity of the shafts of light by switching the blend mode of the adjustment layer to 'Screen'. Adjust the opacity to fine-tune the effect.

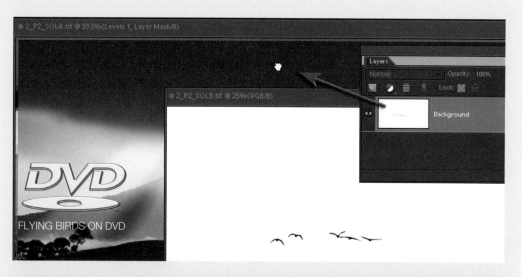

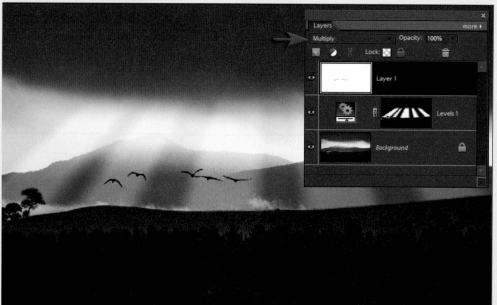

PERFORMANCE TIP

Create a focal point by introducing some birds that will be silhouetted against the shafts of light. Open the second image file and drag the thumbnail from the background layer (in the Layers panel) into the image window of the project. Holding down the Shift key when you let go of the file will center it in the host image. Switching the blend mode to 'Multiply' will render the white background of this layer invisible. Good just got better.

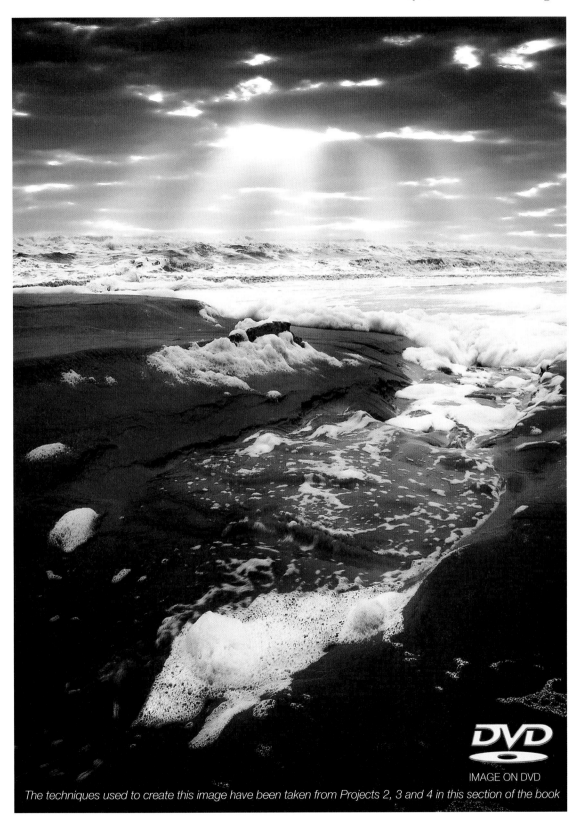

IMAGE ON DVD

The techniques used to create this image have been taken from Projects 2, 3 and 4 in this section of the book

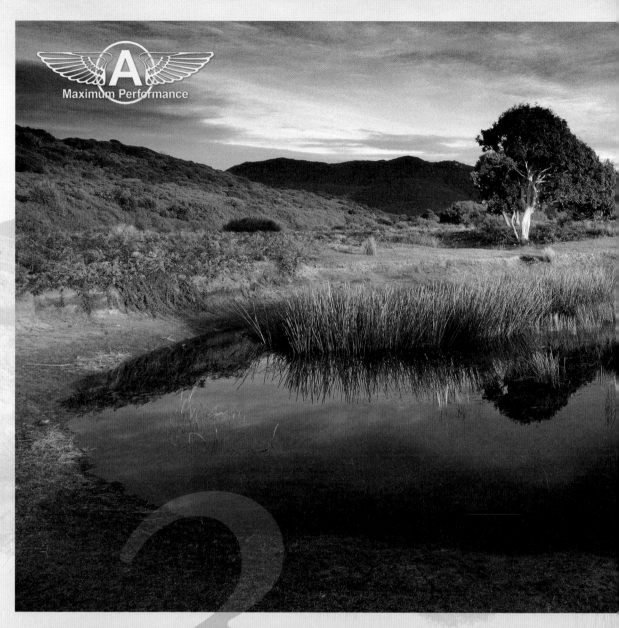

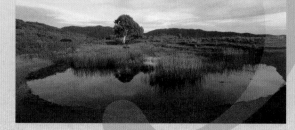

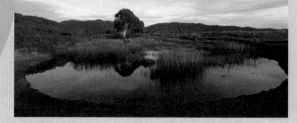

Project 3

The original color image and the result of choosing the less than satisfactory Remove Color command

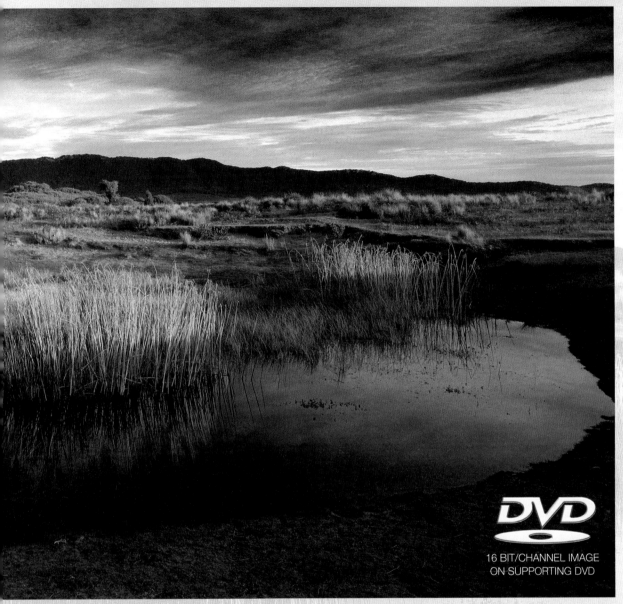

DVD

16 BIT/CHANNEL IMAGE
ON SUPPORTING DVD

Black and white – when 'luminance' is more important than color. Original image by Michael Wennrich

Black and White

When color film arrived over half a century ago the pundits who presumed that black and white images would die a quick death were surprisingly mistaken. Color is all very nice but sometimes the rich tonal qualities that we can see in the work of the photographic artists are something certainly to be savored. Can you imagine an Ansel Adams masterpiece in color? If you can – read no further.

The conversion from color to black and white

The creation of dramatic black and white photographs from your color images is a little more complicated than simply converting your image to Grayscale mode or choosing the Desaturate command. Ask any professional photographer who is skilled in the art of black and white and you will discover that crafting tonally rich images requires a little knowledge about how different color filters affect the resulting tonality of a black and white image.

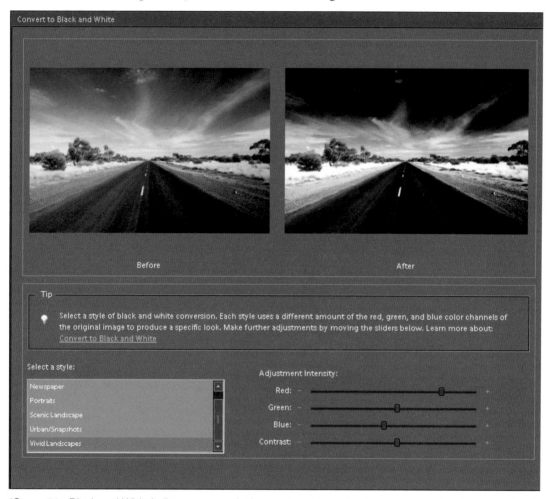

'Convert to Black and White' allows you to mix the tonal differences present in the color channels. Simply select a style and then adjust the intensity sliders to create your own custom conversion

As strange as it may seem, screwing on a color filter for capturing images on black and white film has traditionally been an essential ingredient of the recipe for success. The most popular color filter in the black and white photographer's kit bag, which is used for the most dramatic effect, is the red filter. The effect of the red filter is to lighten all things that are red and darken all things that are not red in the original scene. The result is a print with considerable tonal differences compared to an image shot without a filter. Is this a big deal? Well, yes it is – blue skies are darkened and skin blemishes are lightened. That's a winning combination for most landscape and portrait photographers wanting to create black and white masterpieces.

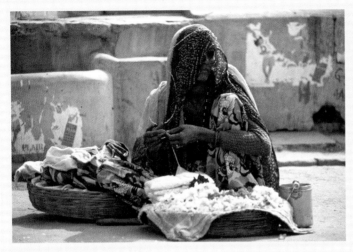

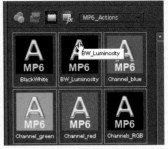

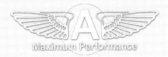

PERFORMANCE TIP

The Maximum Performance Actions included on the DVD includes a series of automated black and white conversions (see the introductory section for installing Maximum Performance Actions). The Black&White_Luminosity action creates a single monochrome layer containing the Luminosity values of the RGB file (usually a superior black and white conversion when compared with the Remove Color command). The Red, Green and Blue channel actions allow you to place one of the three color channels as a black and white layer. These actions would also be useful for accessing the best contrast in order to create a mask, as in the Depth of Field project.

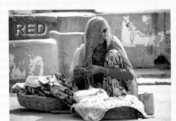
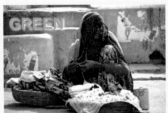
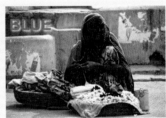

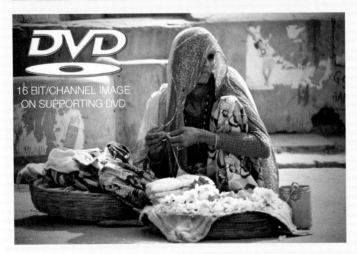

In the image to the left the red channel was used as this offered the best detail in the dark skin tones. The contrast was then increased by duplicating the layer and switching the blend mode to 'Soft Light'. The opacity of this duplicate layer was then dropped to 30%. A vignette was added to complete the project

The Convert to Black and White command (Enhance > Convert to Black and White) allows the user to selectively mix the differences in the tonality present in the three color channels, but unfortunately it is not available as an adjustment layer. This means we are unable to make use of the layer mask that typically comes with an adjustment layer. It also means that we would be unable to modify the color conversion at a later date without returning to the original color file. This approach to the conversion (although vastly superior to anything present in previous versions of the software) limits the usefulness of the technique for those users who wish to extract the maximum amount of control and flexibility over the process of black and white conversion. The famous digital guru, Russell Preston Brown, has come up with a workaround that enables us to retain complete control over the black and white conversion using multiple adjustment layers.

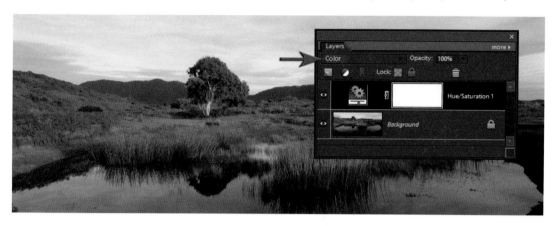

1. Drag the Layers panel from the Panel Bin (this will be your command center for this technique). Click on the Adjustment Layer icon in the Layers panel and scroll down the list to select and create a Hue/Saturation adjustment layer. You will make no adjustments for the time being but simply select OK to close the dialog box. Set the blend mode of this adjustment layer to 'Color'.

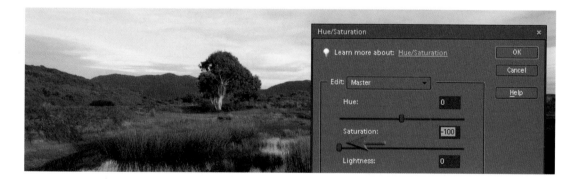

2. Create a second Hue/Saturation adjustment layer. Slide the Saturation slider all the way to the left (−100) to desaturate the image. Select OK. The image will now appear as if you had performed a simple Convert to Grayscale or Desaturate (remove color) command.

Note > This second adjustment layer should be sitting on top of the layers stack.

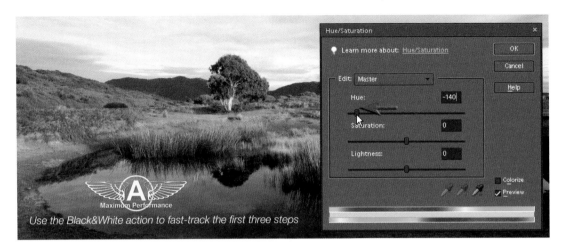

Use the Black&White action to fast-track the first three steps

$3.$ Select the first Hue/Saturation layer that you created and double-click the layer thumbnail to reopen the Hue/Saturation dialog box. Move the Hue slider in this dialog box to the left. Observe the changes to the tonality of the image as you move the slider. Blues will be darkest when the slider is moved to a position around −150. Select OK. The drama of the image will probably have been improved quite dramatically already but we can take this further with some dodging and burning.

Note > A Maximum Performance Action is available to fast-track the first three steps in this project (see the introductory section for installing and using Maximum Performance Actions).

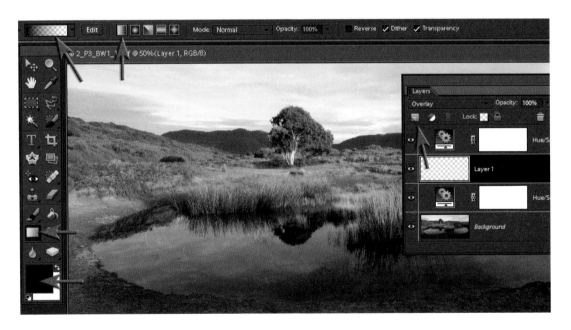

$4.$ Click on the New Layer icon in the Layers panel. Set the blend mode of the layer to 'Overlay'. Set the color swatches in the Tools panel to the default black and white (click on the small black and white swatch icon, or press D on the keyboard). Select the 'Gradient tool' and in the Options bar select the 'Foreground (black) to Transparent' and 'Linear' gradient options.

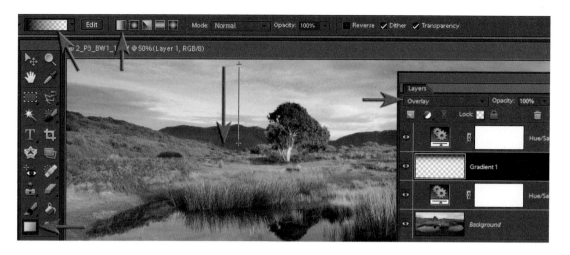

5. Drag a gradient from the top of the image window to the horizon line. This will have the effect of drawing the viewer into the image and will create an increased sense of drama. Lower the opacity of the layer if the effect is too strong and duplicate the layer if you want to increase the drama further.

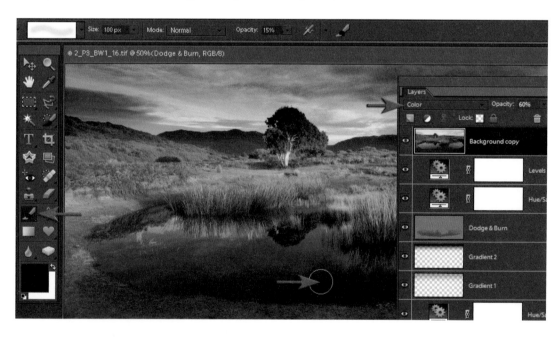

6. Press the Alt key and click on the New Layer icon. In the New Layer dialog box set the blend mode to 'Overlay' and select the Fill with Overlay-neutral color (50% gray) option. Select the 'Brush tool' and select a soft-edged brush from the Options bar and lower the opacity to 10–15%. A layer that is 50% Gray in Overlay or Soft Light mode is invisible. This gray layer will be used to dodge and burn your image non-destructively, i.e. you are not working on the actual pixels of your image. Paint onto the gray layer with black selected as the foreground color to burn (darken) the image in localized areas or switch to white to dodge (lighten) localized areas. You can fill or paint using selections to control the dodging and burning process if required.

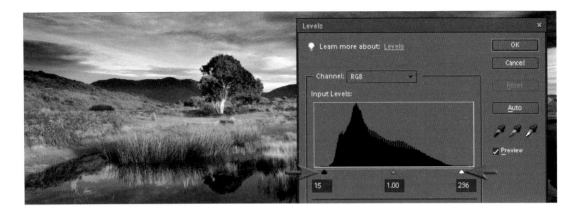

7. Select the top layer and then create a Levels adjustment layer (one adjustment layer to rule them all) to sit above all of the other layers. Make sure the histogram extends all the way between the black and white sliders. Move the sliders in to meet the histogram if this is not the case.

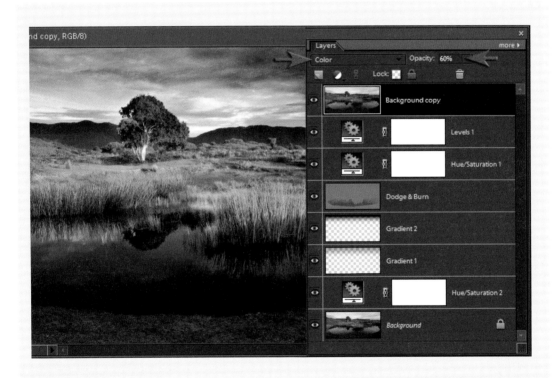

PERFORMANCE TIP

Try experimenting with the introduction of some of the original color. Duplicate the background layer by dragging it to the New Layer icon. Then drag the background copy to the top of the layers stack. Reduce the opacity of this layer and set the blend mode to 'Color' to let the black and white version introduce the drama once more.

Project 4

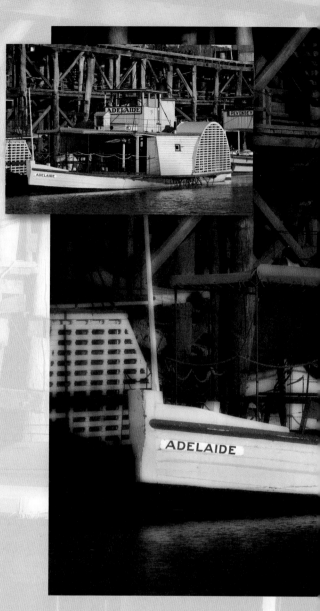

Toning

Burning, toning, split-grade printing and printing through your mother's silk stockings are just some of the wonderful, weird and positively wacky techniques used by the traditional masters of the darkroom waiting to be exposed (or ripped off) in this tantalizing digital project designed to pump up the mood and ambience of the flat and downright dull. The tonality of the project image destined for the toning table will be given a split personality. Shadows and highlights will be gently blurred to add depth and character at the same time as retaining full detail for emphasis and focus. Selected colors will then be mapped to the new tonality to establish the final mood.

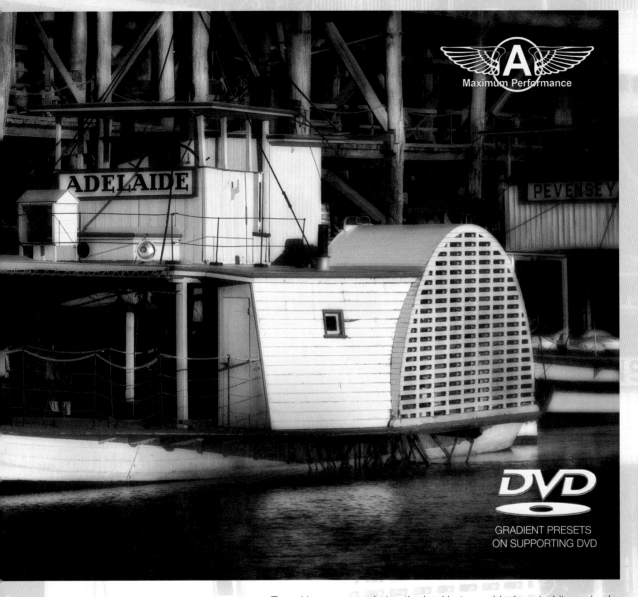

Toned images – exploring the land between black and white and color

It probably comes as no small surprise that 'color' injects images with mood and emotional impact. Photographers, however, frequently work on images that are devoid of color because of the tonal control they are able to achieve in traditional processing and printing techniques. Toning the resulting 'black and white' images keeps the emphasis on the play of light and shade but lets the introduced colors influence the final mood. With the increased sophistication and control that digital image-editing software affords us, we can now explore the 'twilight zone' between color and black and white as never before. The original image has the potential to be more dramatic and carry greater emotional impact through the controlled use of tone and color.

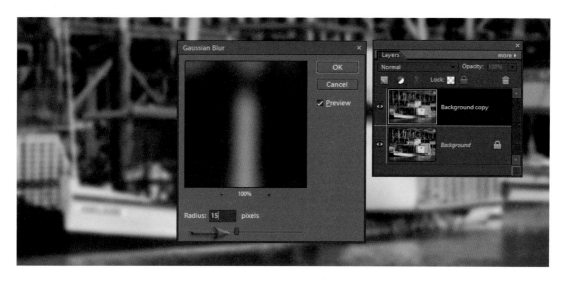

1. This first step will create some soft smooth tones that we can use to recreate the early morning mood. Duplicate the Background layer by dragging it to the Create a new layer icon in the Layers panel. Go to 'Filter > Blur > Gaussian Blur' and increase the Radius to 15 pixels.

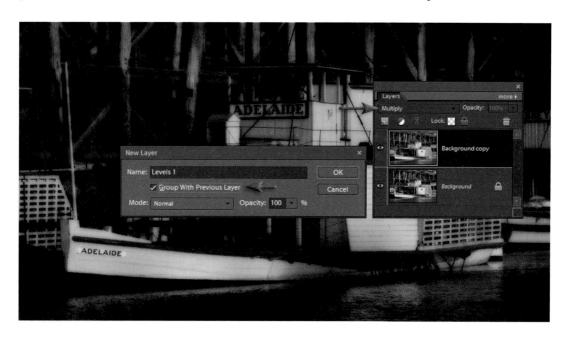

2. Set the mode of the layer to Multiply. The image will appear very dark until we restore the luminance values to the pixels over the next four steps. We can achieve this using a combination of two adjustment layers. Hold down the Alt key while you select a levels adjustment layer from the Create Adjustment Layer menu in the Layers panel. In the New Layer dialog box that opens check the 'Group With Previous Layer' option. This will enable us to modify the tonality of the blur layer without affecting the background layer. Click OK to open the Levels dialog.

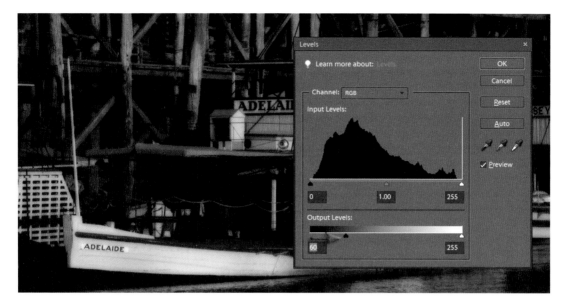

3. Move the Shadow Output slider to the right to prevent the deeper shadow tones from becoming too dark. A value of 60 to 100 depending on how dark shadow values in the image are. We can start with a value of 60 and refine this later after applying the second adjustment layer. Select OK to apply the Levels adjustment.

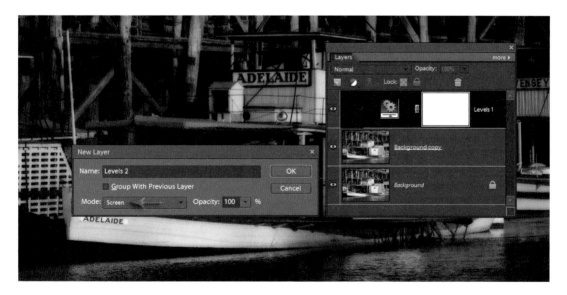

4. Hold down the Alt key while you select a Levels adjustment layer from the Create Adjustment Layer menu in the Layers panel. In the New Layer dialog box that opens set the mode of the new layer to Screen. Select OK to open the second Levels adjustment layer.

Note > We do not need to select the Group With Previous Layer option as we are about to adjust the overall tonality rather than just the Background copy layer.

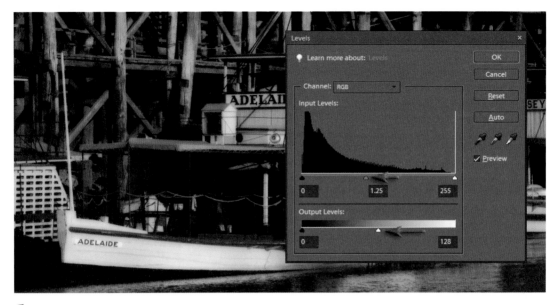

5. The Screen mode applied to this second adjustment layer will lighten all tones. Drag the White output slider to the left to restrict this adjustment to just the shadow tones and midtones (a value of 128 has been used in this project). This will prevent the highlights from becoming too bright. Move the central gamma slider to the left to increase overall brightness in the midtones.

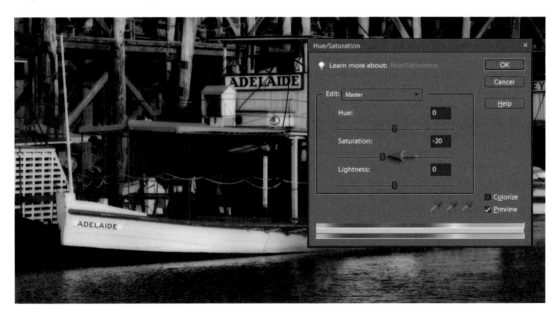

6. The original brightness of the image should now be restored but the saturation values will be slightly higher. Select a Hue/Saturation adjustment layer from the Create Adjustment Layer menu in the Layers panel and lower the saturation to -20.

Note > The Maximum Performance action 'Smooth Tone' can be used to automate the last six steps in this tutorial.

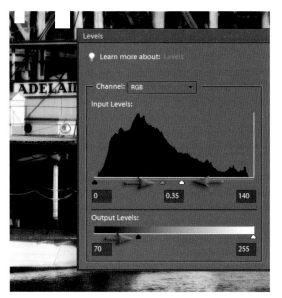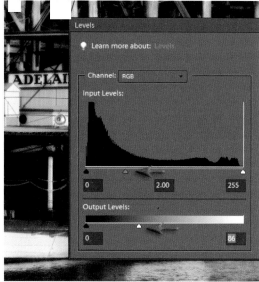

7. At any stage in this project you can modify the impact of the blur layer on the image by adjusting the sliders in the two levels adjustment layers. Double-click the first adjustment layer that is grouped to the background copy layer and drag the White input slider to 140 and the central gamma slider to 0.35 to increase the apparent blur in the image. Select OK to apply the changes. Double-click the second adjustment layer (the one set to the Screen mode) and drag the central gamma slider to 2.00 and the White Output slider to 86 to adjust the overall tonality.

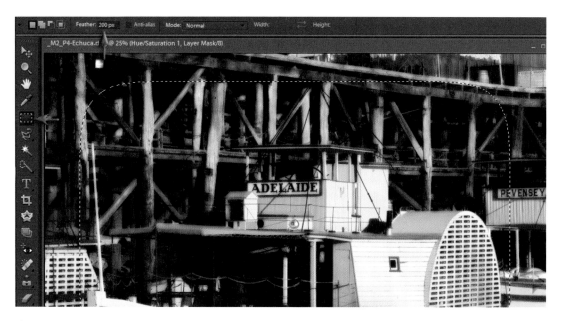

8. We will now add a vignette to this image. Select the Rectangular Marquee Tool in the Tools panel. Set the feather radius to 200 px in the Options bar. Click and drag from the top left-hand corner of the image to the bottom right-hand corner of the image to make a selection.

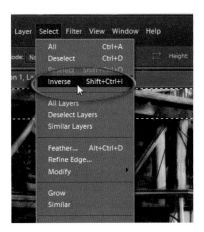 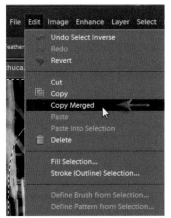 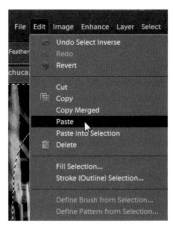

9. From the Select menu choose Inverse so that the edge, rather than the center, of the image is selected. From the Edit menu choose Copy Merged and then from the Edit menu again choose Paste.

Note > The Copy Merged allows you to copy the visible pixels rather than just the pixels on the active layer.

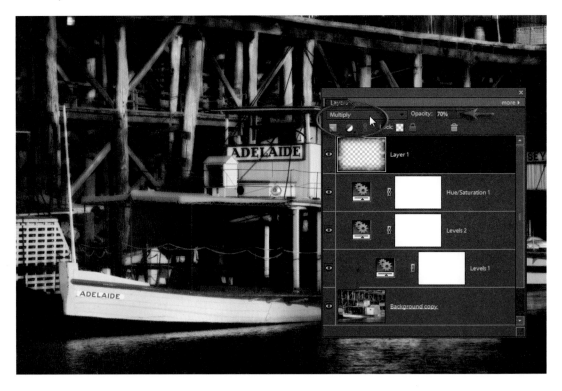

10. The pixels on this new layer (currently making no difference to the appearance of the image) can be used to darken the image by setting the mode of the layer to Multiply. Lower the opacity of the layer if the vignette is too dark using the opacity control in the Layers panel.

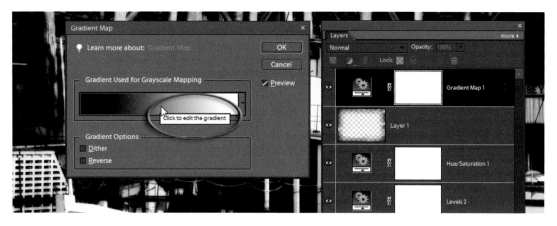

11. Set the foreground colors in the Tools panel to their default black and white settings. Click on the Create Adjustment Layer icon in the Layers panel and choose 'Gradient Map' from the menu. Click on the gradient in the Gradient Map dialog to open the Gradient Editor dialog.

Note > The gradient must start with black and end with white, otherwise your image will not use the full dynamic range possible.

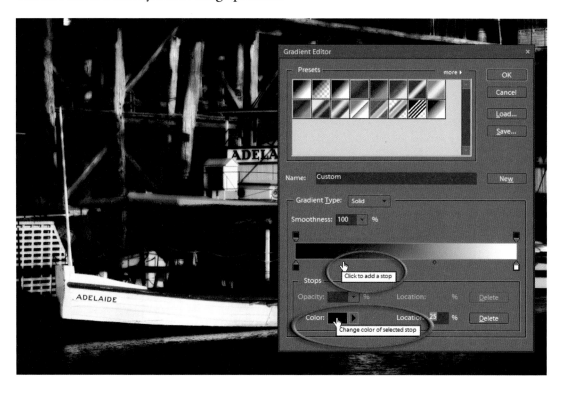

12. The Gradient Editor dialog allows you to assign colors to shadows, midtones and highlights. Click underneath the gradient to create a new color stop. Slide it to a location that reads approximately 25% at the bottom of the dialog. Click on the color swatch to open the Select Stop Color (Color Picker) dialog.

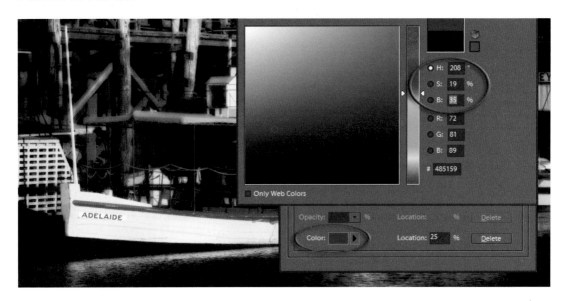

13. Cool colors such as blues or cyans are often chosen to give character to shadow tones. In the project image the HSB values (Hue, Saturation and Brightness) are adjusted to 208°, 19% and 35% (this Brightness value is lighter than the 25% position of the color stop and opens up the dark shadow detail in this image). Select OK in the Select Stop Color dialog to assign this color.

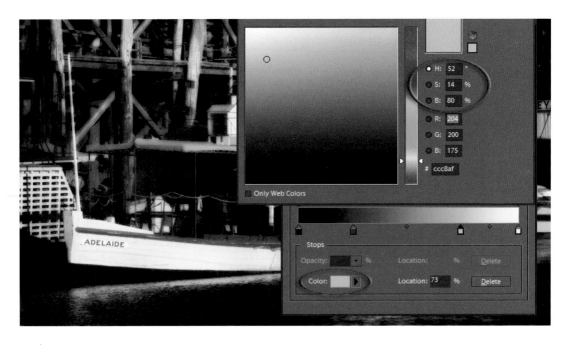

14. Create another stop and move it to a location that reads approximately 75%. This time try choosing a bright warm color to contrast with the blue chosen previously. HSB values of 52°, 14% and 80% have been selected for the project image. Select OK to assign this color to the highlights.

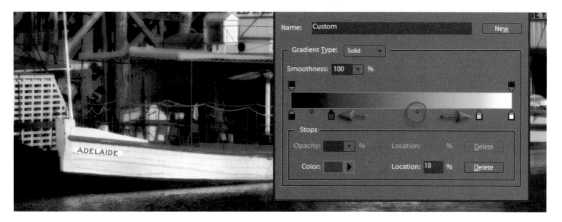

15. The Color stops can be moved to modify the contrast of the image. Pushing the two color stops further apart will reduce the contrast giving increased detail to the shadows and highlights. When a Color Stop is moved Color Midpoints are visible that can also be moved along the color ramp to fine-tune the effects of the gradient on your image.

Note > Avoid moving the color stops or Midpoint too close to each other as this can cause tonal banding or posterization in the image.

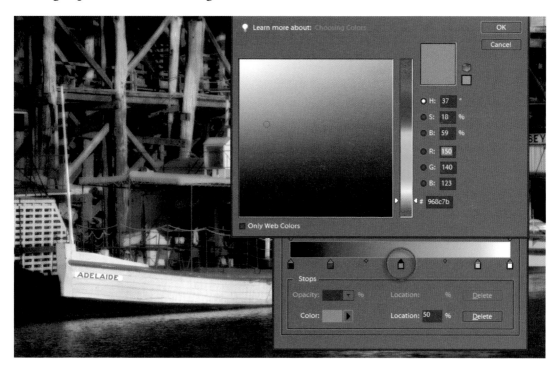

16. Add another Color Stop in the middle of the gradient for maximum control over the toning process. HSB values of 37°, 18% and 59% have been selected for the project image. Select OK to assign this color to the Midtones. This Color Stop increases the warmth in the midtones and completes the toning process.

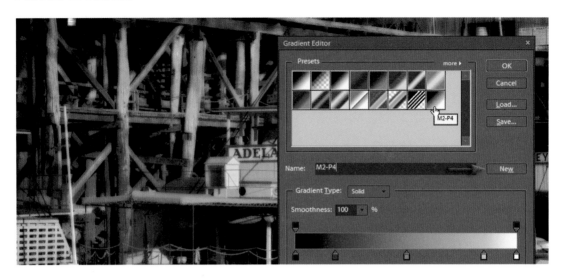

17. A custom gradient can be saved as a Gradient Preset. Enter a name for your gradient and then click on the new Button. The new gradient will appear in the Presets. Gradients can be saved to other locations (such as your desktop or an external drive) so that they can be loaded into imaging projects using a different computer.

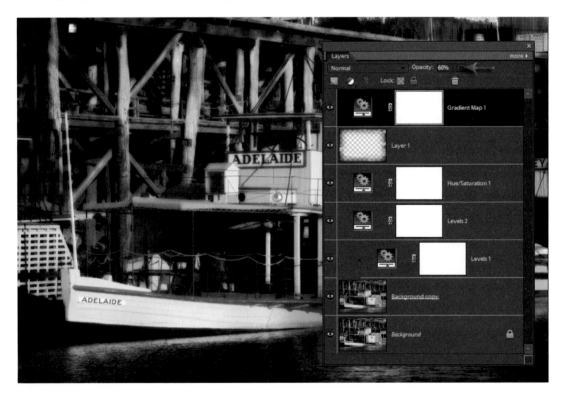

18. Select OK in the Gradient Editor dialog to commit the changes. In the Layers panel reduce the Opacity of the Gradient Map layer to introduce some of the original colors to the image.

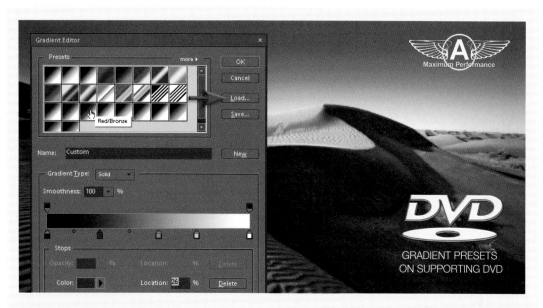

PERFORMANCE TIPS

The gradient map used in this toning project can be downloaded from the supporting DVD and loaded directly from the Gradient Editor dialog or via the Preset Manager (go to 'Edit > Preset Manager > Gradients > Load'). Then browse to the Maximum_Performance.grd preset and select OK. Quick split-tone effects can be accessed via the Maximum Performance split-tone actions available on the DVD.

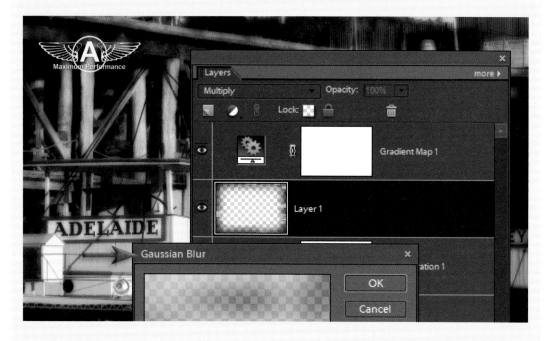

Try blurring the vignette layer by going to Filter > Blur > Gaussian Blur. A 10-pixel blur will give the image an interesting soft-focus effect.

TONAL MAPPING IN ADOBE CAMERA RAW

In the previous toning project we softened the majority of tones and remapped the colors. In contrast to this smooth tone technique there are several techniques for expanding midtone contrast to give you the 'crunchy' look or treatment.

Detail can be boosted by pushing some of the sliders in Adobe Camera Raw to the max. One of the cutting-edge treatments in commercial photography that has been all the rage recently, is where maximum detail and surface texture is expanded along with mid-tone contrast. The final effect is one where the image seems to be part photograph/part illustration. Take a look at http://www.davehillphoto.com/ to get an idea of how this treatment is being applied by one popular US photographer. The effect is also referred to as a HDR effect as this expanded midtone contrast can be created when photographers merge images with different exposures and then map the resulting detail. This effect can, however, be created in Adobe Camera Raw and the main editing space of Photoshop Elements.

To expand the mid-tone contrast and edge detail within the image raise the Recovery, Fill Light, Contrast and Clarity sliders all the way to the right (to a value of +100). Lower the Vibrance slider to reduce the excessive saturation in the image that results from raising the contrast slider.

The massive adjustments may upset the brightness of the image. Click on both of triangles above the histogram to switch the clipping warnings on. Adjust the white point of the image by dragging the Exposure slider to the left or right until thin red lines appear around the edges of the brightest parts of the subject. Adjust the black point of the image by dragging the Blacks slider to the left or right until thin blue lines appear around the edges of the darkest parts of the subject. Drag the Brightness slider to alter the overall brightness of the image and then click the triangles above the histogram to switch the clipping warnings off.

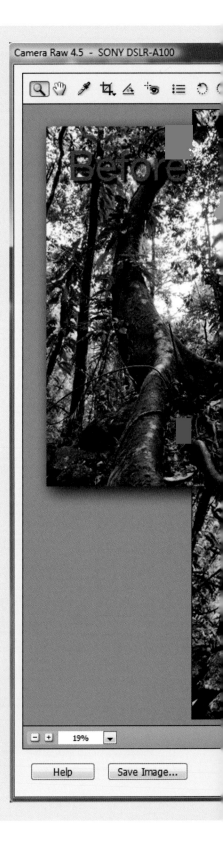

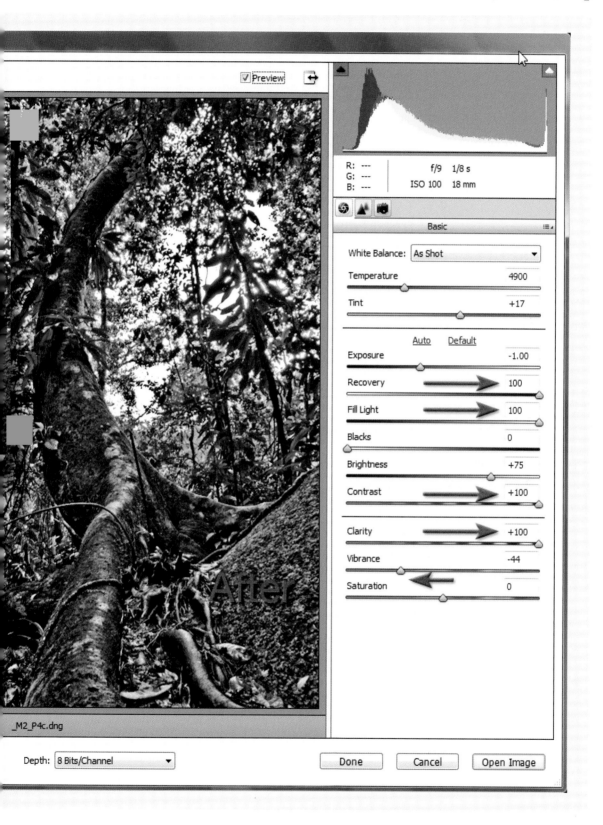

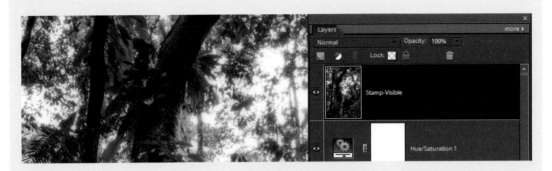

TONAL MAPPING IN THE EDIT SPACE

Midtone contrast can also be applied after first applying the smooth tone technique from the Toning project. Crunchy midtone contrast is even more effective when placed over some tones that have been blurred. Hold down the Ctrl, Alt and Shift modifier keys and then (whilst still holding down the modifier keys) press the letter E. If your new layer 'stamp visible' is not on top of the layers stack, click and drag it to the top of the Layers panel.

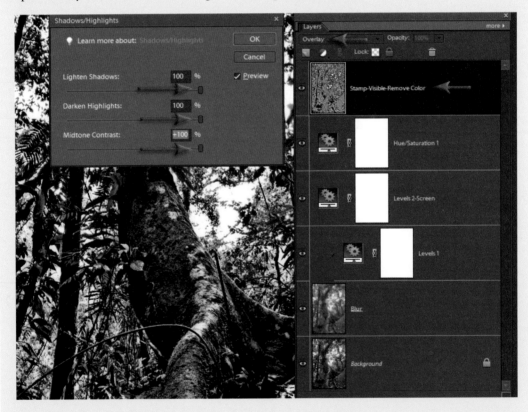

Go to Enhance > Color > Remove Color and set the layer to Soft Light or Overlay mode. Go to Enhance > Lighting > Shadows Highlights and drag all three sliders to 100% to create a similar effect to the one we achieved in Adobe Camera Raw. Select OK and adjust the strength of the effect by lowering the opacity of the layer.

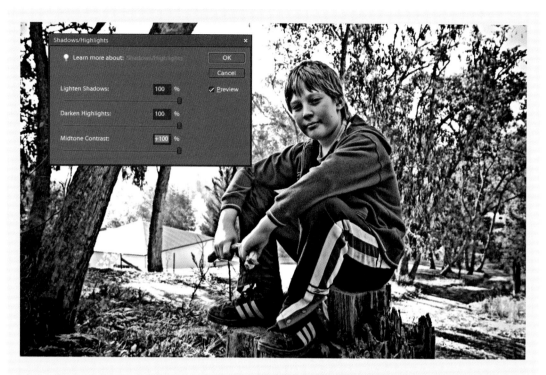

This technique can also be applied in the main Edit space without blurring the image first. Just duplicate the background layer and apply the Shadows Highlights adjustment outlined on the previous page.

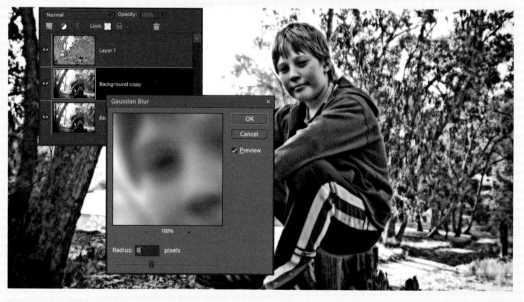

To 'bleed' the underlying colors, duplicate the background layer and apply a 8-pixel Gaussian Blur. Although not as sophisticated as the smooth tone technique outlined in the main tutorial it does work quite well under the midtone contrast layer that ensures the image appears sharp.

Project 5

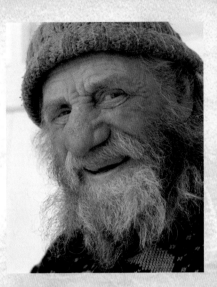

Character Portrait

It is often possible to unleash the hidden potential of an image without going to the hassle of making fiddly selections. This project demonstrates how the tonality of an image can be enriched using duplicated layers, blend modes and a couple of filters to shape and sharpen. Dust off your trophy shelf – I feel an award coming on!

The beauty of these techniques is that we can let Photoshop Elements do all of the hard work and extract an image that has all of the hallmarks of a professionally lit studio-quality portrait from an image illuminated with nothing more than ambient light. The secret to success, if you plan to reuse this recipe on one of your own images, is to start with a razor-sharp image illuminated by soft directional light (diffused window light is ideal).

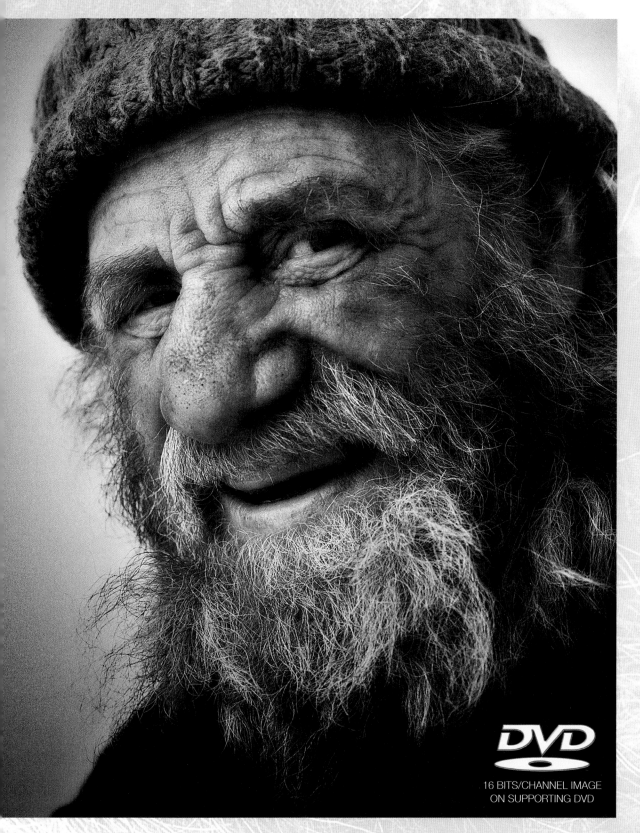

DVD
16 BITS/CHANNEL IMAGE
ON SUPPORTING DVD

Cooking up some character – a recipe for success

Preparing the image

Before we start our culinary masterpiece we should prepare the main ingredient – the image. This should include optimizing the histogram via a manual or auto Levels adjustment (if you have the luxury of accessing a 16 Bit/Channel file via a Raw capture or a 48-bit scan your histogram will appreciate the Levels adjustment prior to hitting the '8 Bits/Channel' option in the Image > Mode submenu). Start the project by removing any distractions in the image so that the viewer's focus will not wander from the *pièce de résistance* – the face containing the character and majesty of our sitter. Keeping it simple is a key to clean and effective design.

1. You can either paint directly on to the background layer or duplicate the layer if you want to preserve the background layer unadjusted. Remember you have the option to undo any brush stroke that is not absolutely effective. In fact Elements allows you to undo 50 steps by default. Check the preferences and adjust the number to suit your own workflow if required. I think 50 is overly generous and this can consume excessive portions of the computer's available RAM that would be best served being made available for the more memory-intensive editing tasks we are about to engage in. There is no need to restart the computer if you decide to lower the number of 'History States' to 20.

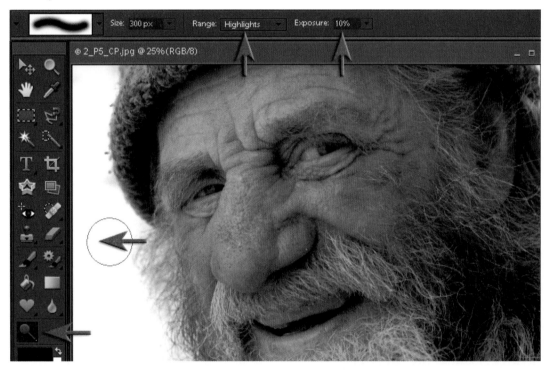

Dodge tool > Use a soft-edged brush and paint with the Dodge tool set to 'Highlights'. Reduce the opacity to around 20–30% to ensure that you lighten the background in the top left-hand corner without unduly affecting the sitter's hat. Lower the opacity to 10% to lighten the rest of the background on this side (around the beard). The following steps will ensure that this backdrop will look like something from a studio (rather than the bus shelter where this image was captured).

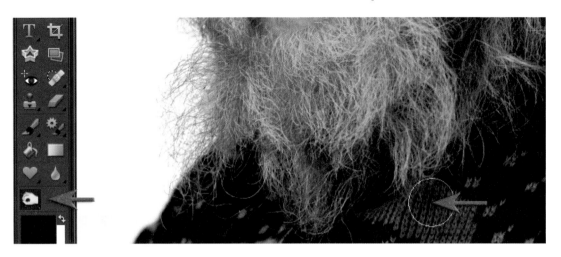

Burn tool > Use a similar soft-edged brush and paint with the Burn tool set to 'Midtones' to reduce the distracting pattern of the clothing. You are not aiming to remove the texture – just subdue it.

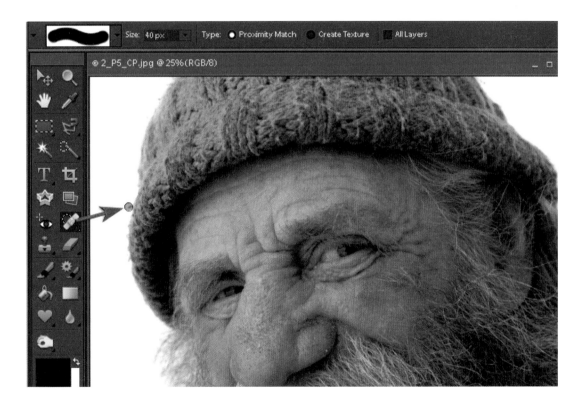

Spot Healing Brush > The Healing Brush tool is the best tool for removing distracting details or dust marks. Use a hard-edged Healing Brush when working in areas of large tonal difference, e.g. removing the dark woollen bobbles that are surrounded by the white background. This will ensure the healing area is not contaminated with the adjacent tones of the nearby hat.

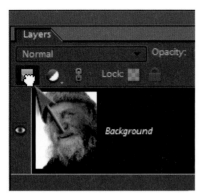
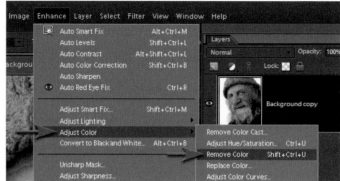

2. To start working on the tonality we need to separate the 'luminance' or brightness values from the color component of the image. Start the process by dragging the background layer to the New Layer icon in the Tools panel to duplicate it (alternatively use the keyboard shortcut Ctrl + J). From the Enhance menu choose the Remove Color command from the Adjust Color submenu. This will create a desaturated layer sitting above the colored background layer.

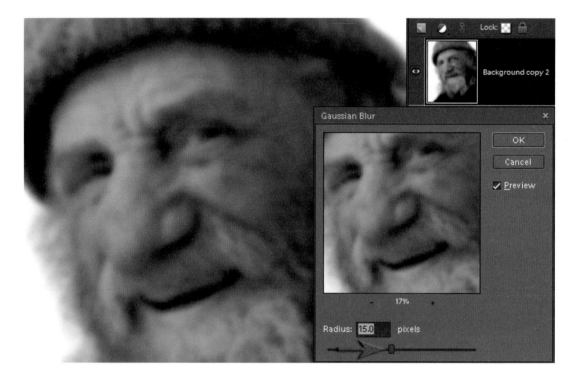

3. The fine detail of this portrait is going to be more pronounced if we create some smooth underlying tones. These smooth tones will also help to increase the three-dimensional quality of the portrait. Duplicate the desaturated layer using the keyboard shortcut Ctrl + J and then go to the Filter menu and choose 'Gaussian Blur' from the Blur submenu. Choose a generous Radius value – one where the skin tones are very smooth but the facial features can still be made out. When the 'Blur Radius' is selected choose OK.

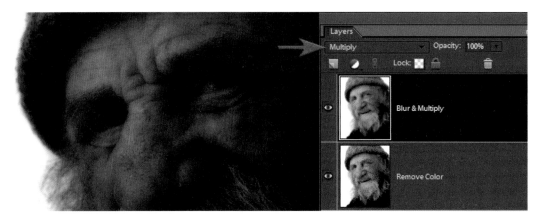

4. Switch the blend mode of the blurred layer to 'Multiply'. The Multiply mode blends the blurred tones back into the sharp detail underneath but renders the image temporarily dark. The shadow information, although very dark, is not lost or 'clipped' by this blending technique. The overall brightness of this image will be restored in the next step so that we can appreciate how effective this technique has been.

Multiply mode > The 'Multiply' blend mode is one of the most useful blend modes for creative editing of digital images. The 'Multiply' blend mode belongs to the 'Darken' family grouping. The brightness values of the pixels on the blend layer and underlying layer are multiplied to create darker tones. Only values that are multiplied with white (level 255) stay the same.

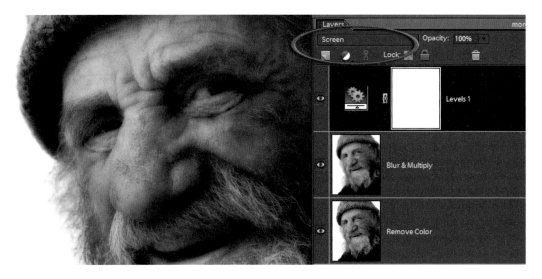

5. To restore the majority of the brightness values to this image simply create a new Levels adjustment layer and switch the blend mode to 'Screen'. The action of first multiplying and then dividing (screening) has, however, incorporated the blur layer into the pixel stew and the visual outcome is altogether different from the start image.

Screen mode > The 'Screen' mode belongs to the 'Lighten' family grouping and has the opposite effect to the 'Multiply' blend mode.

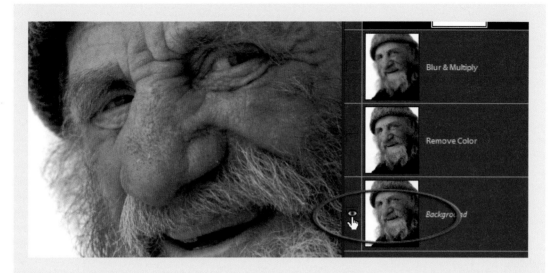

PERFORMANCE TIP - BEFORE AND AFTER

When working on a long project it is often necessary, or reassuring, to perform a quick taste test, i.e. gain a quick reminder of how life started out for this image and whether the techniques you are using are creating positive or negative visual outcomes. Rather than clicking on each Eye icon, on each individual layer, to switch the visibility off (one by one) you can simplify the process by simply holding down the Alt key and clicking only the Eye icon on the background layer. This action switches all of the other layers off in a single click, enabling you to see how life for this image started out. Alt + Click a second time to switch all of the layers back on. Looking good? Then let's proceed.

PERFORMANCE TIP - STAMP VISIBLE

One of the really essential techniques for multilayered image editing is the ability to take all of the combined elements from the visible layers and stamp them to a single new layer. It is so important that Adobe have decided to keep the shortcut a secret. The long way to achieve this stamping process involves choosing 'Select All' from the Select menu, choosing 'Copy Merged' from the Edit menu and then choosing 'Paste', again from the Edit menu.

Stamp Visible – the mother of all keyboard shortcuts

The shortcut is long, very long, but will save you considerable time as this technique is used over and over again in this style of editing. It will also impress the socks off image editors who are self-taught and who are most unlikely to have come across this permutation, as it involves holding down nearly all of the left side of the keyboard! Hold down the Ctrl, Alt and Shift modifier keys and then (whilst still holding down the modifier keys) press the letter E. If your new layer is not on top of the layers stack, click and drag it to the top of the Layers panel.

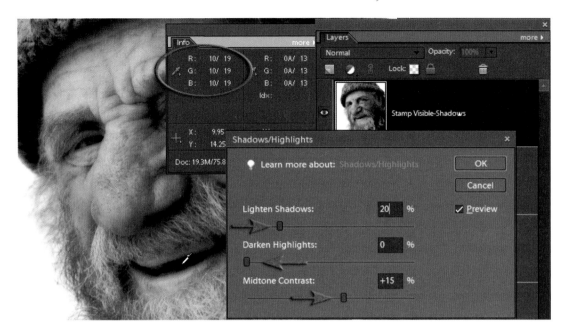

6. Sometimes tones need to be rescued if they are getting too close to 0 or 255. As the shadows are starting to make friends with level 0 and getting a little too close for comfort we must instigate a rescue attempt. We will need to stamp all of the visible elements to a new layer (see previous performance tip) if we are to utilize our good friend and ally – Shadows/Highlights. Choose Enhance > Adjust Lighting > Shadows/Highlights. Move the Lighten Shadows and Midtone Contrast sliders to values that will raise the darkest shadows above level 15.

The Shadows/Highlights adjustment feature is an excellent tool for targeting shadow or highlight tones that need to be massaged in isolation and brought back into the range of tones that can be comfortably printed using an inkjet printer. Although the 'Screen' blend mode did an excellent job of moving the midtones and highlight tones back to their former glory, the shadows of this image are still struggling to emerge above a level where they are likely to print with detail (between level 10 and level 20 depending on the type of paper, ink and printer being used). The adjustment feature can be accessed via the Enhance > Lighting menu. Before accessing the adjustment feature it is probably worth having either the Histogram panel or the Info panel open so that you can gauge when the shadows have been restored to a value that will print on your trusty inkjet printer. Raising the Midtone Contrast slider can also inject some life and drama into the tonality of the image. You may need to do a balancing act between the two sliders whilst observing the numerical or visual effects to your tonal range if you intend to make use of the Midtone Contrast slider.

PERFORMANCE TIP - SHADOWS/HIGHLIGHTS

Shadows/ Highlights > The Shadows/ Highlights adjustment feature is the most sophisticated tool for lowering excessive contrast in Adobe Elements. The tool made a very welcome appearance in Elements 3.0 and forms part of the sophisticated armory of adjustment features that can enable users to edit the tonal qualities of an image with control and confidence.

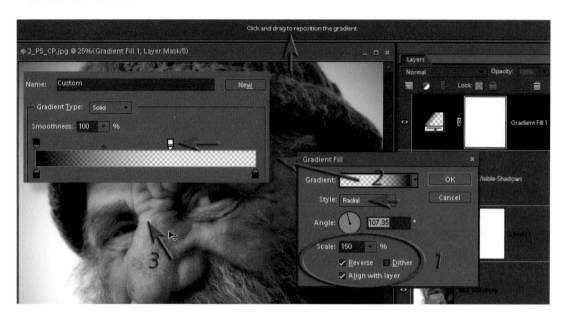

7. The next step involves getting rid of the distracting white background and replacing it with something a little more dramatic. Before creating a gradient make sure that black is the foreground color in the Tools panel (type D on the keyboard to return the color swatches to their default setting). From the Create adjustment layer menu in the Layers panel choose 'Gradient'. The creation of a radial gradient or 'vignette' involves fours steps. First choose the 'Radial' and 'Reverse' options in the Gradient Fill dialog box and enter a value of 150% in the 'Scale' field, and then choose an appropriate angle (I have followed the angle of the face). The second step involves clicking on the gradient to open the Gradient Editor. Choose the 'Foreground to Transparent' preset and move the opacity stop on the far right of the gradient ramp to the left to clear the face of any tone, thereby pushing the starting point of the gradient to the edge of the face. For the third step select OK to close the Gradient Editor and then drag inside the image window to move the center of the gradient to the perfect position. Finally (step 4) select OK and adjust the opacity of the layer to balance the background tone with the portrait.

PERFORMANCE TIP
Gradient layers > One feature short of a full load

Although gradient layers represent an important and powerful editing tool, the good people at Adobe overlooked a very important aspect in this adjustment layer feature. Gradients have a nasty habit of 'banding', either in the screen view and/or in the printed image, giving the tonal transition a posterized appearance that is not at all in keeping with the rich tonal qualities of advanced image-editing techniques. The banding can only partly be reduced by selecting the 'Dither' option (not a default option for the gradients). To ensure this banding does not raise its ugly head the user must add noise to any areas of smooth tone after any gradients have been applied. Gradient layers unfortunately do not contain pixels to which noise can be added, so this can become especially problematic and requires an additional noise layer to resolve the problem.

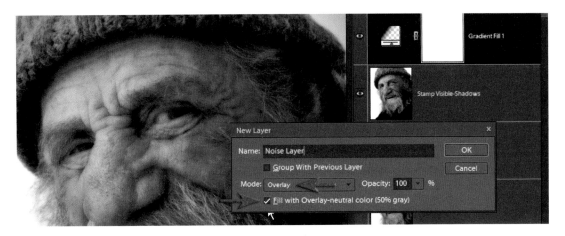

8. Adding noise rather than reducing noise may sound strange. One has to remember, however, that the gradient is completely artificial and completely noiseless – something that cannot be matched even with a low-noise image captured on a digital camera using a low ISO setting. By adding noise we are merely trying to match the noise present in the rest of the image and at the same time eliminate or reduce the problem of banding. You can add noise directly to the Gradient Fill layer but you will have more flexibility and control if the noise is added to a separate layer. To create a Noise layer hold down the Alt key and click on the New Layer icon in the Layers panel. In the New Layer dialog box choose 'Overlay' as the mode and click on the 'Fill with Overlay-neutral color (50% gray)' checkbox.

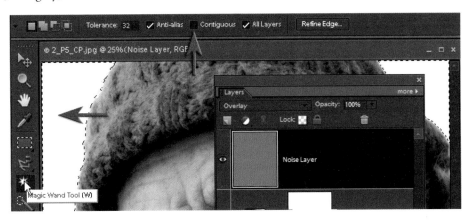

Select OK and then switch off the visibility of the Gradient layer so that we can see the original white background. Only one selection is used in this project and it is used to isolate the background for the noise treatment. Select the 'Magic Wand' from the Tools panel and select the 'Sample All Layers' option in the Options bar. Deselect the 'Contiguous' box and lower the tolerance to 20 to ensure that the selection is painless – a single click should do the trick. You will need to add a generous amount of feather (100 pixels or more) to this mask to create a gradual transition between noise and no noise (Select > Feather). After feathering the selection switch the visibility of the gray overlay layer back on. Zoom in to 100 or 200% (avoid magnifications that do not give an accurate screen view, e.g. 133% etc.).

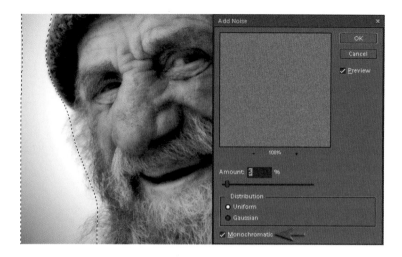

9. With the selection still active select the Add Noise filter from the Filter > Noise submenu. Select the 'Monochromatic' option and choose an amount that will create a noise level that is consistent with the rest of the image file. To check that the noise level is OK hold down the Spacebar to enable you to drag the image between the gradient (with added noise) and the face (with no added noise). When the texture is consistent select OK.

Note > Adding noise is an essential component of using gradients. Think gradient – think noise.

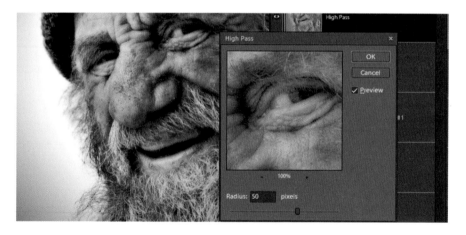

10. The localized contrast is already vastly improved from the original file, but if you want to see how far you can take this tonal manipulation you may like to try the following technique that can add depth and volume to a seemingly lifeless and flat image. Stamp the visible elements yet again to another new layer (Ctrl + Alt + Shift and then type E) and then switch the blend mode to 'Overlay'. From the Filter menu go to the Other submenu and choose the High Pass filter. When this filter is used as an alternative to the Unsharp Mask filter a small radius of between 1 and 5 is usually selected, depending on the resolution of the image file and the output medium, but in this case the Radius slider can be moved to a much higher radius whilst observing the effects to the image file. At the moment the effects may appear a little excessive, but lowering the opacity of the layer and/or switching the blend mode of the layer to 'Soft Light' can refine the overall effect.

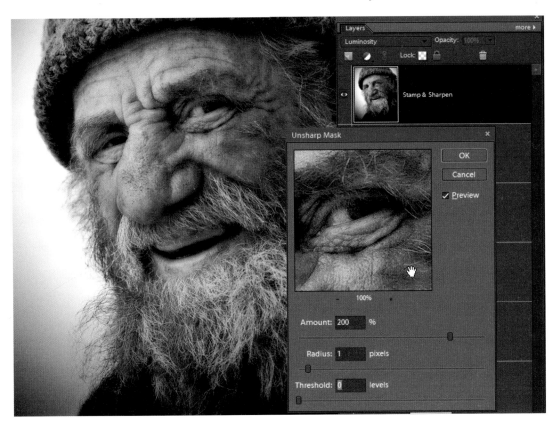

11. The rich tonality will now serve as an excellent canvas for the fine detail that we are about to sharpen. Sharpening should always be done late in the editing process to avoid exaggerating any image artifacts or non-image data. If you are to have maximum control over the sharpening process and the flexibility to adjust the level of sharpening after making a test print (images tend to look a little softer when compared to their screen counterpart – especially when using LCD displays), you need to apply the Unsharp Mask to a Copy Merged layer. You know the drill by now – stamp visible to a new layer. When this has been done you should set the blend mode to 'Luminosity'. Switching the layer to the 'Luminosity' blend mode will have zero effect on the visual outcome of the image at this stage. The advantage of this mode change is when the color is switched back on in the next and final step of the project. If you are used to applying conservative values in the Unsharp Mask filter this is not the time to exercise restraint. Be generous – very generous – with the Amount slider (200 in this project) but keep the Radius slider to the usual amount (no more than 1.5). The Threshold slider, which is usually raised to avoid sharpening minor details, can either be left at 0 so that all of the image information comes under the global sharpening umbrella or raised to around 5 so that the image noise levels are not excessively sharpened. You will need to print a test strip to your favorite paper surface before you can assess whether the amount of sharpening for this image is correct. If the sharpening seems a little excessive simply lower the opacity of the sharpening layer until you find the perfect setting for your paper.

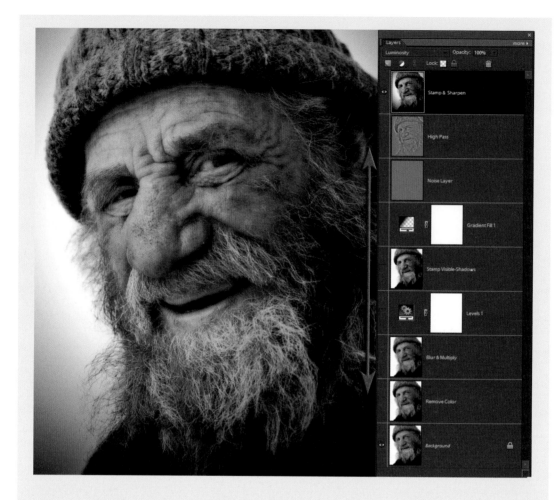

PERFORMANCE TIP

You might be so impressed with the tonal qualities of your monochrome masterpiece that the thought of switching the color back on gives you the shivers. It is important, however, to the learning curve of this project to discover how the luminance values of an image file can be edited independently of the color before being reunited. Color can be a major distraction when editing tonality. Switching off the visibility of the three monochrome or desaturated layers sitting directly above the background layer will allow the top layer in Luminosity mode to merge with the color of the background layer. The blend modes are one of the most under utilized of the editing features to be found in Photoshop Elements. Perhaps it is because of their slightly abstract names and their mathematical approach to multilayered pixel editing, but their creative power and usefulness should not be underestimated. With the digitally remastered dish ready to serve up to your printer you may need to savor both monochrome and color versions over a period of time before your own personal preference helps you make the final decision. Enjoy!

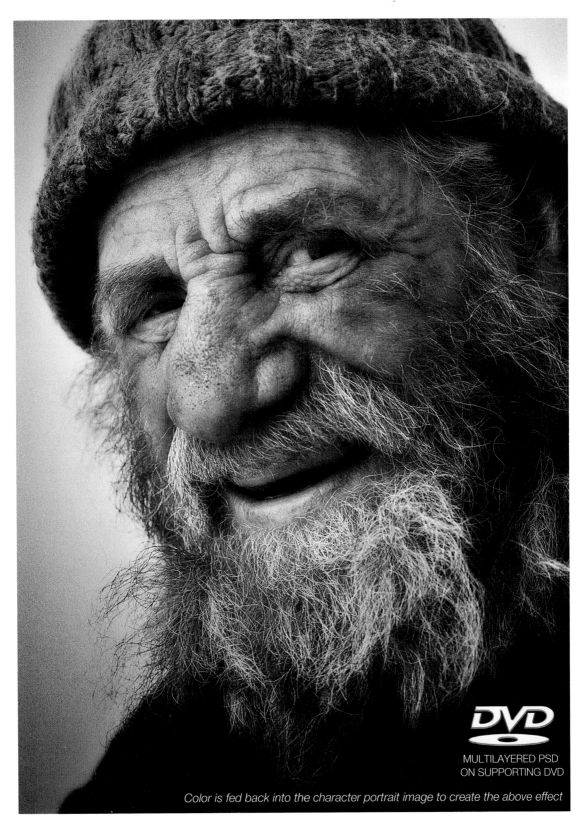

MULTILAYERED PSD
ON SUPPORTING DVD

Color is fed back into the character portrait image to create the above effect

Project 6

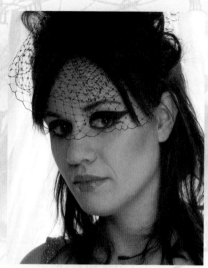

Photograph by Jennifer Stephens

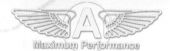

Use the soft focus action to achieve a lightning-fast makeover (minus the heal and liquify steps)

Glamor Portrait

Cheaper (and more fun) than plastic surgery, we explore how pixel surgery can be used to craft perfect portraits that are bound to flatter the sitter every time.

The glamor portrait offers an excellent opportunity to test the effectiveness of a variety of image-editing skills. The portrait is an unforgiving canvas that will show any heavy-handed or poor technique that may be applied. We will start with a color portrait that has been captured using a soft diffused light source.

This project will aim to perfect various features and not to make such changes that the character of the sitter is lost to the technique. The techniques used do not excessively smooth or obliterate the skin texture that would, in turn, lead to an artificial or plastic appearance. The techniques used smooth imperfections without totally eliminating them.

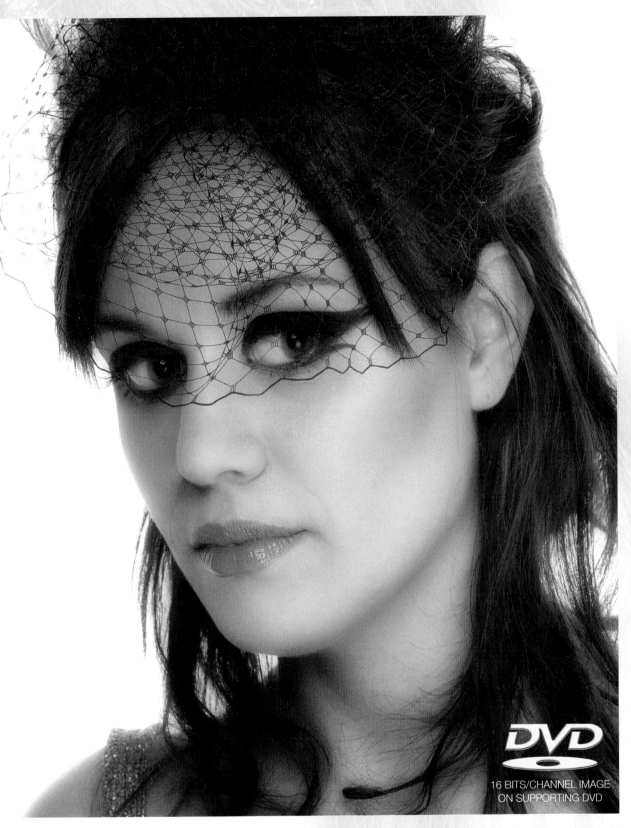

DVD

16 BITS/CHANNEL IMAGE
ON SUPPORTING DVD

The 15-minute (after practice) makeover – techniques designed to flatter your model

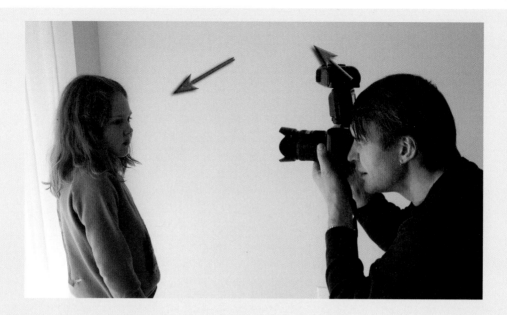

PERFORMANCE TIP

Use window light or diffused flash to obtain a soft low-contrast light source to flatter the subject. Avoid direct flash unless it is diffused with a white umbrella. Stand back from your sitter and zoom in with your lens rather than coming in close and distorting the features of the face (the closer you stand, the bigger the nose of the sitter appears). A perfect white background is difficult to create if you don't have a studio backdrop and multiple lights but, with a little practise, it is possible to get a near white background by capturing the sitter in front of a white translucent curtain against a brightly illuminated window and with a single introduced light source.

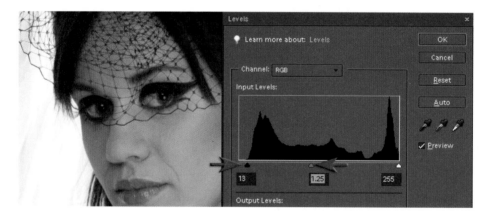

1. If you can capture using the Raw format then you will have the opportunity of perfecting the histogram and color balance in 16 Bits/Channel mode prior to starting the project. Choose Enhance > Adjust Lighting > Levels, then drag the Shadow and Highlight sliders in to meet the histogram or simply click the Auto button. Drop the bit depth once this has been done to 8-bit mode (Image > Mode > 8 Bits/Channel).

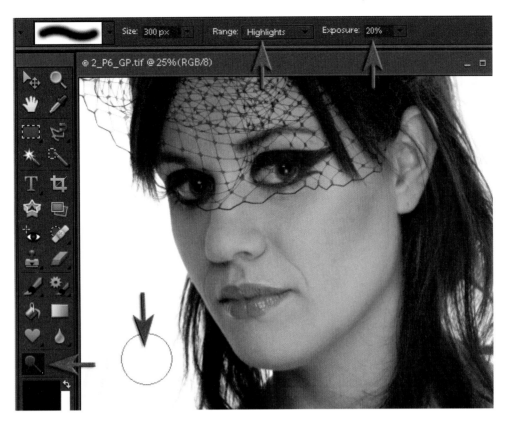

2. Select the 'Dodge tool' in the Tools panel and in the Options bar choose 'Highlights' and an exposure setting of around 20–30%. If you are a little nervous about using this tool on the background layer duplicate the background layer by dragging it to the New Layer icon in the Layers panel. Stroke the background with a large soft brush until any detail or tone present is rendered white. As the Dodge tool in Highlight mode only lightens the brightest tones on the layer, care only needs to be taken if the skin tones or hair next to the white background are also very bright.

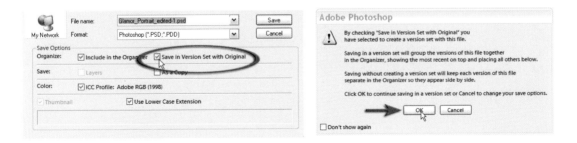

3. As you move through this project it is worth saving consecutive versions. The Organizer in Elements can keep track of these versions (providing the file is already in the Organizer's catalog) and help name them if you click on the 'Save in Version Set with Original' option when you use the Save As command from the File menu.

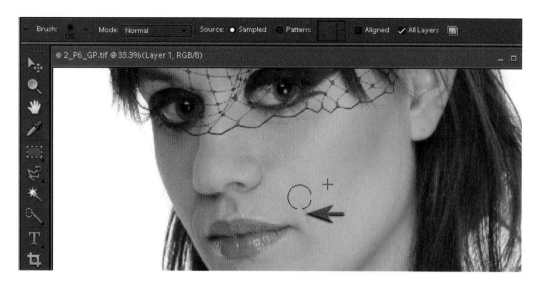

4. Select the Healing Brush from the Tools panel to remove or reduce dark lines on the face. A time-saving technique when working with the Healing Brush tool is to either duplicate the background layer or create a new empty layer before starting the healing process. You can simply fade all of your work at the end of the process by dropping the opacity of the healing layer. If you choose to heal to an empty layer make sure that this is the layer that is selected in the Layers panel and the 'Sample All Layers' option is selected in the Options bar.

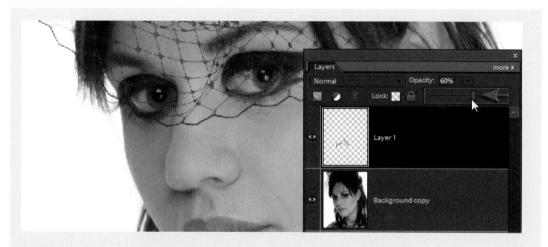

PERFORMANCE TIP

Care must be taken when selecting the size and hardness of the brush. If an overly large soft-edged brush is used near the eyes, lips or hair it can draw in color values that can contaminate the skin tones (a selection can be made prior to using the Healing Brush to isolate the healing area from different colors or tones). If the brush is too hard the edges of the healing area will be visible. Sometimes it is better to use a smaller brush and make several passes rather than trying to complete the section with a single pass. The Healing Brush tool, with its protection of surface texture, is a superior alternative to using the Rubber Stamp tool at a reduced opacity.

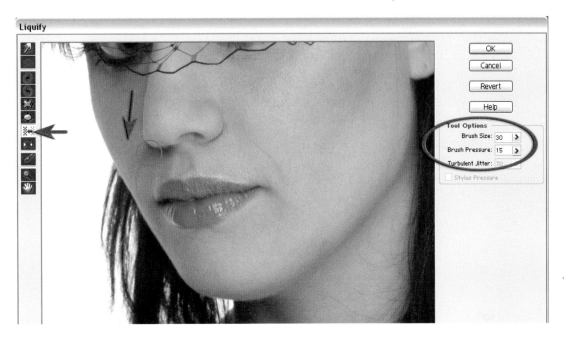

5. Next we're going to alter the facial features. Choose Filter > Distort > Liquify. The Liquify filter is another tool that works directly on your pixels so you may like to duplicate the background layer if you are feeling nervous about the pixel surgery that follows. The various tools in the Liquify filter dialog box can be used to modify the shape or size of the sitter's features. The Pucker tool and Bloat tool can be used to contract or expand various features, e.g. grow eyes or lips and shrink noses. Perhaps the most useful of the Liquify tools, however, is the Shift Pixels tool. This tool can be used to move pixels to the left when stroking down and to the right when stroking up. This tool is ideal for trimming off unsightly fat or reshaping features. In this project the brush pressure is dropped to 15% and an appropriate brush size is selected so that the side of the face is not moved along with the nose. If things start to get ugly just remember the keyboard shortcut Ctrl + Z (undo)!

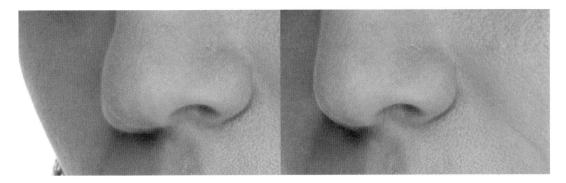

Note > It is important to exercise great restraint when using the Liquify filter, as the face can quickly become a cartoon caricature of itself when taken too far. The filter also softens detail that becomes obvious when overdone.

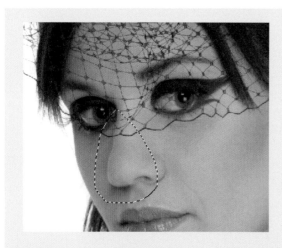
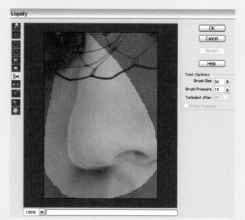

PERFORMANCE TIP

It is possible to 'freeze' pixels to protect them from the actions of the Liquify filter. There is a freeze brush in the Liquify filter of the full version of Photoshop – but not so in Elements. To activate the freeze in Elements simply make a feathered selection prior to selecting the Liquify filter. Select the area to be modified, being careful to leave out sections of the face that should be protected from the pixel surgery. With the selection active open the Liquify dialog box. The areas outside of the selection are now frozen.

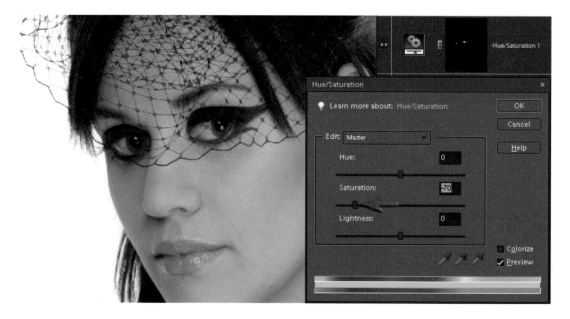

6. Create a Hue/Saturation adjustment layer. Focus your attention on the whites of the eyes and lower the saturation until any discoloring in the eyes is removed. Disregard the effects to the rest of the face for the time being. Select OK and then fill the layer mask with black to conceal the adjustment (Alt + Backspace if black is in the foreground color swatch or Ctrl + Backspace if black is in the background color swatch).

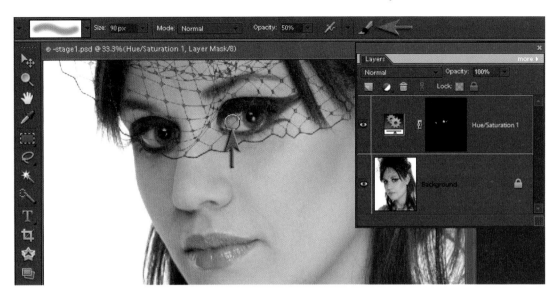

Select the 'Brush tool' from the Tools panel. Choose a soft-edged brush just a little smaller than the eye in the Options bar and lower the opacity to 50%. Choose white as the foreground color in the Tools panel. Stroke the whites of the eyes with the brush until they are appropriately drained of color.

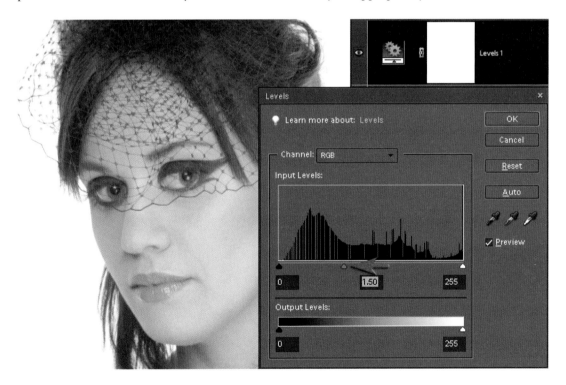

7. Create a Levels adjustment layer and move the Gamma slider to the left to brighten the whites of the eyes. As before, select OK and then fill the layer mask with black to conceal the adjustment once again.

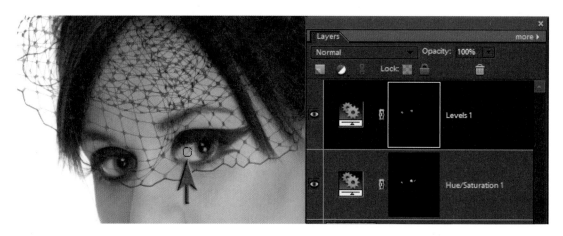

This time brighten the eyes by painting with white at 50% opacity. If you overdo it you can switch colors and paint with black or simply lower the opacity of the adjustment layer.

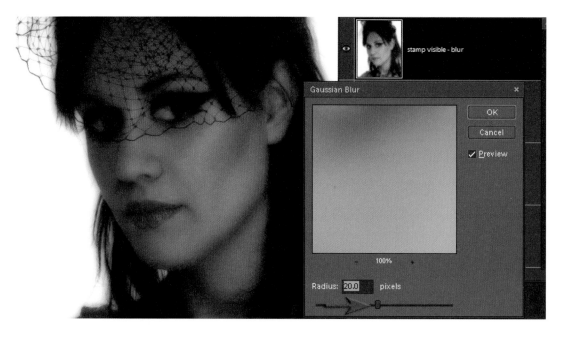

8. The technique to smooth the tones of the face is quick and very effective. The first step is to merge all of the visible elements of this image into a new layer on top of the layers stack (referred to as 'Stamp Visible'). Hold down all of the modifier keys (the Ctrl, Shift and Alt keys) and then type in the letter E. Make sure the resulting layer is on top of the layers stack and set the blend mode of this layer to 'Multiply'. Go to the Filter menu and choose 'Gaussian Blur' from the Blur submenu. Apply a 20-pixel Gaussian Blur.

Visual warning > Now it is going to look like someone turned out some of the lights until we carry out the next stage of the process, but if you use your imagination you can probably already see that the skin tones are now smooth and radiant – if just a tad dark.

PERFORMANCE TIP

The precise pixel radius of the Gaussian Blur filter will vary depending on the resolution of your image. The idea is to bleed the tones, but not so much as to lose the features of the face.

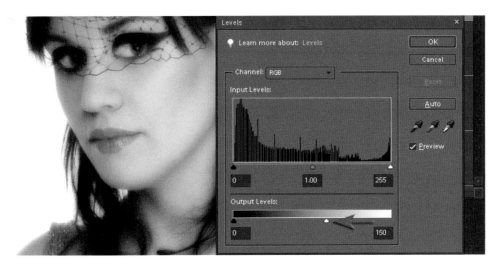

9. Create a Levels adjustment layer and set the blend mode to Screen to lighten the image. If the image is still not light enough drag this adjustment layer to the New Layer icon to duplicate it. The blend mode of this duplicate layer will also be in Screen mode. If this lightens the highlights too much drag the Output highlight slider towards the center of the histogram to restrict the screening effect to the shadows and midtones only.

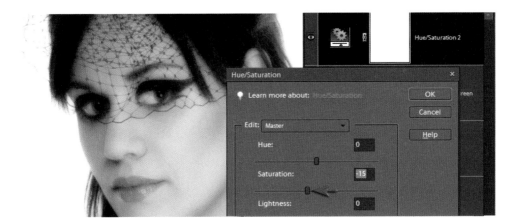

10. Create a Hue/Saturation layer above these screened layers and lower the saturation a little. The side effect to smoothing the skin tones using this technique is that saturation increases. Another problem that will need to be resolved is that the deepest shadow tones may be pushed too dark to print. These important shadow tones will need to be rescued in order to produce a professional result.

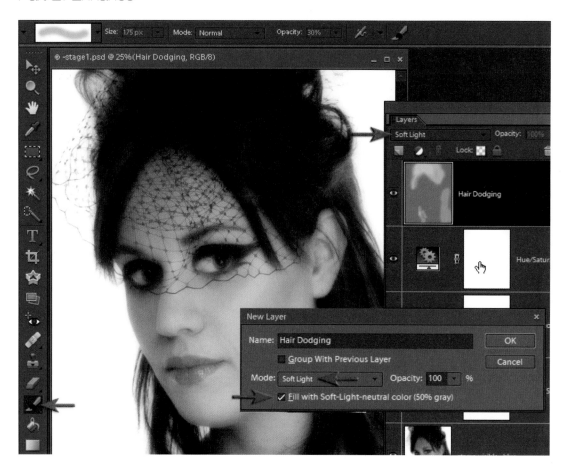

Fine-tuning the tonality

11. There are a number of different ways we can rescue the shadow tones of this image. The first technique uses the non-destructive dodge layer technique. Hold down the Alt key whilst you click on the New Layer icon in the Layers panel. Switch the mode to 'Soft Light' and check the 'Fill with Overlay-neutral color (50% gray)' box. Select OK. This 50% gray layer is invisible in 'Soft Light' mode but can be used to lighten or darken the underlying image. Select 'White' as the foreground color and use a soft-edged brush at 50% opacity to paint the darkest areas of the hair lighter. Several passes at a reduced opacity rather than a single pass at 100% opacity will render the dodging a subtle affair.

PERFORMANCE TIP
Try switching the blend mode of your dodge and burn layer to Overlay mode instead of Soft Light mode for alternative effects when dodging and burning.

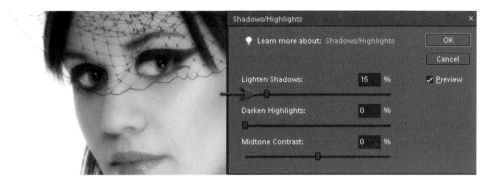

12. The Shadows/Highlights adjustment feature from the Enhance > Adjust Lighting submenu can also be used to target and rescue the darker tones of your image. Stamp Visible to a new layer before implementing the adjustment. When using a layer mask with the Shadows/Highlights adjustment command it is possible to pump up the level of lightening and midtone contrast without affecting the midtones or highlights in the image.

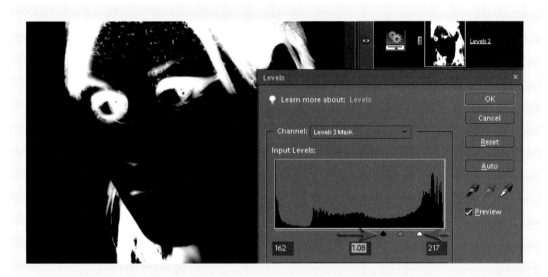

PERFORMANCE TIP

The Shadows/Highlights is a very powerful adjustment feature. Use a layer mask to further limit or restrict the effects of the Shadows/Highlights adjustment. Create a Levels adjustment layer without making any adjustment (simply click OK). Copy the image to the clipboard (Edit > Copy Merged) and paste it into the layer mask of this adjustment layer. In order to paste the image into the layer mask you must first Alt + Click the layer mask. When you Alt + Click an empty layer mask the image window will appear completely white. From the Edit menu choose 'Paste'. If this action is not taken the copied pixels will be pasted to a new layer. To restrict the adjustment to just the darkest tones of the image you must first invert the image in the layer mask (Ctrl + I) and then perform a Levels adjustment (Ctrl + L) to this layer mask. Move the Shadow slider to the right to restrict the lightening process to just the darkest shadows. Move the Highlight slider to the left to increase the effect of the Shadows adjustment.

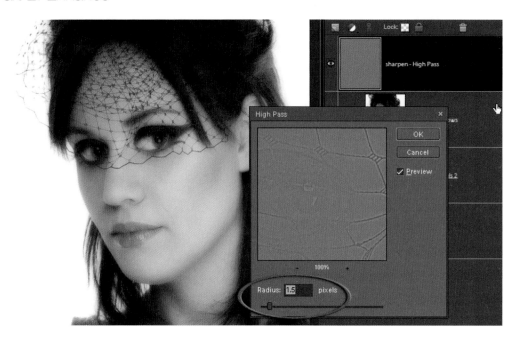

13. Smooth skin tones can be unduly sensitive to the application of the Unsharp Mask. It is usual to raise the Threshold slider sufficiently so that areas of smooth tonal gradation are left unaffected. Film grain, image sensor noise and minor skin defects all come in for the sharpening treatment if the threshold is left too low. If the sharpening process is proving problematic using the Unsharp Mask, a selective sharpening technique should be considered. Stamp Visible to a new layer, set the blend mode to 'Overlay' and apply the High Pass filter (Filter > Other > High Pass). At this stage the sharpening is global but it can be restricted by using a layer mask borrowed from an adjustment layer or by painting directly into this High Pass layer using 50% gray to eliminate sharpening.

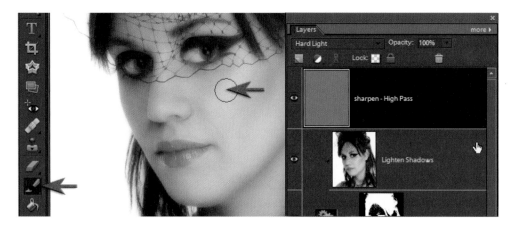

Click on a 50% gray swatch in the Swatches panel or click on the foreground color swatch in the Tools panel and set the HSB values to 0, 0 and 50. With 50% gray as your foreground color you can now proceed to paint the smoother areas of skin to ensure they escape the sharpening process.

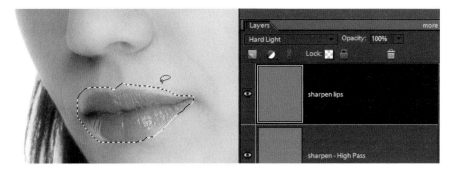

14. You can add a little lip-gloss (or extra sparkle to the eyes) by duplicating the High Pass layer and filling the rest of the image with 50% gray. Make selections of the lips and/or eyes and then invert the selection. Then choose 'Fill Selection' from the Edit menu and choose 50% gray. Switching the mode of the layer to 'Hard Light' will pump up the effect to maximum.

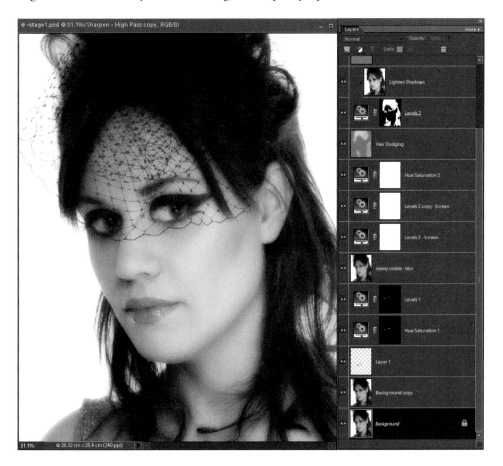

It might seem like a long road to the final result but this technique can be surprisingly quick when you get into the swing of things. It avoids excessive selections and fiddly work, and a lot of minor blemishes are nuked via the blurred layer set to Multiply mode. Of course the real reward will be the admiration of your photographic skills by the sitter – who will be eternally grateful.

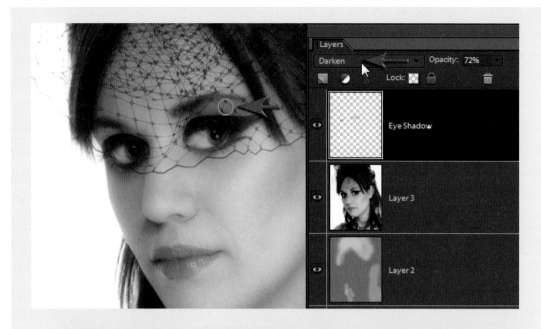

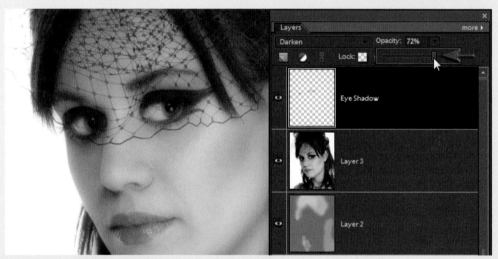

PERFORMANCE TIP

If you can't leave well enough alone, or would just like to explore different approaches to the make-up the model is using, then you can add your own make-up in post-production instead of pre-production. Add a new empty layer set to Darken or Multiply mode. Using a soft paint brush set to 50% opacity build up some eye shadow, rouge or lipstick and then lower the opacity of the layer until you create the right effect.

Try grouping a Hue/Saturation slider with the make-up layer and move the Hue and Saturation slider to explore alternative shades quickly and easily. If only getting ready to go out for the evening was this simple!

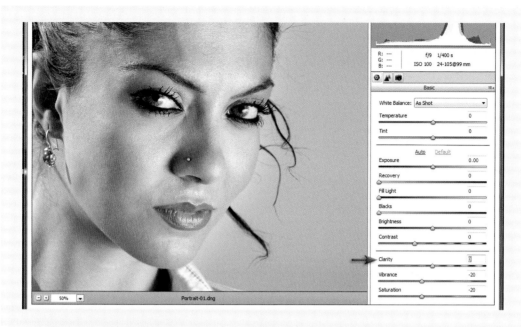

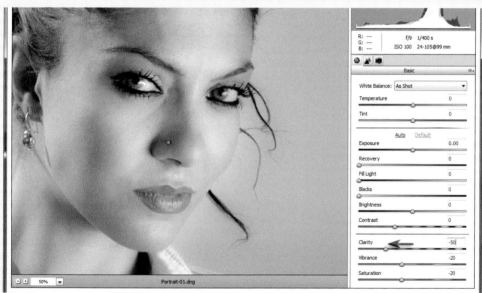

Ozgurdonmaz (www.iStockphoto.com - image number 4875147)

NEGATIVE CLARITY IN ADOBE CAMERA RAW

Softening the skin tones on a model's face that had to be performed in the main editing space can now be carried out much faster in Adobe Camera Raw (ACR). In Adobe Camera Raw 4.5 and later we now have the option to use a 'Negative Clarity' adjustment. This is useful to soften and suppress detail and texture. In the example above the Clarity slider has been dropped to −50 to illustrate how the adjustment can be used to reduce the excessive detail in the model's skin. Be careful, as excessive amounts of negative clarity will lower the contrast of the image.

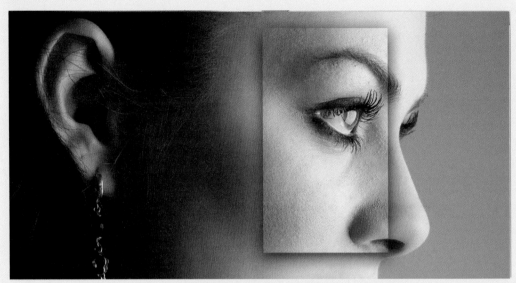

Ozgurdonmaz (www.iStockphoto.com - image number 5009631)

SURFACE BLUR FILTER (NEW TO PHOTOSHOP ELEMENTS 7)

This filter, unlike the Gaussian Blur filter, has a 'Threshold' slider that, if used correctly, will leave edges crisp and sharp whilst blurring the surfaces inside the edges. This will ensure there are no nasty haloes around the edges of your subject as a result of the blurring process.

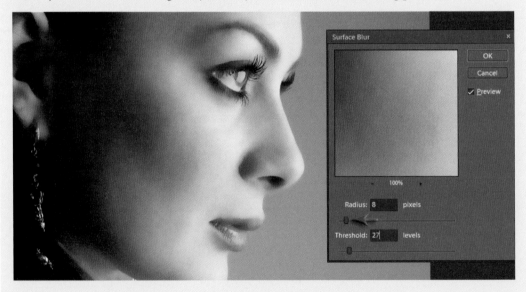

It is important to get the balance right between the Radius and the Threshold slider settings for each and every image (there is no one 'perfect recipe' that suits every image). To get a feel for what these two sliders do, set them both to a value between 20 and 25. Now move the Radius slider lower until you detect the surface tone becoming 'mottled' or 'blotchy' and then move it higher again until the surface appears very smooth. Finding the minimum radius that renders the surface smooth is your goal here.

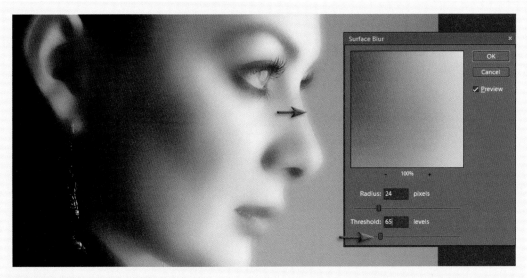

Now drag the Threshold slider higher until you see haloes appear around the edges of your subject. Back the slider off to a point where all of the haloes disappear. If you continue to move the slider lower, after the haloes have disappeared, you will start to re-introduce the finer detail that was removed by the Radius slider. Try to make the surface as smooth as possible at this stage as some of the texture and detail can be made visible by lowering the opacity of this layer.

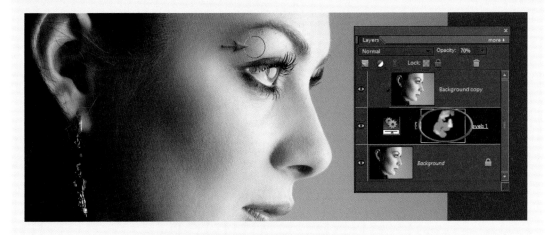

Select OK to apply the Surface Blur filter. Create an adjustment layer below this copy layer and group the background copy layer to the adjustment layer (Layer > Group with Previous). Fill the adjustment layer mask with black to conceal the surface blur. Select white as the foreground color in the Tools panel and then choose a soft-edged brush and set the opacity to 60-80% in the Options bar. Paint to reveal the blur in the areas of the skin only. You do not need to be too critical about accuracy as areas of fine detail such as the eyelashes and the contours of the face have already been preserved on the Surface Blur layer. You will, however need to avoid painting over areas such as the lips to ensure fine detail is not lost in these areas. Paint a second time to reveal additional softening where needed.

Project 7

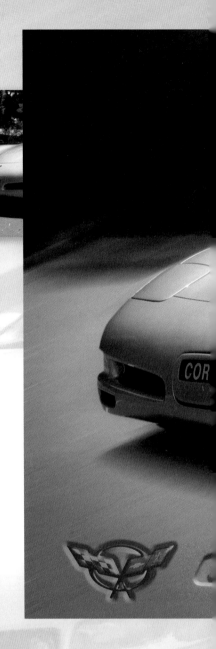

Motion Blur

If you have a need for speed and would like to 'move it, move it' this project shows you how to get some ooomph into your stationary wagon.

To get some motion magic happening we need to start with nothing more than a half-decent parked car. The example used in this project may look like your professional car shoot but was in fact captured using a fixed lens digicam in a school car park. With little more than a selection, a couple of blur filters and a little know-how the static becomes dramatic.

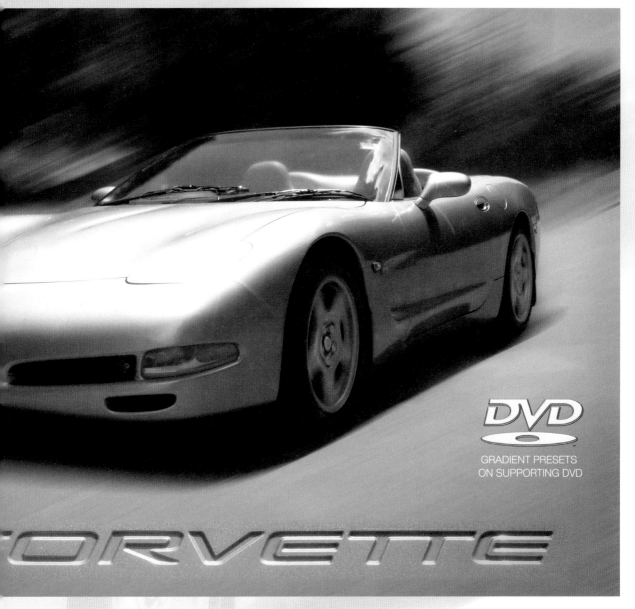

CORVETTE

GRADIENT PRESETS
ON SUPPORTING DVD

A 1999 Corvette is polished and taken for a spin in this classic car makeover

The post-production editing or 'car makeover' is simplified when there are not too many reflections in the bodywork or chrome of the car that you capture. Busy reflections will either detract from the final quality or increase the time you spend removing the unwanted detail. In this tutorial you will learn how to smooth out the bodywork, streak the background and spin the wheels, and finally put the icing on the corporate cake by applying the logos to give the image that advertising look.

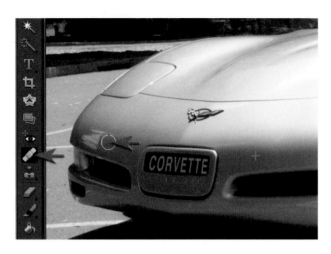 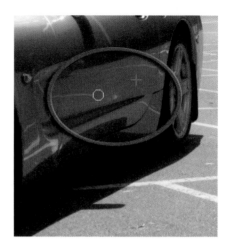

Stage 1 - Cleaning the paintwork

1. If you are not experienced using the Healing Brush tool and Clone Stamp tool I would recommend duplicating the background layer by dragging it to the New Layer icon in the Layers panel. This will give you the option of trashing the layer if all goes horribly wrong. Hold down the Alt key and click on an area of good paintwork and then paint over any scratches, blemishes or damaged areas. Vary both the size and the hardness of the brush to get the best results. If you are working in the middle of a panel the Healing Brush tool usually gives the best results. If you are working close to an edge you may want to try increasing the hardness of the brush in the Options bar or switching to the Clone Stamp tool. Double-click on the layer name in the Layers panel and name it 'Clean' to differentiate it from the background layer.

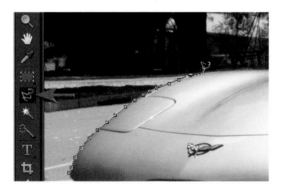 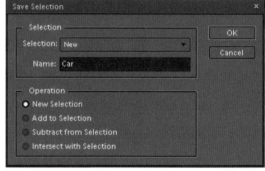

2. Make a selection of the car using one of the tools from the Lasso group (the edge contrast is a little too low for the Quick Selection tool). The Magnetic Lasso tool will do a good job of selecting most of the car. Select only the car, excluding its shadow. Click on an edge of the car with the Magnetic Lasso tool and move the tool slowly along the edge to start the process. You will notice that the tool lays down anchor points. When moving the tool over an edge with poor contrast you can help Photoshop along a little by clicking to add an anchor point manually (Photoshop cannot see some edges due to the poor contrast). Alternatively you can fine-tune the sensitivity of the tool by experimenting with the settings in the Options bar. From the Select menu choose 'Save Selection', give your selection a name such as 'Car' and click OK.

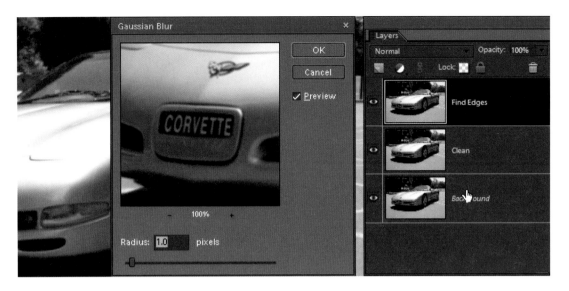

3. The next part of the process involves separating the edges of the car from the broader areas of paintwork. This will allow us to smooth out the paintwork whilst retaining the definition and detail of the edges. Duplicate the layer you have just cleaned and healed (if you duplicated the background layer in the first step you will now have three layers in your Layers panel) and apply a 1-pixel Gaussian Blur (Filter > Blur > Gaussian Blur). This prepares the file for the filter used in the next step.

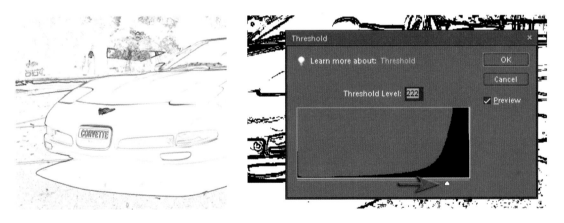

4. Choose the Find Edges filter found in the Stylize submenu (Filter > Stylize > Find Edges) to reduce this layer to the edges only. To increase the contrast and width of the edges we can apply the Threshold filter from the Adjustments submenu (Filter > Adjustments > Threshold). Drag the slider in the Threshold dialog box to the right until you have well-defined black lines and limited detail visible in the panels. Name the layer you have been working on to save any possible confusion later. I have called mine 'Find Edges'.

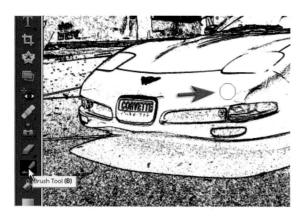
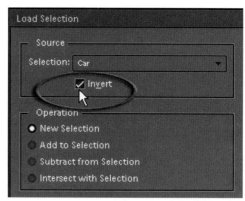

5. Select the 'Brush tool' in the Tools panel and 'White' as the foreground color (press the letter D on your keyboard to set the colors to their default settings and then press the letter X to switch the foreground and background colors). Paint to remove any detail in the paintwork that is not required, i.e. anything that is not the edge of a panel or important detail that needs to be pin sharp. Load the selection (Select > Load Selection) that you saved earlier in step 2. Check the Invert box and then select OK. The background should now be selected.

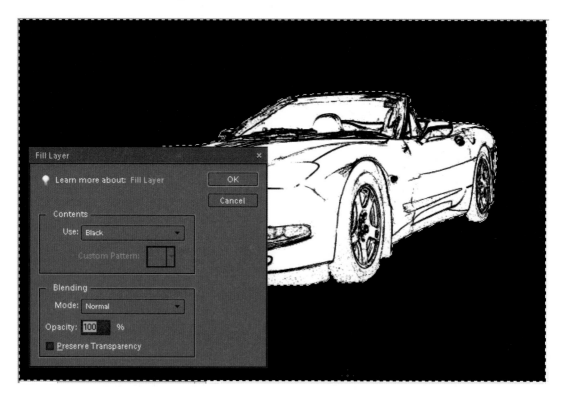

6. Choose 'Fill Selection' from the Edit menu and select 'Black' for the contents color. Select OK. Your image should now appear as a line drawing of the car with a black background. Choose 'Deselect' from the Select menu.

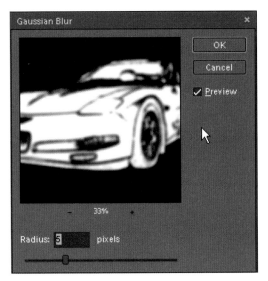
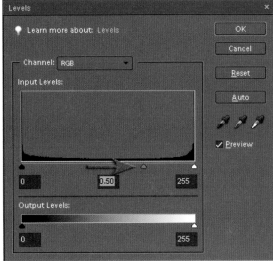

7. To soften the lines so that detail of the edges fades gradually into the smooth paintwork we must apply a small amount of Gaussian Blur to this layer. Although softening the edges the Gaussian Blur may also reduce the density of the lines, so follow the Gaussian Blur with a Levels adjustment (Enhance > Adjust Lighting > Levels). In the Levels dialog box move the central Gamma slider underneath the histogram to the right until the lines once again appear black. This is now the resource for our mask that we will use to protect the important detail when we smooth out the superfluous detail in the bodywork.

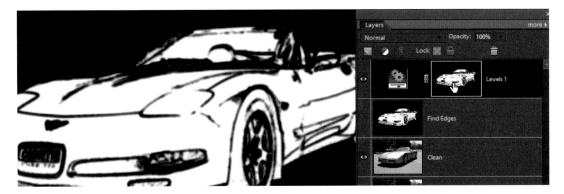

8. To transfer this layer to a mask we need to choose 'All' from the Select menu. Photoshop Elements cannot add a layer mask to a pixel layer so we will need to borrow a mask from an adjustment layer. Create a Levels adjustment layer and then select OK without making any adjustment. Hold down the Alt key and click on the layer mask of this adjustment layer in the Layers panel. The image window will appear white (you are now viewing the contents of the layer mask, and as yet there is nothing in there). Now choose 'Paste' from the Edit menu and the line drawing of your car should now appear. Alt-click the layer mask a second time and choose 'Deselect' from the Select menu. Although it appears you are still viewing the layer mask you are in fact viewing the layer beneath, which is identical.

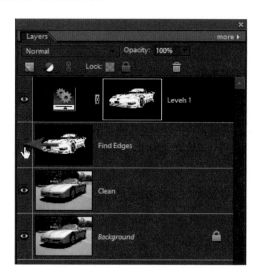 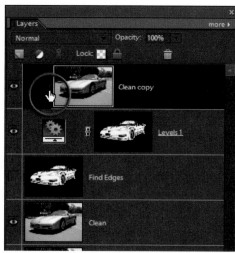

9. Click on the Eye icon to hide the visibility of the mask resource layer I have called 'Find Edges' (the one below the adjustment layer) or discard it by dragging it to the Trashcan icon in the Layers panel. Create a duplicate of the layer that you cleaned in step 1 by holding down the Alt key and dragging it to the top of the layers stack. Group this layer with the adjustment layer supporting your layer mask by going to the Layer menu and choosing the command Group with Previous.

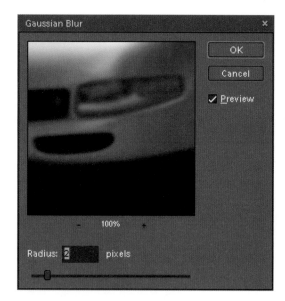 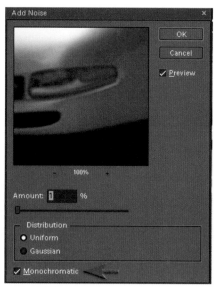

10. Apply a small amount of Gaussian Blur to this Clean Copy layer – 1 or 2 pixels is usually required if you are using a file from a fixed lens digital compact or prosumer camera. This step will create smooth paintwork by removing superfluous detail and image noise. The important detail such as the crisp edges to the bodywork and panels will not be affected due to the actions of the mask below. If you have used more than 1-pixel Gaussian Blur to smooth the paintwork you may need to add 1% noise to this layer to prevent possible tonal banding or posterization (visual steps of tone instead of a smooth transition of tone).

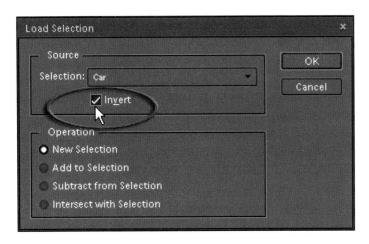

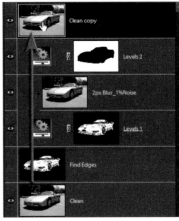

Stage 2 - Blurring the background

11. Now that the car looks brand new we can add the dramatic element in this project. Load the selection of your car, ensuring the Invert box is checked again (Select > Load Selection). Create another adjustment layer with the selection still active. There is no need to make any adjustment. We are again just using the adjustment layer to access its layer mask. The active selection will create its own layer mask. Again whilst holding down the Alt key, drag a copy of the clean layer to the top of the layers stack. You may want to rename your previous clean copy layer to save any possible confusion or to remember any settings you have used.

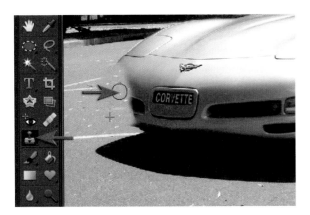

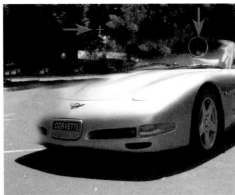

12. Before we apply the Motion Blur filter to this copy layer we must prepare the layer so that the car is not streaked into the background, thereby creating a ghost image of itself. Select the 'Clone Stamp tool' from the Tools panel. Choose a large soft-edged brush set to 100% opacity in the Options bar. Clone away the front and the rear of the car by setting a source point in the road in the lower right-hand corner of the image. To set the source point hold down the Alt key and click your mouse. Clone away the top of the car by moving the source point to the trees above the windscreen. There is no need to be overly precise with this work, as any imperfections will be hidden when the Motion Blur filter is applied in the next step.

Important > Do not clone away any of the shadow of the car.

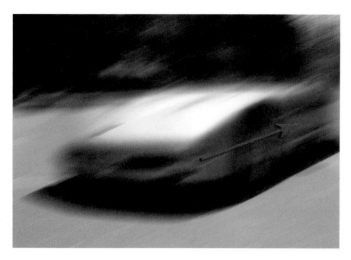
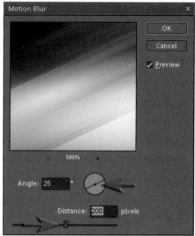

13. Go to the Filter menu and choose 'Motion Blur' from the Blur submenu. Drag the Distance slider to the right to increase the apparent speed of the car. Adjust the angle using the little wheel or by entering a figure in the field so that the streaked lines of the blurred background appear to line up with the angle of the car and then select OK. Group the motion blur layer with the adjustment layer beneath by choosing the Group with Previous command from the Layer menu. Although we now have an impressive result the image is not yet perfect.

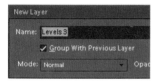
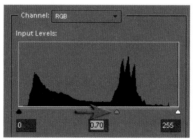
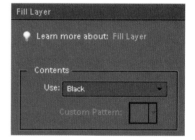

14. We must now turn our attention to the shadows. The Motion Blur filter may drag lighter tones underneath where the wheels make contact with the ground. This will give the illusion that the car is floating above the road instead of in contact with it. To darken the road immediately next to the tires we can use an adjustment layer. To prevent the adjustment layer from lightening the entire image we simply need to add the adjustment layer to the group. Hold down the Alt key as you click on the Adjustment Layer icon in the Layers panel and select a Levels adjustment layer. When the New Layer dialog box opens check the Group With Previous Layer box and select OK. When the Levels dialog box opens move the central Gamma slider underneath the histogram to the right to darken the road. Pay particular attention to the road directly in front of the rear wheel. Select OK when the tones match. To restrict this darkening process to just a small area around the wheels we must fill the layer mask with black. Go to the Edit menu and choose 'Fill Layer'. Select 'Black' as the contents and select OK. The effects of the adjustment layer will momentarily disappear.

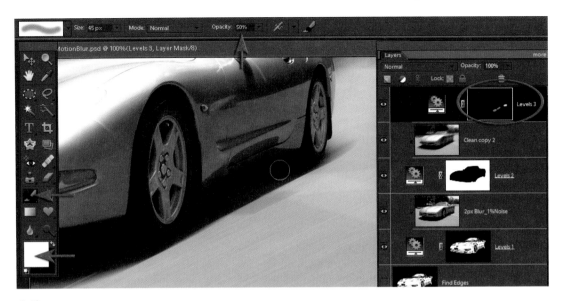

15. Now choose the 'Brush tool' in the Tools panel and select 'White' as the foreground color. Drop the opacity of the brush to 50% and paint where the road requires darkening. Make several strokes with the brush (letting go of the mouse button after each stroke) until the road is darkened sufficiently.

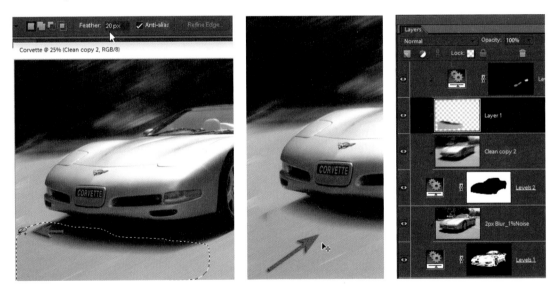

16. The act of adding motion blur to the shadow has made it too long in front of the car so we need to reposition it. Make a selection of the soft leading edge of the shadow using the Lasso tool with a 20-pixel feather selected in the Options bar. Select 'Copy' from the Edit menu and then select 'Paste' from the Edit menu. Group this layer with the Layer group underneath (Layer > Group with Previous). Select the 'Move tool' and drag the shadow back underneath the car. Ignore the original shadow that may appear to the left, as this will be removed in the next step.

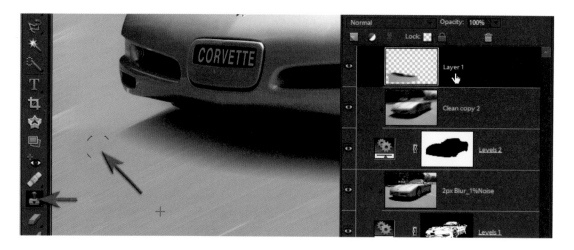

17. To remove any evidence of the original shadow select the 'Clone Stamp tool' and check the Sample All Layers box in the Options bar. This option will allow you to select the pixels from the layer underneath without first selecting it. Choose a sample point by holding down the Alt key and clicking the mouse. Now the Motion Blur will be convincing and the car will look like it is neither floating nor parked.

Stage 3 - Spinning the wheels

If you examine the pin-sharp wheels of the car you will probably appreciate that there is still more work to do before we can hide the fact that this car is actually static. We must apply a small amount of Motion Blur to the wheels but this needs to be a radial instead of linear Motion Blur.

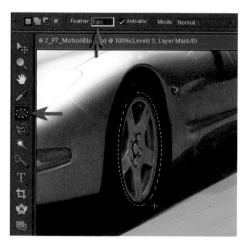 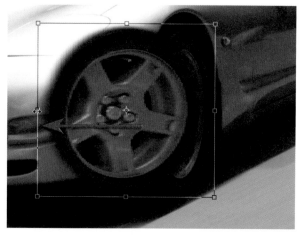

18. Make a selection with the Circular Marquee tool using a 5-pixel feather. If you need to move the selection before it is complete (letting go of the mouse button will complete the selection) you can press the Spacebar and slide the selection to a better position. Copy the wheel using the Copy Merged command from the Edit menu. The Copy Merged command will copy all of the visible pixels instead of the pixels on the currently selected layer. Choose 'Paste' from the Edit menu to paste a copy of the wheel to a new layer. From the Select menu choose Reselect.

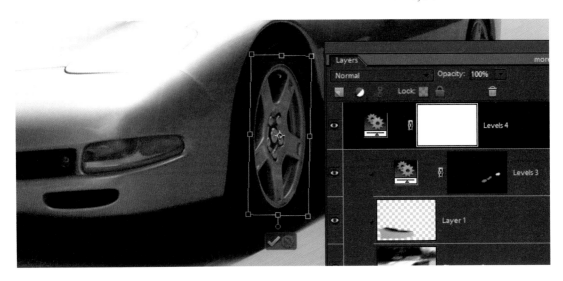

Note > If the ellipse of the selection is slightly crooked when compared to the ellipse of the wheel that you are trying to select you can rotate the selection by using the Transform command (Image > Transform > Free Transform). You must, however, select an adjustment layer with an empty layer mask to ensure that no pixels are rotated when the elliptical selection is rotated. As none are currently available in this project you would have to create one.

Choose the Transform command (Image > Transform > Free Transform) and drag the side handle of the bounding box until the wheel appears as a circle instead of an ellipse. To get the best result from the Radial Blur filter we must present the wheel on the same plane to the one in which the filter works, i.e. front on.

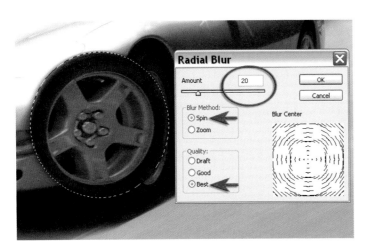
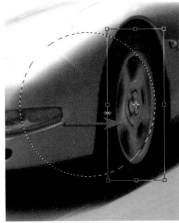

19. From the Blur group of Filters choose the Radial Blur filter. Check the radio buttons 'Spin' and 'Best' and start with a value of around 20 pixels before clicking OK. If the radial blur is excessive or insufficient choose 'Undo' from the Edit menu and then try the filter using an alternative amount. When you have applied the filter choose the Transform command again and return the wheel to its original elliptical shape. Repeat the process with the rear wheel.

Stage 4 - Adding the graphics

A classic car shot such as this would look great with a little window dressing. Rather than create the graphics from scratch a couple of extra close-up images were taken of the car model name and its distinctive logo of crossed flags.

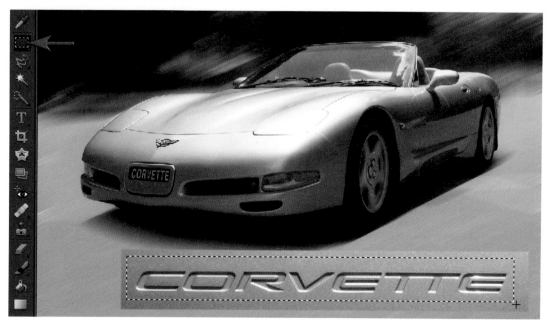

20. Open the image 'Logo1' and then click and drag the background layer thumbnail in the Layers panel from this new image file into the window of the car image. Use the Move tool to drag it into position below the car. Set the layer to Luminosity mode in the Layers panel so the background behind the text adopts the same color as the road. You can create a softer edge to the background by using the rectangular Marquee tool and making a feathered selection around the name. I have used a 30-pixel feather in this project.

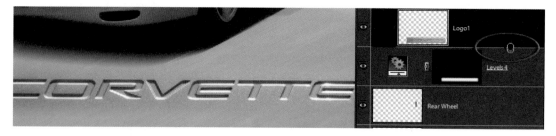

21. Select the layer beneath the Logo1 layer and then create a Levels adjustment layer (no adjustment required). The active selection will create a mask that we can use to soften the edge of the logo. To make use of this mask select the logo layer and then choose 'Group with Previous' from the Layer menu. We can disguise the tonal difference of the background by grouping a Levels adjustment layer with the logo layer (hold down the Alt key and check the option in the New Layer dialog box as in step 14).

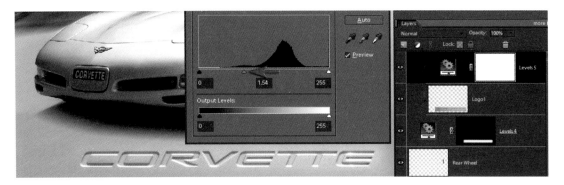

22. Move the Gamma slider until the left side of the logo's background appears the same tone as the road (ignore the fact that the right side is now lighter than the road) and then select OK.

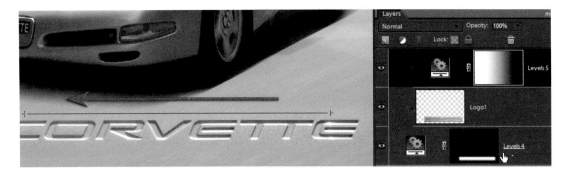

23. Select the 'Gradient tool' in the Tools panel and choose the 'Black', 'White gradient' and 'Linear' options in the Options bar. Click and drag a straight line from the end of the logo to the start of the logo (hold down the Shift key whilst dragging your line to constrain the gradient to a straight line). This will shield the right side of the gradient from the excessive effects of the adjustment and create a tonal balance or uniformity along the width of the logo.

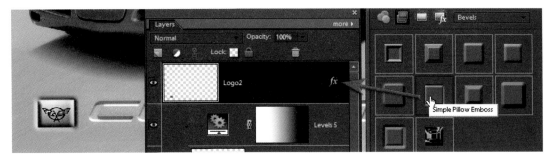

24. Open and drag in the second logo file. Use the Transform command to rescale the logo and move it into position. In the Effects panel choose the Layer Styles icon and the Bevels subcategory, and apply the Simple Pillow Emboss style by double-clicking its icon in the panel. This will ensure the logo matches the style of the embossed letters. Delete the background surrounding this second logo if you wish to emboss only the flags instead of the entire layer.

Stage 5 - Completing the image

At last we are on the home straight. All we have to do is add a vignette to focus the attention on the car and then, as always, an appropriate amount of sharpening just prior to printing.

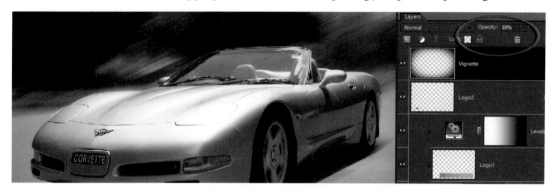

25. Create a new layer and make sure it is positioned above all other layers in the Layers panel. Choose the 'Circular Marquee tool' and select a 200-pixel Radius in the Options bar. Drag from the top left-hand corner of the image to the bottom right-hand corner of the image. Choose 'Inverse' from the Select menu and sample some of the dark green foliage using the Eyedropper tool. Then choose 'Fill Selection' from the Edit menu and select 'Foreground Color' as the contents. Drop the opacity of the vignette layer to create the right effect and set the mode of this layer to Multiply.

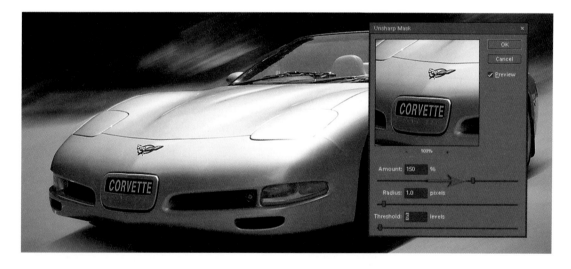

26. Complete the project by sharpening the image. Select the top layer in the Layers panel and then hold down the Ctrl + Alt + Shift keys and type the letter N followed by the letter E. This keyboard shortcut will copy all of the visible layers and paste them to a new layer. Use a generous amount of sharpening (150 to 200) but keep the radius low (0.8 to 1.5). Threshold can be raised slightly (3 to 6) when using files from a digital compact rather than a digital SLR. Print the image to assess the appropriate amount of sharpening. If the sharpening is excessive lower the opacity of the unsharp mask layer. Perfection on a plate – well almost. For even more realism don't forget to add that quintessential ingredient that I missed in this project – the driver!

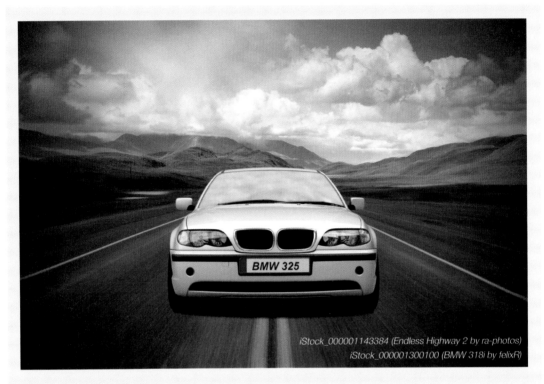

iStock_000001143384 (Endless Highway 2 by ra-photos)
iStock_000001300100 (BMW 318i by felixR)

PERFORMANCE TIP

When the movement is towards the camera the illusion of movement can be created by using the Radial Blur filter instead of the Motion Blur filter. To reduce the effects of the blur in the distance the filter can first be applied to a duplicate layer and this duplicate layer can then be grouped with an adjustment layer that contains a radial gradient. The sky was also masked using a linear gradient in Multiply mode.

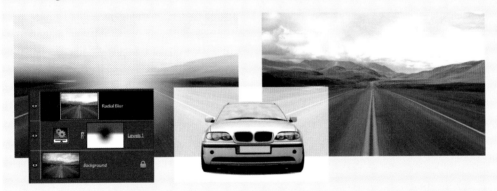

The car in this illustration came from a separate image and was masked using techniques outlined in Project 1 of the Montage section (Part 3) in this book. The original shadow was preserved using the techniques outlined in Project 6 of the Montage section. The images used in this Performance Tip are courtesy of iStockphoto (www.iStockphoto.com).

Project 8

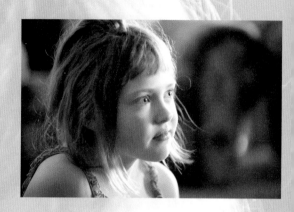

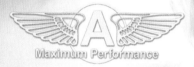

Low Key

A low-key image is where the dark tones dominate the photograph. Small bright highlights punctuate the shadow areas, creating the characteristic mood of a low-key image. The position of the light source for a typical low-key image is behind the subject or behind and off to one side so that deep shadows are created. In the olden (pre-digital) days the appropriate exposure usually centered around how far the photographer could reduce the exposure before the highlights appeared dull. In the digital age this approach to exposure at the time of capture should be avoided at all costs, especially when black velvet-like tones are your benchmark for quality.

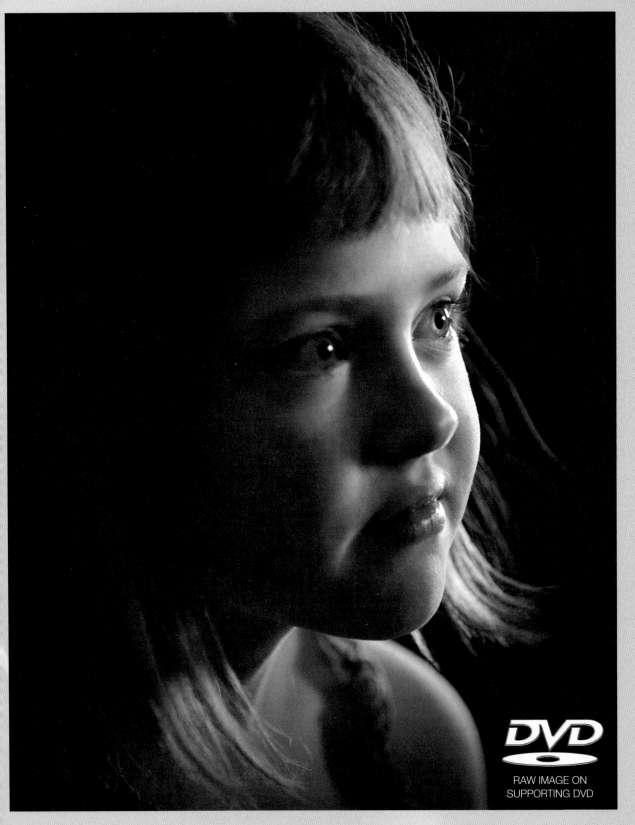

RAW IMAGE ON
SUPPORTING DVD

The classic low-key image – redefining exposure for a digital age

Exposure for low-key images

For those digital photographers interested in the dark side, an old SLR loaded with a fine-grain black and white film is a hard act to follow. The liquid smooth transitions and black velvet-like quality of dark low-key prints of yesteryear is something that digital capture is hard pressed to match. The sad reality of digital capture is that underexposure in low light produces noise and banding (steps rather than smooth transitions of tone) in abundance. The answer, however, is surprisingly simple for those who have access to a DSLR and have selected the Raw format from the Quality menu settings in their camera. The next step is to be generous with your exposure to the point of clipping or overexposing your highlights and only attempt to lower the exposure of the shadows in Adobe Camera Raw.

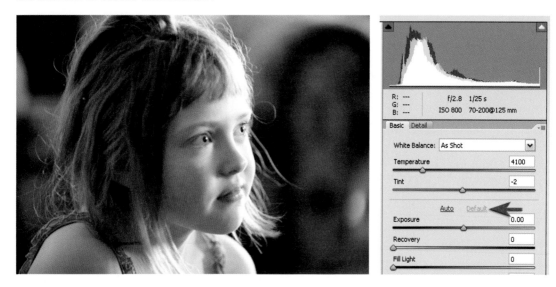

1. The first step is the most difficult to master for those who are used to using Auto or Program exposure modes. Although the final outcome may require deep shadow tones, the aim in digital low-key exposure is to first get the shadow tones away from the left-hand wall of the histogram by increasing and NOT decreasing the exposure. It is vitally important, however, not to increase the exposure so far that you lose or clip highlight detail. The original exposure of the image used in this project reveals that the shadow tones (visible as the highest peaks in the histogram) have had a generous exposure in-camera so that noise and banding have been avoided (the tones have moved well to the right in the histogram). The highlights, however, look as though they have become clipped or overexposed. The feedback from the histogram on the camera's LCD would have confirmed the clipping at the time of exposure (the tall peak on the extreme right-hand side of the histogram) and if you had your camera set to warn you of overexposure the highlights would have been merrily flashing at you to ridicule you of your sad attempts to expose this image. The typical DSLR camera is, however, a pessimist when it comes to clipped highlights and ignorant of what is possible in Adobe Camera Raw. Adobe Camera Raw can recover at least one stop of extra highlight information when the Exposure slider is dragged to the left (as long as the photographer has used a DSLR camera that has a broader dynamic range than your typical fixed lens compact digicam).

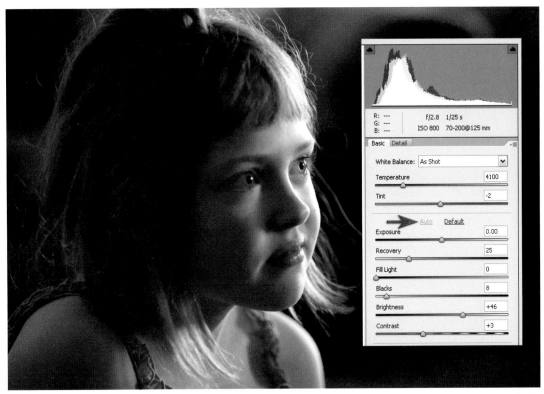

Adobe Camera Raw rescues the highlights – sometimes automatically

'Exposing right'

When the Auto checkbox in the Exposure slider is checked Adobe Camera Raw often attempts to rescue overexposed highlights automatically. With a little knowledge and some attention to the histogram during the capture stage you can master the art of pushing your highlights to the edge. So if your model is not in a hurry (mine is watching a half-hour TV show) you can take an initial exposure on Auto and then check your camera for overexposure. Increase the exposure using the exposure compensation dial on the camera until you see the flashing highlights. When the flashing highlights start to appear you can still add around one extra stop to the exposure before the highlights can no longer be recovered in Adobe Camera Raw. The popular term for this peculiar behavior is called 'exposing right'.

PERFORMANCE TIP

If the highlights are merrily flashing and the shadows are still banked up against the left-hand wall of the histogram the solution is to increase the amount of fill light, i.e. reduce the difference in brightness between the main light source and the fill light. If using flash as the source of your fill light it would be important to drop the power of the flash by at least two stops and choose the 'Slow-Sync' setting (a camera flash setting that balances both the ambient light exposure and flash exposure) so that the flash light does not overpower the main light source positioned behind your subject.

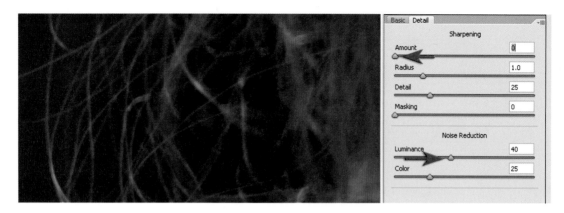

2. Before we massage the tones to create our low-key image we must first check that our tones are smooth and free from color and luminance noise. Zoom in to 100% magnification for an accurate preview and look for any problems in the smooth dark-toned areas. Setting both the Luminance Smoothing and Color Noise Reduction sliders to 25 (found in the Detail tab) removes the noise in this image. I would also recommend that the Sharpness slider be set to 0 at this point. Selective sharpening in the main editing space may help to keep the tones as smooth as possible rather than committing to global sharpening using the Adobe Camera Raw dialog box.

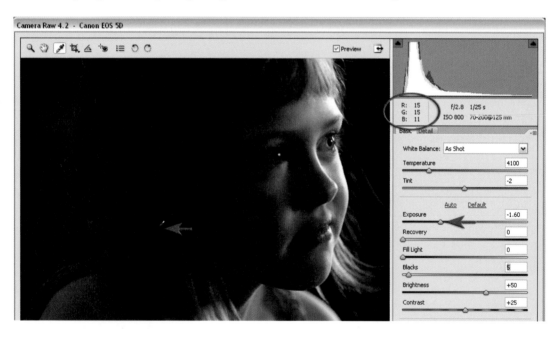

3. Create the low-key look by dropping the Exposure and/or the Brightness sliders in the Adjust tab. You can continue to drop these sliders until the highlights start to move away from the right-hand wall of the histogram. Select the 'White Balance tool' and move your mouse cursor over the deeper shadows – this will give you an idea of the RGB values you are likely to get when this image is opened into the editing space. Once you approach an average of 15 to 20 in all three channels the low-key look should have been achieved.

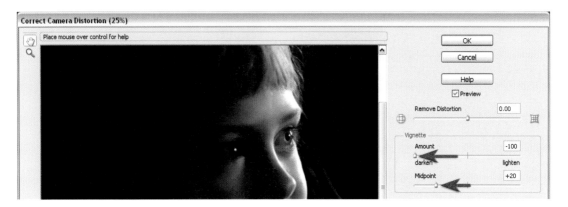

4. To enhance this image further a vignette has been added. This can be achieved in the Adobe Camera Raw dialog box in the full version of Photoshop but in Photoshop Elements the vignette has to be added in the main editing space. In Photoshop Elements the Correct Camera Distortion filter can be used to add the vignette. Just drag the Amount slider to the left to darken the corners. Dragging the Midpoint slider to the left will slowly move the darkening effect towards the center of the image.

Note > If you are in 8 Bits/Channel mode and you want to add a vignette using layers, first create a new layer in Multiply mode and fill this layer with white. Hold down the Alt key as you click on the New Layer icon in the Layers panel to access the New Layer dialog box to give you these options.

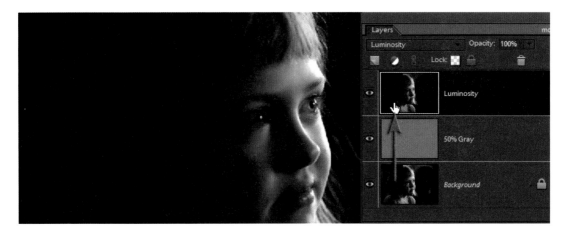

5. To drop the RGB to Black and White I have used a technique that extracts the luminance values from the RGB file. I usually find that this gives a superior result to lowering the saturation or choosing the Remove Color command. Simply click the New Layer icon in the Layers panel and from the Fill Layer dialog box choose '50% Gray' as the contents color (Edit > Fill Layer > 50% Gray). Create a duplicate of the background layer (or merge the contents if you have placed the vignette on a separate layer) and then move this duplicate background layer to the top of the layers stack. Switch the mode of the background copy layer to 'Luminosity' to create a black and white image from the Luminance values.

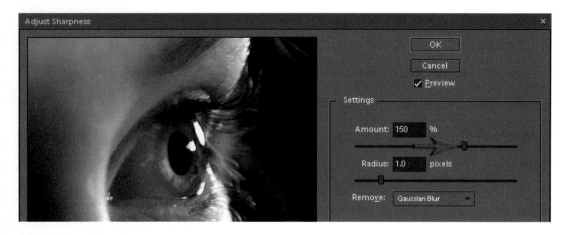

6. To complete the project the file should be sharpened for printing. Photoshop Elements has two alternative sharpening filters. Adjust Sharpness (Enhance > Adjust Sharpness) is an excellent alternative to the Unsharp Mask for sharpening images that have little to no noise. To ensure the image does not appear over-sharpened be sure to restrict the Radius to nothing higher than 1.5. The image preview in this dialog will appear in color as the layer itself has not been dropped to black and white.

Note > If the Adjust Sharpness is making the smoother soft-focus tones appear anything but liquid smooth then consider a localized sharpening technique as described below.

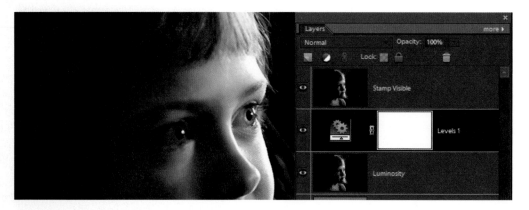

7. Create a stamp visible layer (hold down the Ctrl, Shift and Alt keys and press the E key). Apply a generous amount of sharpening using either Unsharp Mask or Adjust Sharpness (be generous with the Amount slider but restrict the Radius slider to nothing greater than 1.5).

8. Click on the layer beneath the layer you have just sharpened, to make this the active layer. Then click on the Create Adjustment Layer icon in the Layers panel and choose a Levels adjustment layer from the pull-down menu. When the Levels dialog opens make no adjustment – just click OK. Make sure this adjustment layer is below the layer you have sharpened. Click and drag it into position if it needs to move.

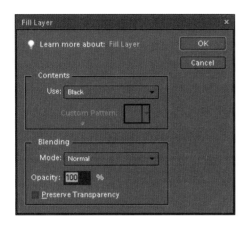

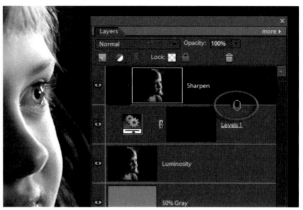

9. Fill the adjustment layer mask with black (Edit > Fill Layer > Black).

10. Click on the sharpened layer to make this the active layer. From the Layer menu choose 'Group with Previous'.

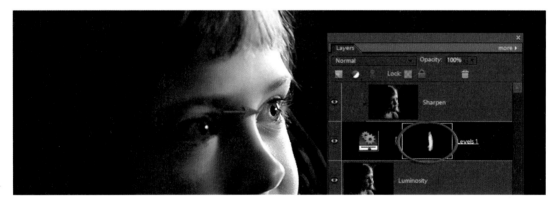

11. Select the Brush tool from the Tools panel. Select 'White' as the foreground color. Choose a soft brush from the Options bar and drop the opacity of the brush to 50%.

12. Click on the layer mask in the Layers panel to make this active and then move your attention to the main image window. Zoom the image to either 50% or Actual Pixels (100%). Paint in the areas where you would like to increase the sharpness of the image. Painting several times in the same region will slowly build up the sharpness of the image.

PERFORMANCE TIP - A FINAL WORD OF WARNING
To extract the maximum quality from your low-key image you will need to print this image on premium quality photo paper or have the image printed at a professional quality print service provider. All the work will be for nothing if the printer or surface quality of the paper cannot handle all of these smooth dark tones. If printed well the print will stand up to close – really close – scrutiny at close range.

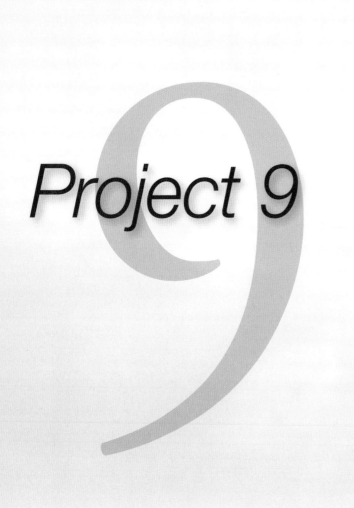

Project 9

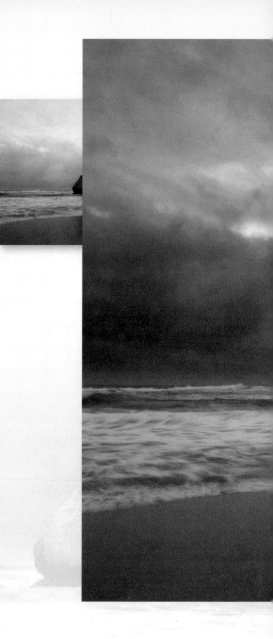

Channels

You can spend a long time making pointless selections when all Elements needs is to be shown the differences between 'that which must be changed' and the pixels that need to be left alone, based on hue, saturation or brightness. I have learnt to resist the temptation to jump in early with the lasso or tragic wand tool and instead learn to utilize and exploit the differences that may be lurking beneath the RGB surface of the image. The differences that Photoshop Elements thrives on for selection-free editing can usually be found in the component channels of the RGB image.

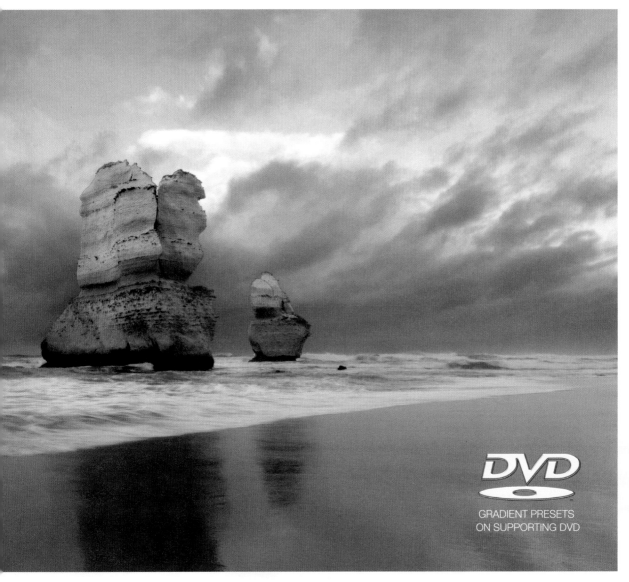

The Apostles – The finished image together with the start image and the red and blue channels. The red channel is employed to enhance the sky whilst using the blue channel to mask its effects.

The red channel in this seascape image is information-rich in the sky, whilst the blue channel has excellent contrast that could be utilized for the creation of a mask to control localized adjustments. Users of the full version of Photoshop have this information available in the Channels panel. The Photoshop Elements user must find another way, as the Channels panel is out of bounds. Although Photoshop Elements uses the three primary color channels to create the RGB image, Adobe feels that the Photoshop Elements user does not need to see the component information. Just because you can't see the channels doesn't mean you can't use them.

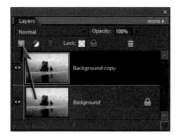
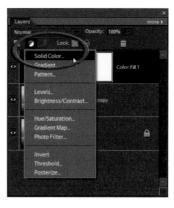
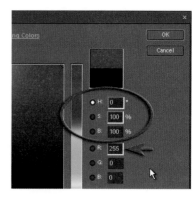

Part 1 - Extracting the red channel

1. To start the ball rolling duplicate the background layer by dragging it to the New Layer icon in the Layers panel and then add a Solid Color adjustment layer from the Create Adjustment Layers menu in the Layers panel. Select Red in the Color Picker (255 Red, 0 Green, 0 Blue).

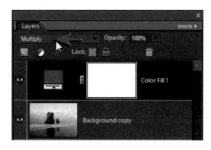
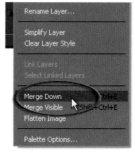

2. Set the blending mode for the layer to Multiply and then choose Merge Down from the Layer menu. It will probably come as no surprise, but your image has just turned bright red.

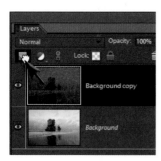
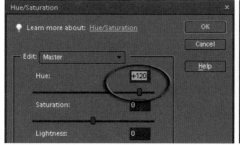
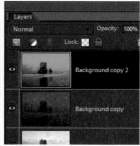

3. Duplicate the Red layer (background copy) by dragging it to the New Layer icon and from the Enhance menu choose 'Adjust Hue/Saturation' from the Adjust Color submenu (Enhance > Adjust Color > Adjust Hue/Saturation, or use the keyboard shortcut Ctrl + U. Move the Hue slider to +120. Your 'Background copy 2' layer is now bright green.

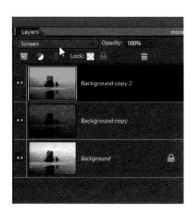
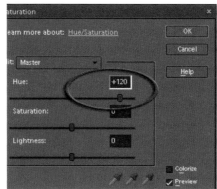
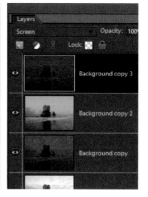

4. Change the blend mode of this green layer (Background copy 2) to Screen (this will turn the main image yellow as the filtering process begins to take place) and then drag the green Background copy 2 layer to the New Layer icon to copy it. Use the Hue/Saturation adjustment again to change the hue to blue by dragging the Hue slider to +120. The image in your main image window should now appear as a black and white image – these are not just any shades of gray but the gray values that are only present in the red channel of your image. It is a bit too early for the round of applause as we are currently using three layers to achieve this effect.

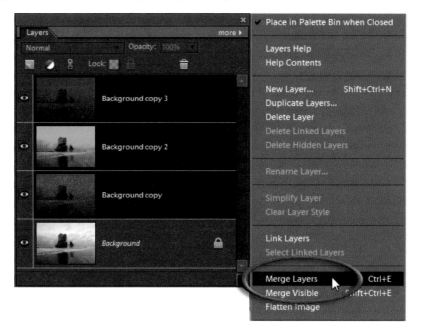

5. Select all three colored layers by holding down the Ctrl key and click on each layer in turn so that all three colored layers are highlighted. From the Layer menu choose Merge Layers. This red layer (dropped to grayscale values) is a useful way to create dramatic black and white images, due to the fact that red filtration of a full color scene makes blue skies darker without darkening any clouds that may be present in the sky. We will, however, take this a few steps further if you are able to stay along for the ride.

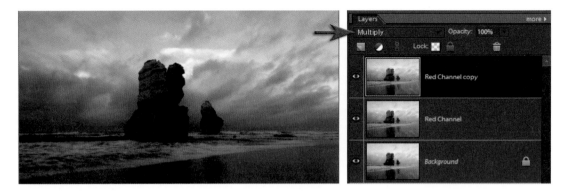

Part 2 - Using the red channel layer to darken the sky

6. I have named the background copy layer as the Red Channel (really a layer) by clicking on its name in the Layers panel (just so things don't get too confusing). Duplicate the Red Channel layer by dragging it to the New Layer icon and change the blend mode to Multiply. This step is designed to darken the sky and create a lot more drama. Choose 'Merge Down' from the Layer menu to create a single darkened red channel layer. Now click on the background layer in the Layers panel to select it and then from the Create Adjustment Layer icon in the Layers panel choose 'Levels'. Don't make any adjustment, just click 'OK' in the Levels dialog box. We will use the adjustment layer mask on this adjustment layer to mask or hide everything in the Red Channel layer except the sky, which we will leave visible in order to darken the sky below.

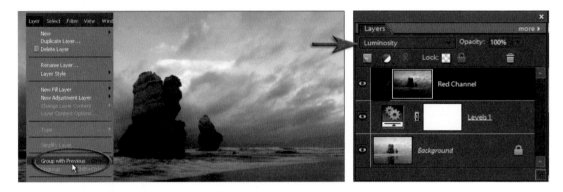

7. Click on the Red Channel layer to make it active and then from the Layer menu choose 'Group with Previous'. Change the blend mode of the Red Channel layer to Luminosity. The Luminosity blend mode will allow all of the color from the background layer to become visible but retain the brightness or 'luminance' values of the Red Channel layer. The mask beneath can hide any of the luminance values that are not required. Adjust the opacity of the Red Channel layer if the drama needs to be lowered a little. Now you could just paint in the mask to hide the unwanted luminance values but the idea behind this tutorial is to let Photoshop do all of the work – we are just providing the brains. My brain cells tell me that a mask for those rocks probably already exists in the blue channel of this RGB file. We will typically find that the sky is very light in the blue channel and everything that has no blue component will be dark, i.e. the rocks and foreground beach.

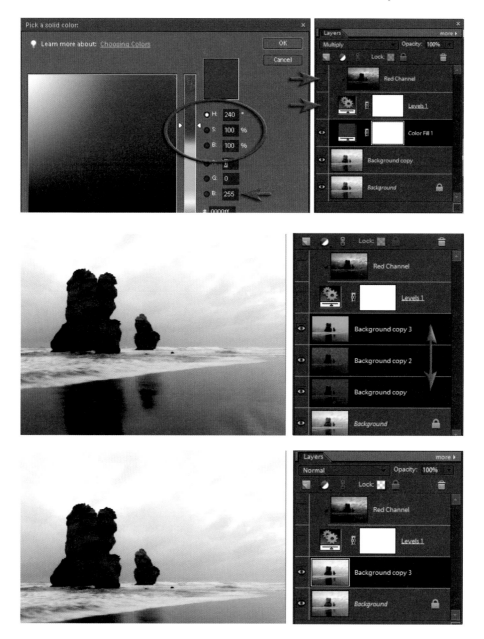

Part 3 - Channel masking

8. Switch off the visibility of the top two layers by clicking on the eye icon next to the layer thumbnail. Using the same technique as in Part 1 of this tutorial create a blue channel layer. Instead of selecting Red as the Solid Color in step 1 choose 255 Blue (the other two channels should be set to 0 in the Color Picker). The rest of the procedure is identical (hallelujah!) using the same +120 Hue value in the Hue/Saturation dialog box each time and the same sequence of blend modes (first apply the Multiply mode to the blue solid color adjustment layer, apply the Screen mode to the subsequent color layers and then Merge Layers).

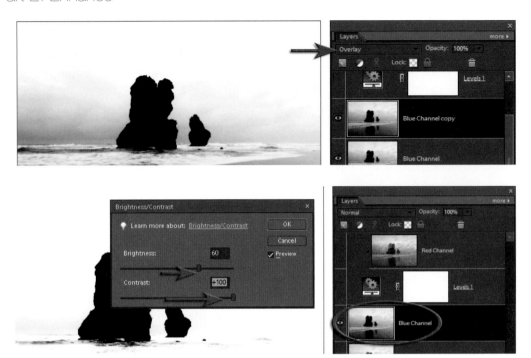

9. After merging the three color layers to create a Blue Channel layer you should see that the rocks in the sea are very dark against the bright sky (the basis of a really effective mask) – the contrast, however, is not quite high enough to act as a layer mask just yet. The aim is to render all of the sky white and the rocks black. To increase the contrast duplicate the Blue Channel layer and then set the duplicate layer to Overlay mode. Then choose Merge Down from the Layers menu. Apply the Brightness/Contrast adjustment feature (Enhance > Adjust Lighting > Brightness/Contrast) to render the sky mostly white and the rocks mostly black.

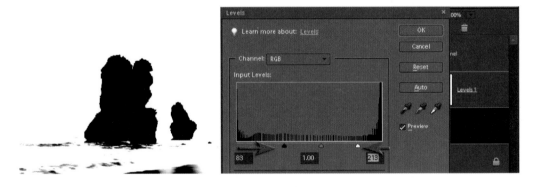

10. Apply a Levels adjustment to this layer (Enhance > Adjust Lighting > Levels) and drag the white slider underneath the histogram to the left until no traces of gray sky are left. Drag the black slider underneath the histogram to the right until the rocks are solid black. Click OK to apply the changes and create your mask – the only problem now is that it needs to be in the layer mask above and not in its own layer.

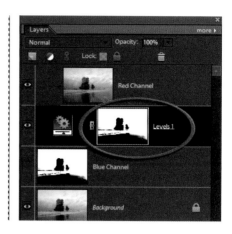

11. To transfer this high-contrast Blue Channel layer to the layer mask above select 'All' from the Select menu and then choose 'Copy' from the Edit menu. Hold down the Alt key and click on the adjustment layer mask thumbnail on the Levels 1 layer. The main image window should momentarily appear white, as you are now viewing the empty contents of this layer mask. Choose 'Paste' from the Edit menu to paste the contents of the clipboard into this layer mask. Hold down the Alt key again and click on the layer mask thumbnail one more time to switch off the layer mask view. Nothing will have appeared to have changed until you then switch off the visibility of the Blue Channel layer by clicking on the eye icon next to the layer thumbnail. Don't expect perfection just yet as the water and the reflections on the beach will appear slightly weird at this point in time.

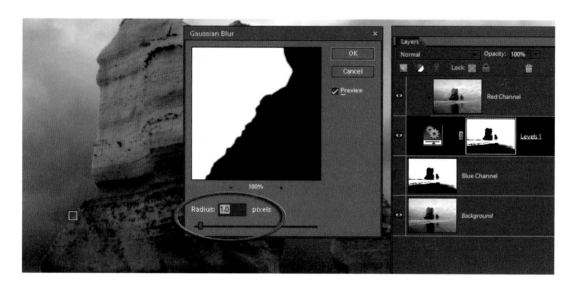

12. Apart from some strange tones in the water and on the beach you will probably also notice a halo, or white line, appearing around the rocks where the sky has not been darkened. To remove this halo, first apply a 1- or 2-pixel Gaussian Blur filter to the layer mask to soften the edge (Filter > Blur > Gaussian Blur). This step serves to soften the edge whilst the next step will attempt to realign the edge.

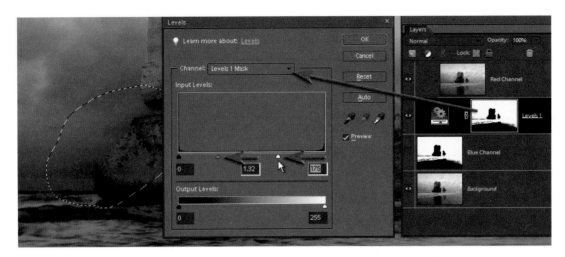

13. Make a selection with the Lasso tool around any edges that have a thin white halo around them. Apply a Levels adjustment to the mask. Moving the central Gamma slider underneath the histogram in the Levels dialog box to the left and moving the white Highlight slider to the left should remove the halo.

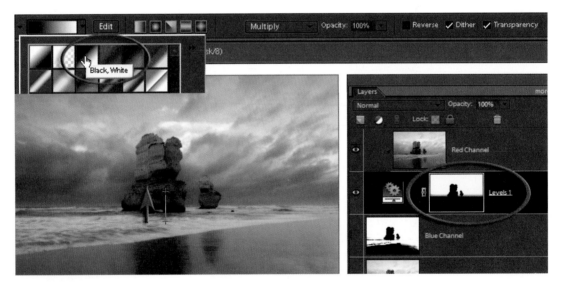

14. To finish off this edit we must hide the foreground pixels in the Red Channel, in order to return normal viewing to both the water and the reflections on the beach. Select the Gradient tool in the Tools panel and choose the 'Black, White' gradient in the Options bar and set the Opacity to 100%. Make sure the Linear gradient option is also selected and change the blend mode to Multiply. Move your mouse cursor into the main image window (this is the only painting tool used in the entire edit) and click just around the base of the central rock and drag a short stroke to a point around halfway up the rock. Let go of the mouse clicker to apply the gradient to the layer mask. As the blend mode of the Gradient tool is set to Multiply this gradient will be added to the existing mask rather than replacing it.

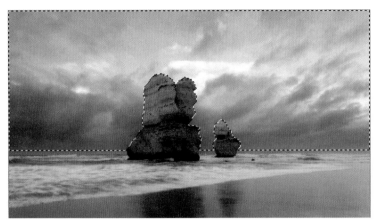

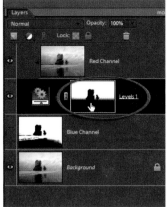

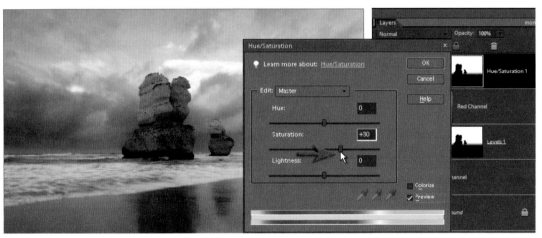

15. The last step of this edit is to replace some of the saturation in the sky that was upset when we changed the Red Channel layer to Luminosity mode. It is a really painless process to pick up the selection from the layer mask we have just crafted. Hold down the Ctrl key and click on the layer mask thumbnail. This will load the mask as a selection. With the active selection simply select a Hue/Saturation adjustment layer from the Create Adjustment Layer menu in the Layers panel and increase the intensity of the color to taste.

Not convinced?

You may be thinking that this is a very long process to simply darken the sky of this image. I have, however, learnt all the keyboard shortcuts for every step of this process (including all of the blend modes and merge commands) and I reckon most people would only be halfway around the first rock with their Lasso tool before I had completed this entire editing procedure (all 15 steps). This image edit would normally only take you three or four minutes when you know where you are going. If this is not fast enough be sure to check out the action with this book. Remember – just one click and you have all three channels as layers installed in the Layers panel. A little more brains and a little less playing with your tools now will pay dividends in the amount of time you save later.

part

3

montage

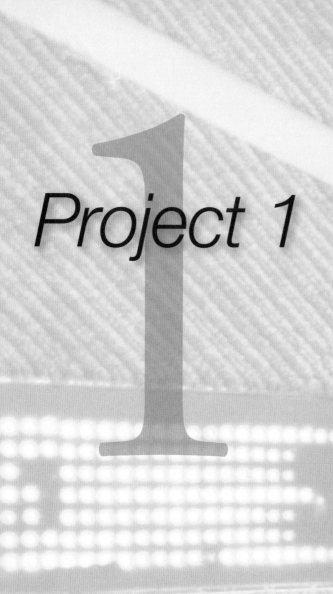
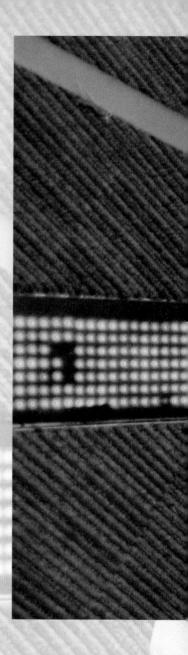

Project 1

Creative Montage

Masks can be used to control which pixels are concealed or revealed on any image layer except the background layer. If the mask layer that has been used to conceal pixels is then discarded the original pixels reappear. This approach to montage work is termed 'non-destructive'. In the full version of Photoshop the mask can be applied to any layer. In Photoshop Elements layer masks are only available on adjustment layers, but these can be used to mask the pixels on the layer, or layers, above.

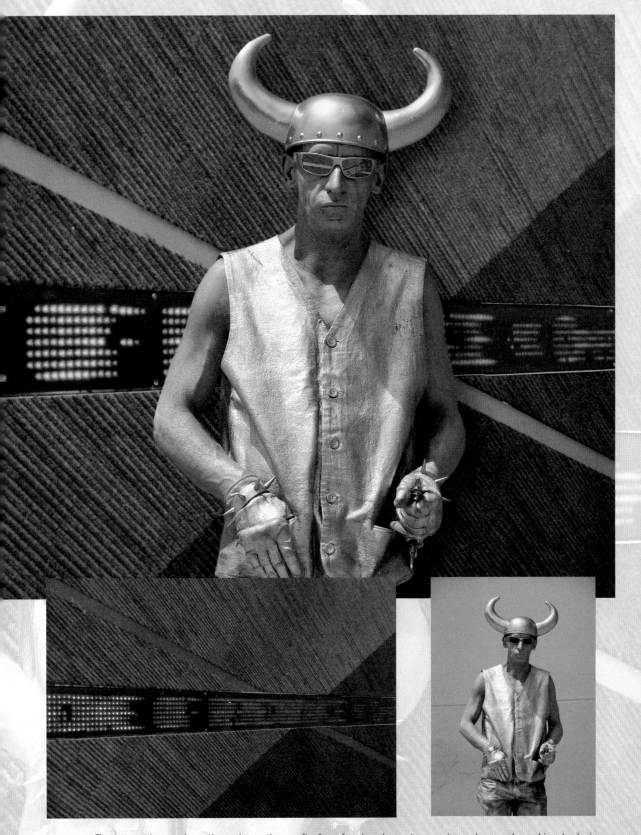

Forget cutting and pasting – learn the craft of professional montage using advanced masking techniques

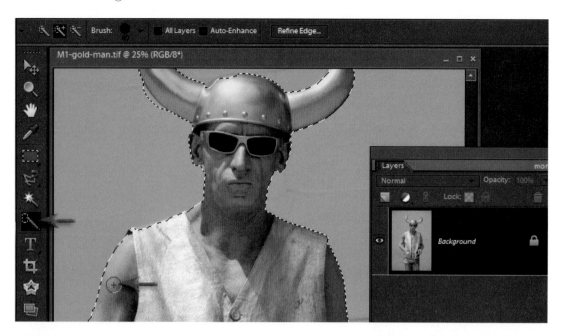

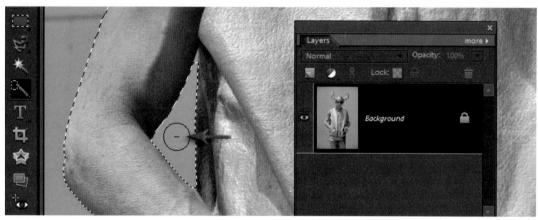

1. Select the Quick Selection Tool in the Tools panel and then deselect the Auto Enhance option in the Options bar. With subjects that are easy to select, the Auto Enhance option can save you time as the edge quality will be refined as you select. The edge contrast in this subject is low in places and no one tool can easily select the entire subject in this image. When this is the case it is better to turn the Auto Enhance feature off and refine the edge later. After selecting the gold man you will notice the selection may not be perfect. You will almost certainly have to remove the areas from under the arms and between the legs from the selection. To do this hold down the Alt key and click and drag over these areas. You may need to reduce the size of the brush when painting over these regions. Do not spend too long trying to perfect difficult regions of the selection using the Quick Selection Tool as we will use additional techniques to complete the process.

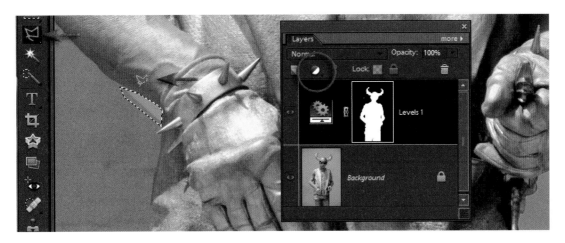

2. With the selection active go to the Layers panel and add a Levels adjustment layer from the Create adjustment layer menu. Select OK without making any adjustment. The selection will have been converted into a layer mask. We can use this layer mask to perfect the selection. Hold down the Alt and Shift keys and click on the Adjustment layer mask to view the mask and the image at the same time. The mask is currently indicating the area that is not selected. The mask can be converted back into a selection when we have finished editing the mask with painting tools or selection tools. Select the Polygonal Lasso Tool from the Tools panel and set the feather value to 0 pixels in the Options bar. Click around any area where the mask color needs to be extended to meet the edge of the gold man. Check that you have black as the foreground color in the Tools panel and then use the keyboard shortcut Alt + Backspace to fill the selected area with the mask color.

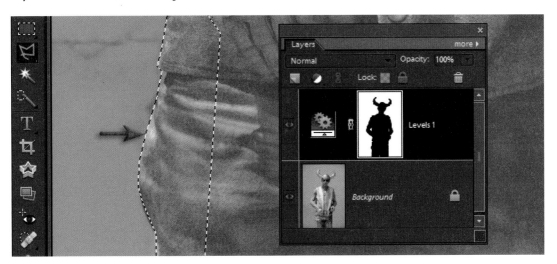

3. To create the perfect selection it will be necessary to remove any mask color that appears over the subject. To do this make a selection and fill with the Background color (Ctrl + Backspace). When the edge is difficult to see because the mask color extends over the edge of the subject go to Filter > Adjustments > Invert (Ctrl + I). Now you will be able to see the edge clearly you can then make your selection and fill with the Foreground color.

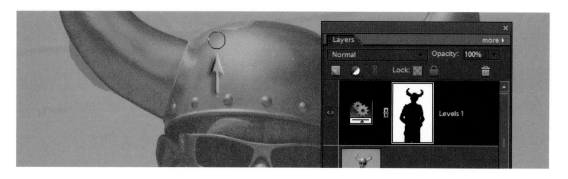

4. If you have a steady hand you can also choose to paint directly into the mask using the Brush Tool. Choose a Brush setting of 100% hardness in the Options bar and then paint with Black to add to the mask or with white to remove the mask color. Zoom in to the image (Ctrl + Spacebar) to ensure the mask is accurate and use the Spacebar to access the hand tool that will enable you to drag around the image while you are zoomed in. Alternatively use the Navigator panel to navigate around the edge of your subject. Before leaving the mask view make sure that the background is covered in the mask color rather than the gold man (Ctrl + I will invert the mask if required). Alt + Shift click the layer mask to return to the normal view.

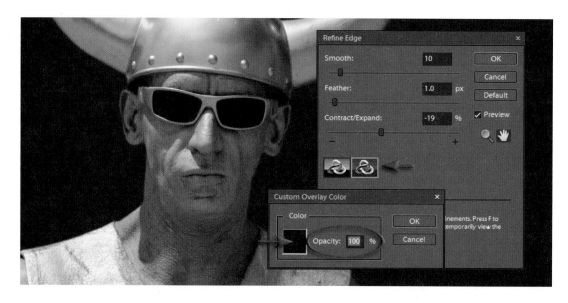

5. The edges of the mask will need to be refined before the mask can be used for a high quality montage. Select Refine Edge from the Select menu and from the View menu choose Selection to hide the selection edge. Double-click the Custom Overlay Color option in the panel to open the options dialog and set the Color to dark gray and the Opacity to 100%. Select OK to apply the color change. Set the Smooth slider to 10, the Feather slider to 1.0 and slide the Contract/Expand slider to the left to conceal the white edge that surrounds your subject.

Note > If the subject is gray instead of the background you need to cancel the process and Invert the mask before choosing the Refine Edge command.

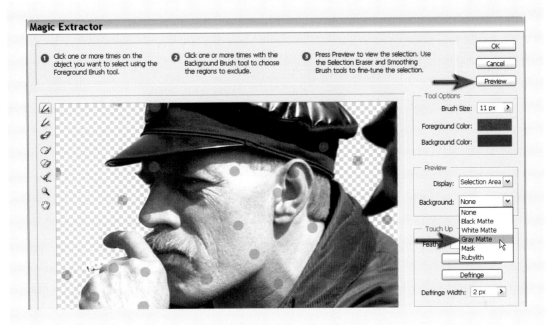

PERFORMANCE TIP

The fact of life is that some extractions can be as painful as pulling teeth! With this in mind Adobe offers you even more magic – the Magic Extractor (Image > Magic Extractor). This is yet another alternative for getting rid of problematic backgrounds. This tool takes a little more time than the Quick Selection tool and is destructive in nature (it deletes the pixels you select with the Background Brush tool) so I would advise duplicating this layer before proceeding. You make little marks or squiggles to advise Photoshop which regions of the image you would like to keep and which regions you would like to delete. Click on the Preview button to see how Photoshop does the hard maths to extract your subject from the background. From the Preview menu choose a matte color to view your extracted subject (choose a different tone to the original background or one that is similar to the new background).

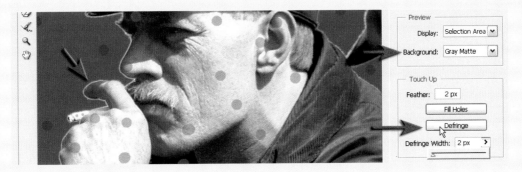

In the Touch Up section of the dialog box select a Feather value (usually 1 or 2 pixels) and then choose a 'Defringe Width' to remove any of the remaining background. Not a bad job – if you don't mind losing the background pixels.

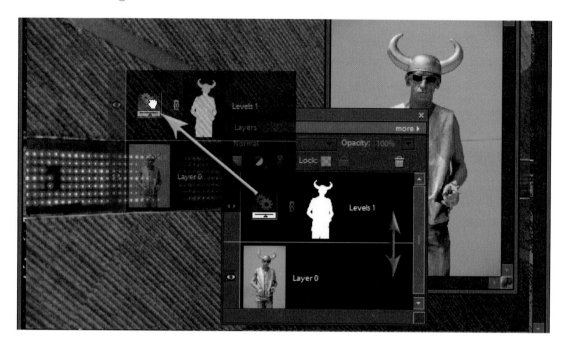

6. Open the new background image and place the two image files along side each other. Select both layers in the gold man file (hold down the Ctrl key and click on each layer) and then drag the layers into the new background file to create a file containing all three layers.

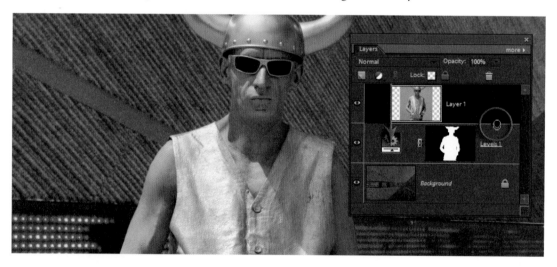

7. Drag the adjustment layer in the Layers panel so that it is under the layer of the gold man. Select the Layer containing the gold man and then choose Group with Previous from the Layer menu. Alternatively you can take your mouse cursor to the dividing line between the two layers, hold down the Alt key until you see the clipping mask icon appear and the click to group them. The original background behind the gold man will now be hidden from view and you will be able to see the new background on the background layer.

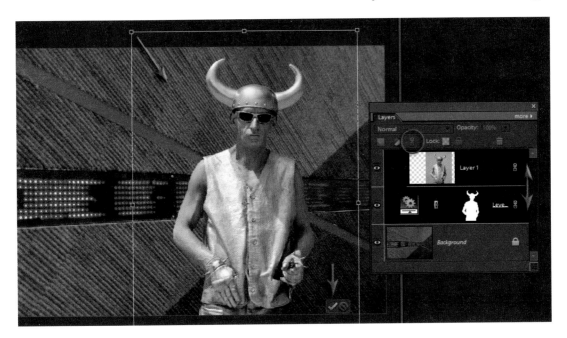

8. Select the top two layers (Ctrl-click each layer) and then select the Link Layers option in the Layers panel. This will ensure the size and position of the mask will match the subject above. Go to 'Image > Transform > Free Transform' (Ctrl + T). Use the keyboard shortcut Ctrl + 0 to fit the Transform bounding box on the screen. Drag a corner handle to re-size the image so that it sits nicely against the new background (you will not require all of the legs to replicate the framing in this project). Press the 'Commit' icon or Enter key to apply the transformation.

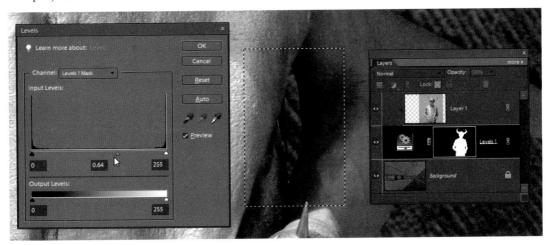

9. Zoom in and take a close look at the edges You may notice a white halo along some of the edges (the old background). This can be removed by making a selection of a the problem area (use a 5-pixel feather if your selection crosses the edge of your subject) and then applying a Levels adjustment (Enhance > Adjust Lighting > Levels or Ctrl + L) to move the edge of the mask. Move the central gamma slider to the right to remove any of the old lighter background that may still be visible on the layer above.

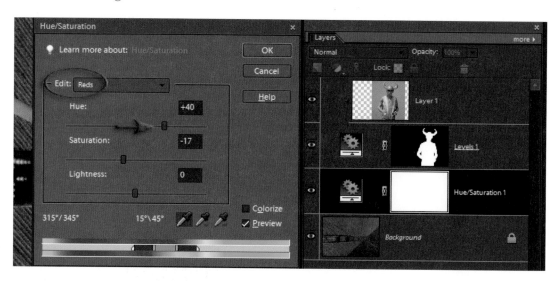

10. Click on the background layer in the Layers panel and then choose a Hue/Saturation adjustment layer from the Create Adjustment layer menu. Select Reds from the Edit menu in the Hue/Saturation dialog and move the Hue slider to the right until the Red stripes in the image turn yellow. Adjust the saturation to taste and then Select OK to apply the changes.

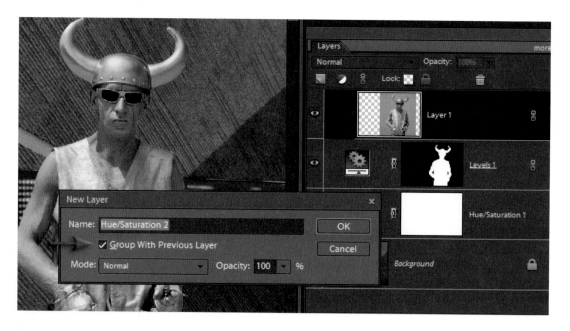

11. Select the top layer in the Layers panel (the one with the gold man). Hold down the Alt key and select another Hue/Saturation adjustment layer. Holding down the Alt key as you select the adjustment layer will open the New Layer dialog. Choose the Group with previous option in this dialog and select OK. Grouping the Hue/Saturation adjustment layer to the layer below will ensure the adjustments do not flow down and affect the colors on the background layer.

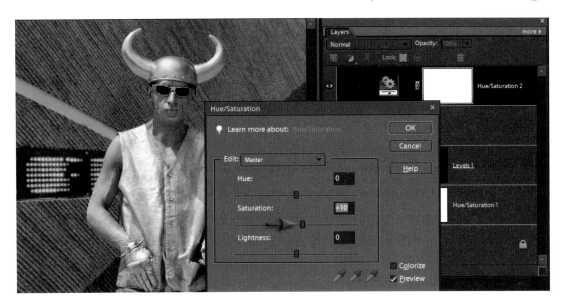

12. Adjust the saturation of the gold man to match the saturation of the yellows on the background layer. Notice how the adjustments are only affecting the layer below. Select OK to apply the changes. The ability to match the color and tonality of a number of different layers in a composite image is an essential skill for montage work.

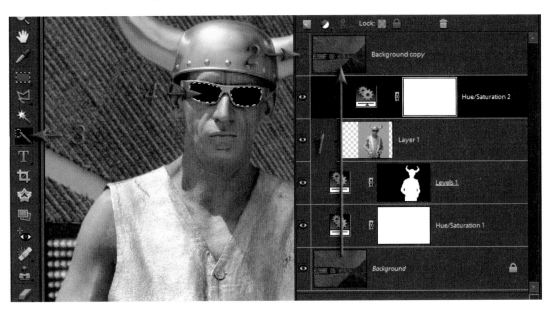

13. The basic task of replacing the background is complete. We will now paste a copy of the background layer in the lenses of the dark glasses. Duplicate the background layer (Ctrl + J) and then drag this copy layer to the top of the layers stack. Switch off the visibility of this copy layer by clicking on the visibility icon. Select the Quick Selection Tool in the Tools panel and select the All Layers option in the Options bar and the Auto Enhance option. Click on each lens in turn to select them.

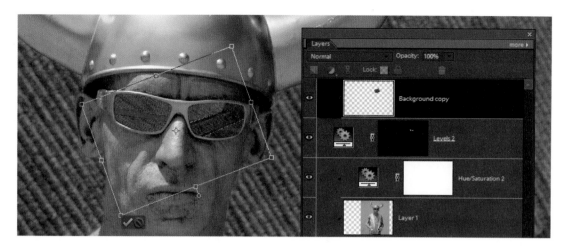

14. Create a Levels adjustment layer below the background copy layer. Select OK without making any adjustment. The selection will create a layer mask we can use. Select the background copy layer and then group the background copy layer with the adjustment layer. Select 'Free Transform' from the Edit menu and then scale and rotate the layer so that the red stripes appear in the lenses of the sunglasses. You have the option to lower the opacity of the layer in the Layers panel if required.

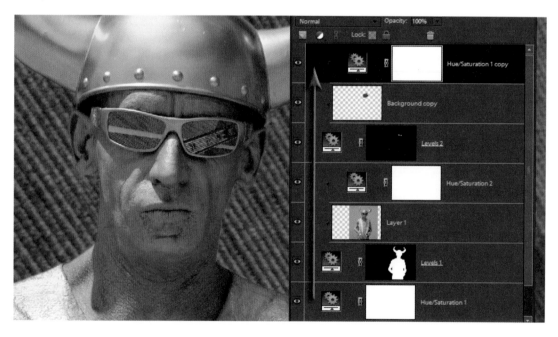

15. Hold down the Alt key and click and drag the Hue/Saturation 1 adjustment layer to the top of the layers stack. This action will copy the adjustment layer and change the red stripes to yellow but it will also affect the color of the golden Viking. To limit the changes to the reflections in the glasses group this with the layer below (the transformed background copy layer). Note how you can have more that two layers in a clipping group.

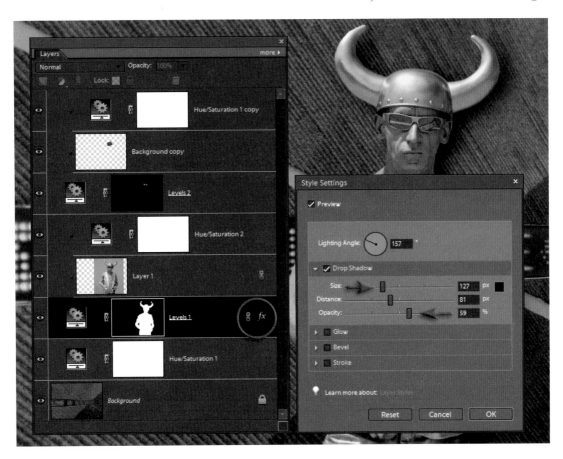

16. Select the Levels 1 adjustment layer in the Layers panel. Go to the Effects panel (Windows > Effects) and click on the Layer Styles icon (two overlapping window frames). Choose Drop Shadows from the drop-down menu. Double-click on the style 'high' to apply the style to the adjustment layer. You will see a drop shadow appear behind the gold man and a blue 'fx' icon appear on the layer (next to the link icon). Double-click the 'fx' icon to open the Style Settings dialog. Move your mouse cursor into the image window and drag the shadow to the right side of the image (the left side of the gold man) to match the direction of the light source in this image. Adjust the Opacity and Size sliders to create the perfect shadow and select OK to apply the changes.

Note > This project has introduced a completely non-destructive approach to montage. Any aspect of the composite image can be re-edited as no pixels were permanently changed or deleted on any layer during the process. The techniques outlined in this project work around the fact that layer masks are only supported on adjustment layers in Elements (unlike the full version of Photoshop which supports masks on all layers). We are effectively hijacking the adjustment layers on grouped adjustment layers to serve this purpose. Although there is a mask option when using the Selection Brush Tool, you are prevented from using the Lasso tools in Elements when working in this mask mode – hence the work we carried out directly on the adjustment layer mask with the mask visible. Same result as the full version of Photoshop – slightly different workflow required to get there.

Project 2

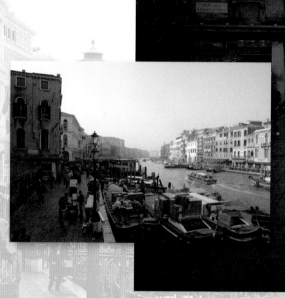

Replacing a Sky

For people who seem to find themselves in the right place at the wrong time!
Have you ever traveled long and far to get to a scenic vista only to find that the
lighting is useless and the sky is a little short of inspiring? Do you make camp and
wait for the weather to change or reluctantly and humiliatingly buy the postcard?
Before you hit the Delete button or assign these 'almost rans' to a never-to-be-
opened-again folder to collect digital dust, consider the post-production alternatives.
Photoshop Elements lets you revisit these uninspired digital vistas to inject the mood
that you were looking for when you first whipped the camera out from its case.

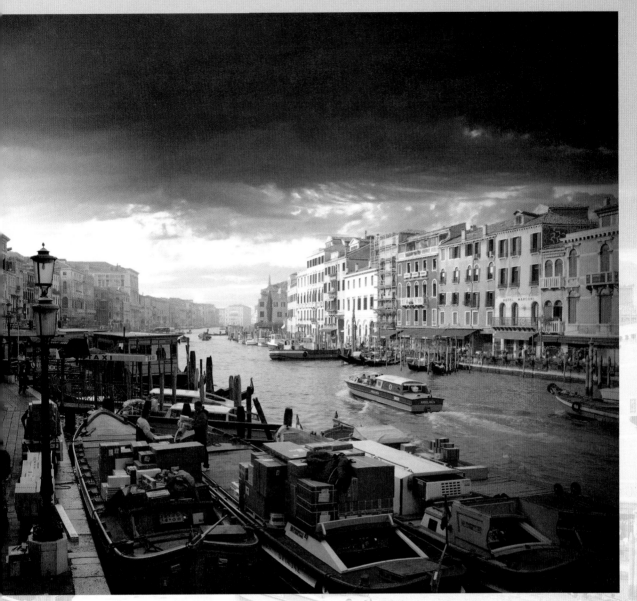

Drama in Venice – change the sky to change the weather

I think every photographer can relate to the intrepid explorers of the Australian Outback who, after scaling the highest peak in the area with great expectations, decided to call it Mount Disappointment! One can only conclude that they were expecting to see something that was simply not there. This something extra could be made real so that all of your landscapes live up to your high expectations – with just a little digital help.

Check out the supporting DVD to access an extensive stock library of royalty-free skies

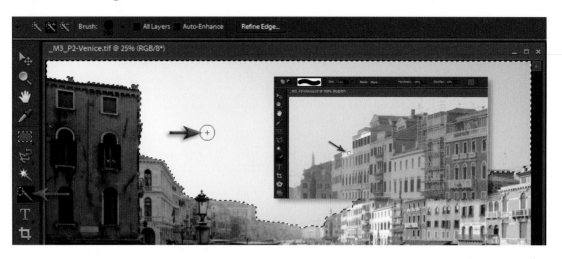

1. Select the Quick Selection Tool from the Tools panel and deselect the Auto Enhance option in the Options bar. Zoom in to 100% or 'Actual Pixels' and select Selection Brush Tool from the Tools panel and the mask option in the Options bar. Paint to add the tops of the buildings that were not included in the mask because of the overzealous behavior of the Quick Selection Tool. Exclude the scaffolding and the TV aerials from the mask. Choose the Selection option in the Options bar when this work is finished.

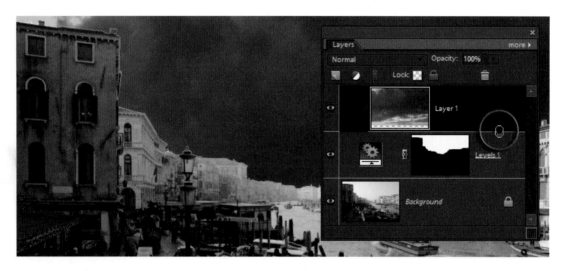

2. From the Layers panel choose Levels adjustment from the Create adjustment layer menu. Select the Sky image used in this project and from the Select menu choose All. From the Edit menu choose Copy. Return to the Venice image and from the Edit menu choose Paste. From the Layer menu choose Group with previous or hold down the Alt key and click on the dividing line between the sky layer and the adjustment layer below to group the two layers. Don't be alarmed at how bad it looks at the moment, we have several more steps to go before things start to look OK. For the moment we must be content that the sky was captured at a similar time of day to the Venice image and the direction of light is also similar.

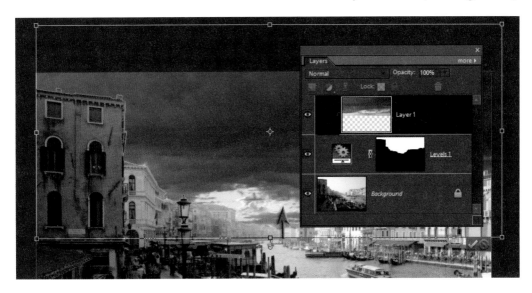

3. Make sure the image rather than the mask is the active component of the layer and then go to Image > Transform > Free Transform (Ctrl + T). Click and drag inside the Transform bounding box to raise the sky into position. Click and drag on the top-center handle to further enhance the location and shape of the sky to fit the host image. Press the Enter key to commit the transformation.

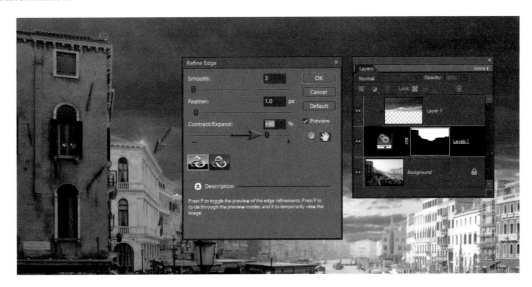

4. Click on the layer mask to make it active and then go to Select > Refine Edge. Choose a setting of 3 for the Smooth slider, a 1-pixel Feather and then move the contract/expand slider to the right until the light halo from around the majority of the buildings has disappeared. It is not possible to remove the halo around the buildings on the extreme left-hand side of the image without removing too much edge detail from the rest of the skyline. The halos around these building can be fully corrected using the Levels adjustment technique as outlined in Project 1 of this section.

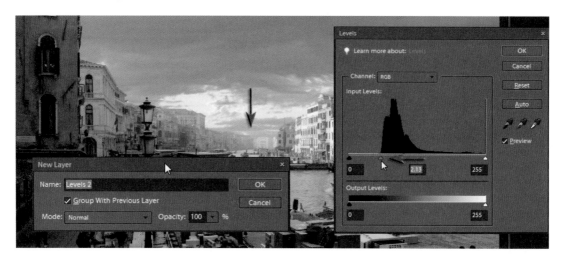

5. Hold down the Alt key and select a Levels adjustment from the Create adjustment layer menu. Select the group with previous option in the New Layer dialog. Move the central gamma slider underneath the histogram to the left to render both the highlights and midtones of the sky very bright so that they match the tones of the distant buildings. Skies that have been captured in less humid conditions will always require this adjustment if they are to look at home in a location where there is reduced contrast together with lighter tones in the distant subject matter. Select OK to apply the changes.

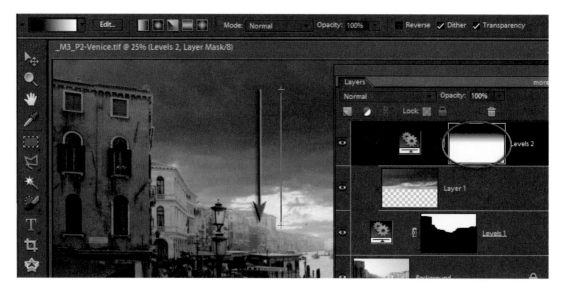

6. Select the Gradient Tool from the Tools panel. In the Options bar choose the Black, White and Linear gradient options and an Opacity setting of 100%. Click and drag a gradient from the top of the image to a position just above the horizon line. Hold down the Shift key to constrain the gradient. This will give the sky depth and ensure the sky retains its drama above the buildings in the foreground.

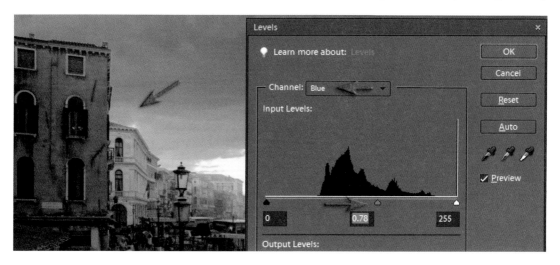

7. Create a second Levels adjustment and group this to the layer below. The purpose of this second adjustment layer is to increase the intensity of the light on the left side of the image. This will help establish the light source that is bathing the buildings on the right side of the image in a warm afternoon glow and help establish a realistic effect. Increase the warmth by moving the gamma slider to the right in the red channel and moving the gamma slider to the right in the blue channel. Raise the overall brightness in the RGB channel. Observe the effect above the foreground buildings on the left side of the image.

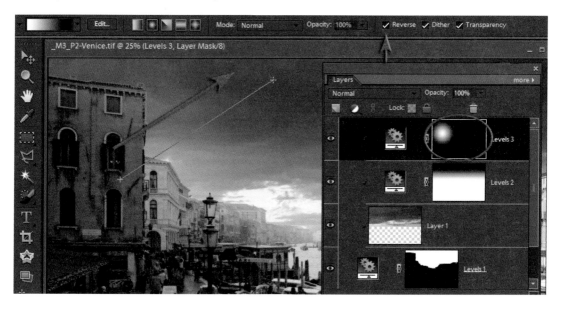

8. Select the Gradient Tool from the Tools panel. Select the Black, White and Radial options. Select the Reverse checkbox in the Options bar. Drag a short gradient from behind the buildings on the left side of the image to the top-center of the image. This gradient will enhance the effect of the setting sun.

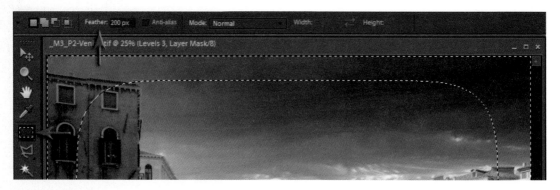

9. Select the Rectangular Marquee Tool in the Tools panel and set the feather to 200 pixels in the Options bar. Click and drag a selection from the upper right-hand corner of the image to the lower left-hand corner of the image. Go to Select > Inverse or use the keyboard shortcut Shift + Ctrl + I. From the Edit menu choose Copy Merged and from the Edit menu choose Paste.

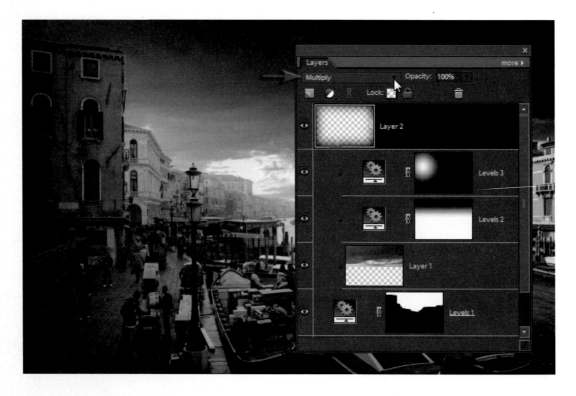

10. Using the information from the file itself to create a vignette prevents the highlights at the edges of the image from excessive darkening. Set the mode of this new layer to Multiply and adjust the opacity of the layer to make the vignette a little more subtle. The project is now complete and the scene carries all of the mood of an old Venetian painting courtesy of a dramatic sky.

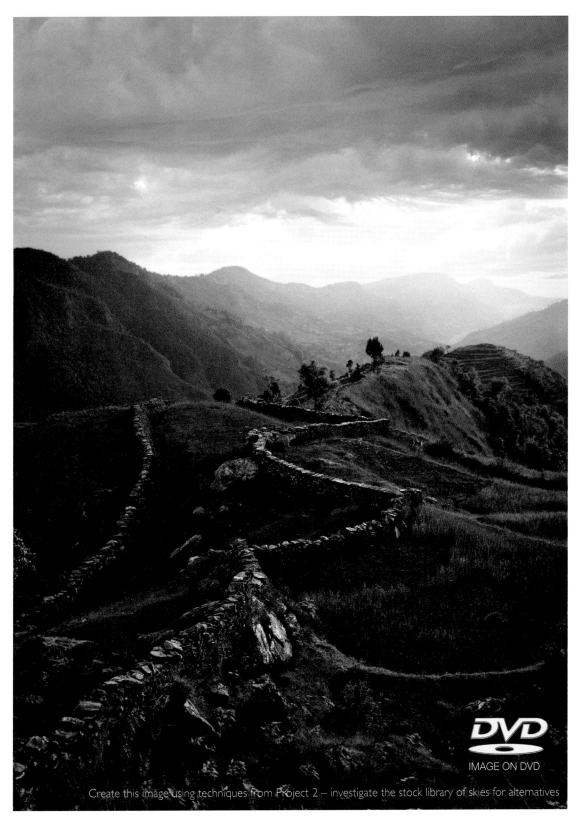

IMAGE ON DVD

Create this image using techniques from Project 2 – investigate the stock library of skies for alternatives

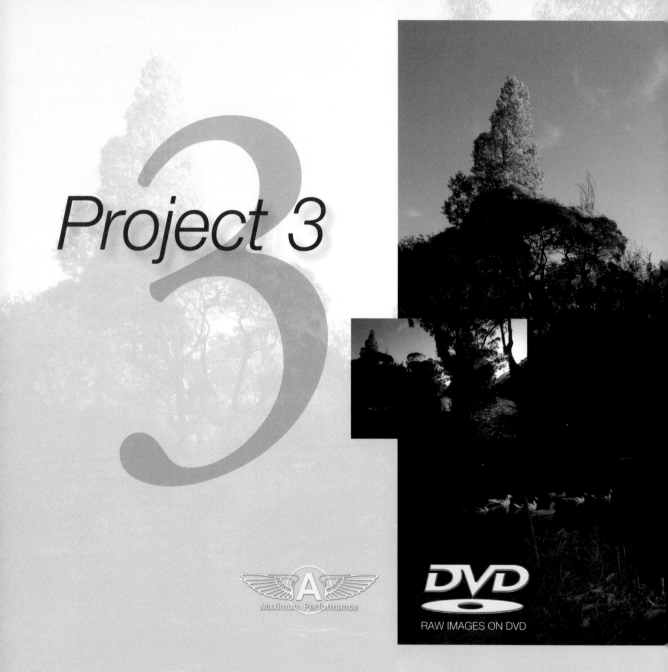

Project 3

High Dynamic Range

Contrary to popular opinion, what you see is not always what you get. You may be able to see the detail in those dark shadows and bright highlights when the sun is shining – but can your image sensor? Contrast in a scene is often a photographer's worst enemy. Contrast is a sneak thief that steals away the detail in the highlights or shadows (sometimes both).

Maximum Performance

DVD

RAW IMAGES ON DVD

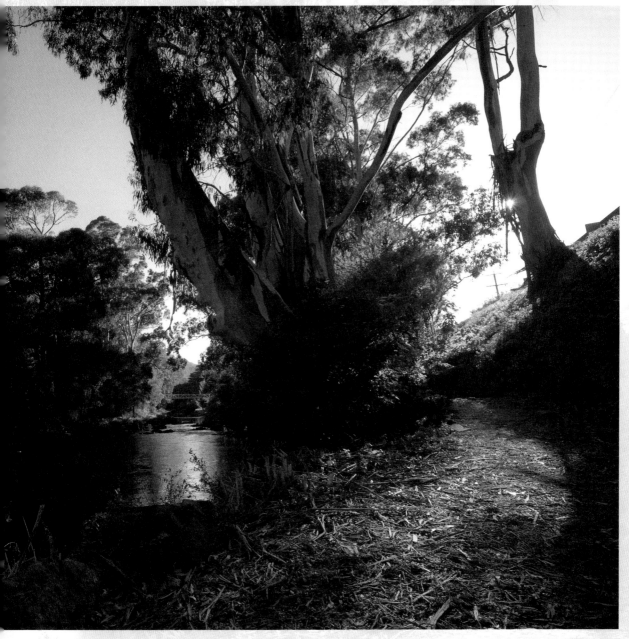

Contrast no problem – discover the secrets to limitless dynamic range

Wedding photographers will deal with the problem of contrast by using fill flash to lower the subject contrast; commercial photographers diffuse their own light source or use additional fill lighting and check for missing detail using the Histogram or a Polaroid. Landscape photographers, however, have drawn the short straw when it comes to solving the contrast problem. For the landscape photographer there is no 'quick fix'. A reflector that can fill the shadows of the Grand Canyon has yet to be made and diffusing the sun's light is only going to happen if the clouds are prepared to play ball.

Method 1 - using a single Camera Raw file

The first technique the photographer can use to combat extreme subject contrast utilizes the flexibility of the Camera Raw format (an image format that can be selected in most high-end digicams and all DSLR cameras). If you are able to capture in Raw mode you will be able to exploit the full dynamic range that your image sensor is capable of. Choosing the JPEG format in your camera when photographing high-contrast subjects may result in the loss of shadow and highlight detail (*see* Part 1, Project 3: Camera Raw, page 22). Part 2 of this project offers an option for merging two separate exposures to restore highlight and shadow detail.

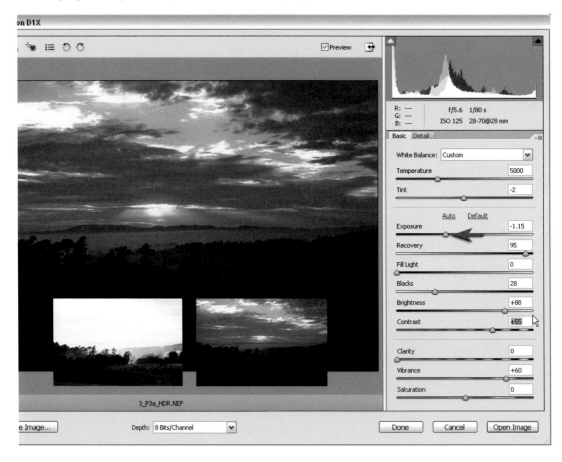

When the Raw file is opened in Photoshop Elements, moving the Exposure slider allows you to take advantage of the extra information in the Camera Raw file to simulate an increase or decrease of exposure in the camera. This allows the photographer to access either increased highlight information or increased shadow information after the image has been captured. It is possible to open multiple versions of the same Raw file and combine them in the main editing space of Photoshop Elements.

Note > When the Raw information is processed the preview and thumbnail of the Raw file reflects these preferences but the Raw data cannot itself be modified. Raw files can be processed multiple times using different settings for exposure, color, sharpness, etc.

To achieve the optimum dynamic range that is possible from the information recorded by the image sensor (increased shadow detail AND increased highlight detail) we can open two images from the same Raw file, each file being optimized for a different end of the exposure range. In Photoshop Elements we can then simply merge the two exposures together. Some would call this manipulation when in reality all we are doing is restoring the tonality back to how our human vision first saw the scene rather than how the camera interpreted it.

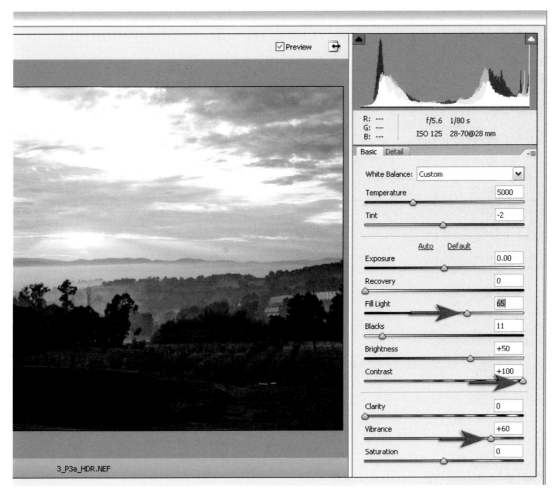

1. Open your Camera Raw file in the Adobe Camera Raw dialog box. Move the Exposure slider or Fill Light slider to the right until the shadow detail has opened up and the detail is clearly visible. Pay no attention to the highlights that may now appear overexposed. Notice how the tall peaks on the left-hand side of the histogram move away from the left side as you move the Exposure or Fill Light sliders to the right. If the shadows are rich in detail but appear flat and gray you can compensate for these by raising both the Contrast and Vibrance sliders. Zoom in to 100% and check the shadows for excessive noise. If noise is a problem proceed to the Detail tab and raise the Luminance Smoothing and Color Noise Reduction sliders to the right until the noise is sufficiently suppressed. Set the 'Depth' in the bottom of the dialog box to 8 Bits/Channel and select 'Open Image'.

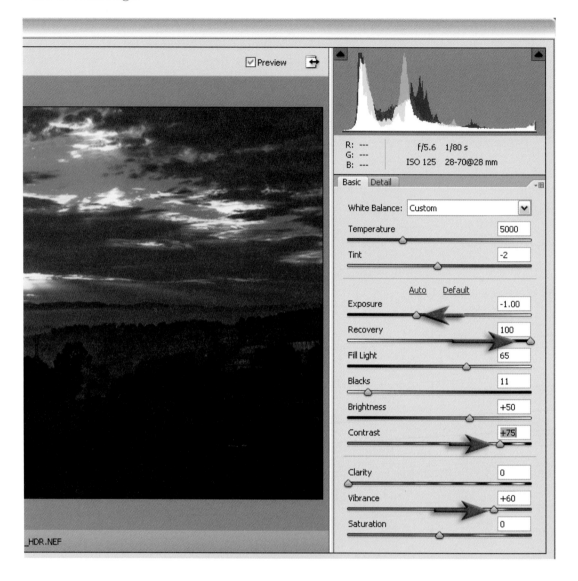

_HDR.NEF

2. Go to File > Place and browse to the same Raw file that you have just opened. Open the file into the Raw dialog box for the second time and now move the Exposure slider to the left to optimize the image for the highlight detail. Drag the Recovery slider all the way to the right and then choose appropriate settings for the Contrast and Vibrance sliders and select the OK button. This second 'interpretation' from the Raw data will be placed on a layer above the first. Commit the transform bounding box without altering the size so that both layers will align perfectly.

PERFORMANCE TIP

In the example some of the highlights are only just recoverable. If you are presented with a landscape with even more contrast the only way of achieving additional information in the highlights or shadows is to bracket the exposures (covered in the next part of this project).

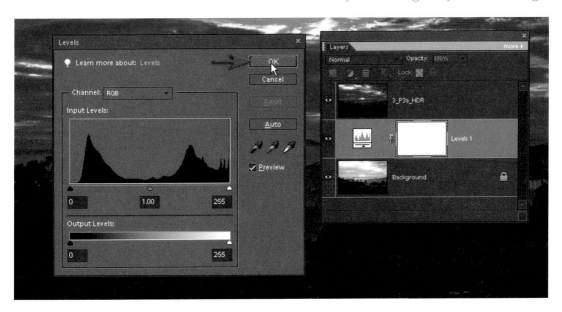

3. The next step involves adding a layer mask that will be used to conceal the darker features of the top layer. To create an adjustment layer for this purpose first select the background layer in the Layers palette and then click on the Create Adjustment Layer icon and choose 'Levels'. Do not make any adjustment in this dialog box but simply select OK.

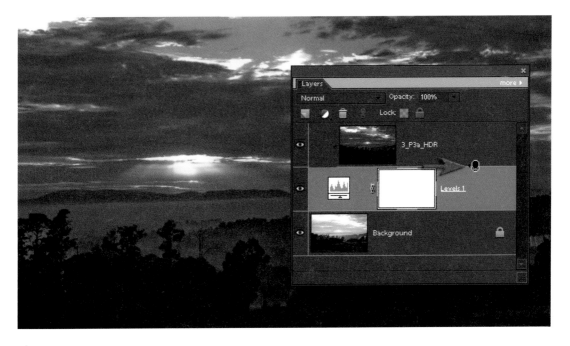

4. Group the top layer with this adjustment layer to link the layer mask to this image layer. Click on the top layer to make this the active layer and then from the Layer menu choose 'Group with Previous'.

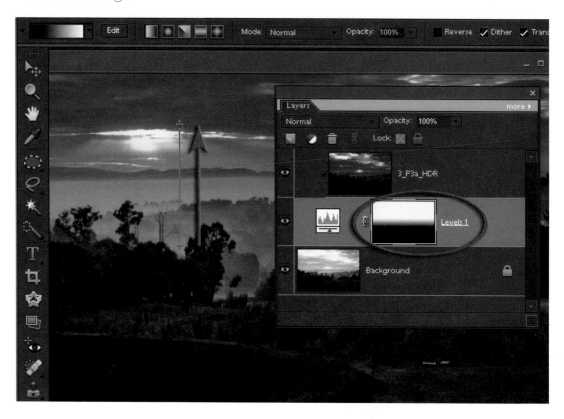

5. In the Tools palette choose the 'Gradient tool' and from the Options bar choose the 'Black, White' gradient, 'Linear' option with an opacity of 100%. Click on the layer mask to make this the active component of the layer. Move the cursor into the image window and click just below the horizon line. Hold down the Shift key and drag the gradient to a position just above the sun and then let go of the mouse button. This action will add a gradient to the layer mask and will act to hide the darker foreground pixels in the top layer. We will now be able to view the sky from the image with the decreased exposure, and the foreground from the image with the increased exposure.

PERFORMANCE TIP

A more complex mask is often called for when the subject is not so clearly defined as a bright sky and a dark foreground. If this is the case you can paint directly into the mask using a soft-edged brush with the foreground color set to 'Black' and the opacity dropped to 50%.

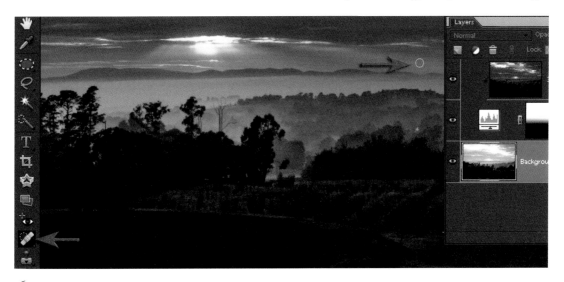

6. The camera used to capture this image has a dust mark on the sensor. It is visible in the sky on the right side of the image, just above the distant hills. Select the Spot Healing Brush Tool and then, with a small soft-edged brush, click in the sky to repair the damage. You may need to perform this task on both the top layer and the background layer depending on where you have drawn your gradient.

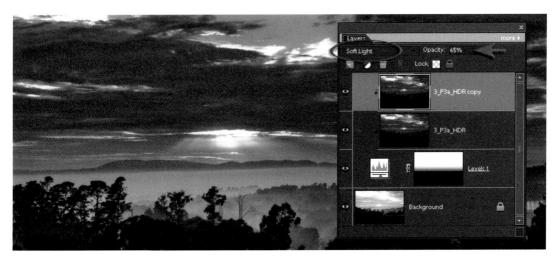

7. To create the right balance between the foreground and background it may be necessary to fine-tune the image. We could have increased the contrast and saturation of the decreased exposure in the Raw dialog box but it was difficult to gain an idea of what the two images would look like when combined at this stage of the process. In this project it was decided to duplicate the top layer (drag the layer to the New Layer icon in the Layers palette) and then switch the mode to 'Soft Light'. You will notice that the duplicated layer is still part of the group and so the mask shields this layer as well as the layer beneath. The 'Soft Light' blend mode has the effect of increasing both the contrast and the saturation of the sky. The effect is that the image now looks like how I remembered the scene when I first raised the camera to my eye.

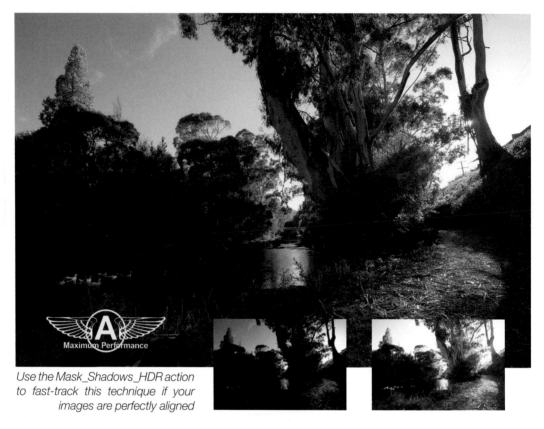

Use the Mask_Shadows_HDR action to fast-track this technique if your images are perfectly aligned

Method 2 - bracketing exposures

$1.$ If we can't fit all the goodies in one exposure, then we'll just have to take two or more. The idea is to montage, or blend, the best of both worlds (the light and dark sides of the camera's not-quite all-seeing eye). To make the post-production easier we need to take a little care in the pre-production, i.e. mount the camera securely on a sturdy tripod. Take two exposures – one overexposing from the auto reading and the other underexposing from the auto reading. One or two stops either side of the meter-indicated exposure should cover most high-contrast situations.

PERFORMANCE TIP

Setting your camera to 'auto bracket exposure mode' means that you don't have to touch the camera between the two exposures, thereby ensuring the first and second exposures can be exactly aligned with the minimum of fuss. Unfortunately for me, the little Fuji FinePix s7000 I was using for this image has auto bracket exposure but it is not operational in Raw capture mode – the only respectable format for self-respecting landscape photographers. This is where you dig out your infrared remote or trusty cable release (if you have somewhere to screw it into). The only other movement to be aware of is something beyond your control. If there is a gale blowing (or even a moderate gust) you are not going to get the leaves on the trees to align perfectly in post-production. This also goes for fast-moving clouds and anything else that is likely to be zooming around in the fraction of a second between the first and second exposures.

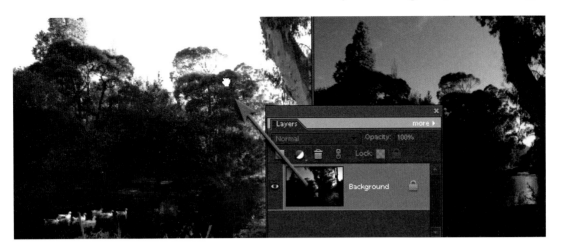

2. Click on the dark underexposed image to make it the active image window and then drag the layer thumbnail (in the Layers palette) into the window of the lighter overexposed image. Holding down the Shift key as you let go of the image will align the two layers (but not necessarily the two images).

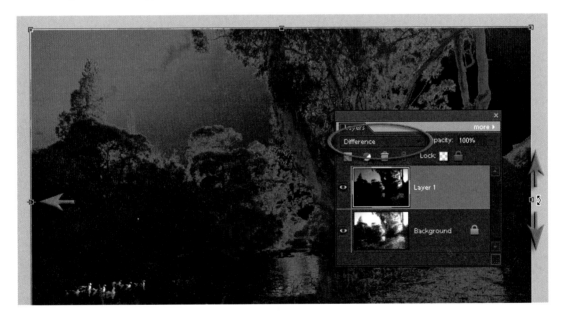

3. In the Layers palette set the blend mode of the top layer to 'Difference' to check the alignment of the two images. If they align, no white edges will be apparent (usually the case if the tripod was sturdy and the two exposures were made via an auto feature or cable release). If you had to resort to a friend's right shoulder you will now spend the time you thought you had saved earlier. To make a perfect alignment you need to select 'Free Transform' from the Image > Transform menu. Nudge the left side into alignment and then move the reference·point location in the Options bar to the left-hand side of the square. Highlight the numbers in the rotation field in the Options bar and then rotate the image into final alignment by pressing the up or down arrow keys on the keyboard.

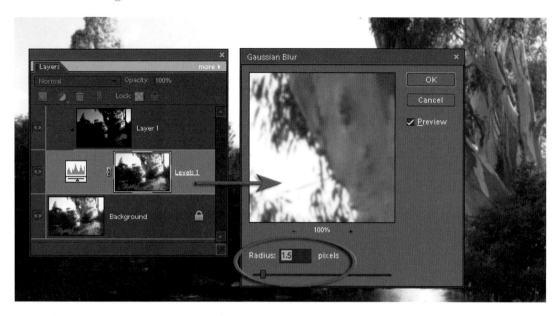

4. Add a Levels adjustment layer above the background layer. Make no adjustments as only the mask is required. Group the top layer with this adjustment layer (hold down the Alt key as you click on the dividing line between the two layers). Click on the background layer and choose 'All' from the Select menu (Ctrl + A). Copy to the clipboard and then Alt + Click the adjustment layer thumbnail. The image window should appear white as the layer mask is empty. Now choose 'Paste' from the edit menu (Ctrl + V). Apply a small amount of Gaussian Blur to this mask before Alt + Clicking once again to return to the normal view.

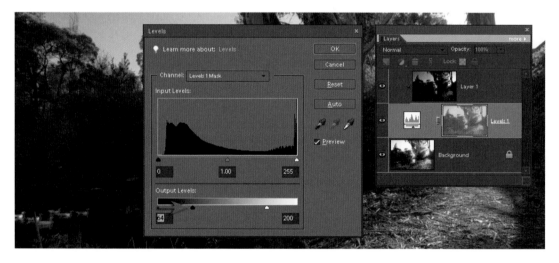

5. It is important to recreate the expanded contrast of the original scene, otherwise the image will look slightly surreal if the overall contrast is low. The first technique to expand the contrast is to apply a Levels adjustment to this layer mask (Ctrl + L). Drag in the Output sliders (directly beneath the Shadow and Highlight sliders) until the final contrast appears high but not clipped (lowering the contrast of the mask increases the contrast of the final image).

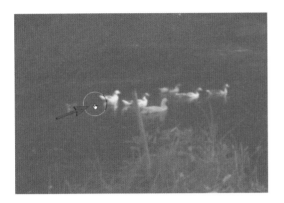 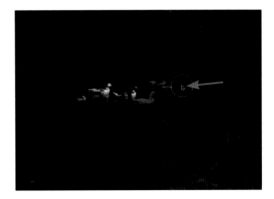

6. The observant amongst us will have noticed the ducks have been breeding. The ghost images can be removed by painting or cloning them out on both the top layer and the layer mask beneath. If using a soft-edged brush to paint them out you should first sample an adjacent color by holding down the Alt key and clicking on the surrounding tone. Alt + click the layer mask to get a clear idea of what you are doing.

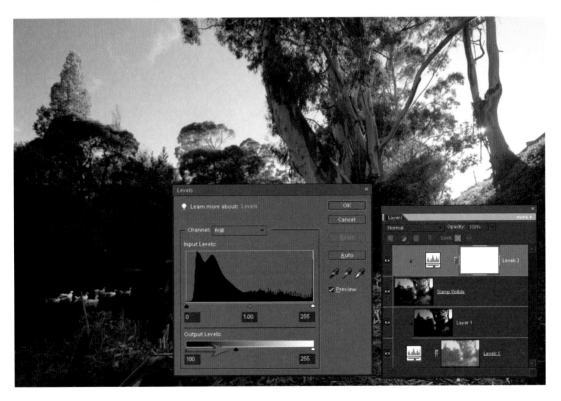

7. In order to achieve the final contrast setting for this image, stamp the visible elements to a new layer (Ctrl + Alt + Shift then type the letter E) and place this new layer in Overlay or Soft Light mode. Adjust the opacity of this layer until the required effect is created. If the shadow tones are rendered too dark by this process, a Levels adjustment layer can be grouped with this layer and the Shadows Output slider raised to restrict the increase in contrast to just the midtones and highlight tones.

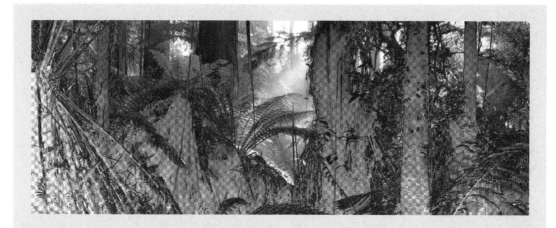

PERFORMANCE TIP

In the full version of Photoshop the user has access to the 'Advanced Blending Options'. In this dialog box it is possible to reduce the opacity of the shadow tones on the top layer to reveal the shadow tones beneath. The effect can be faded in gradually, creating a blend of the optimum highlights from the top layer and the optimum shadow tones of the background layer. The advanced blending options are only available to users of the full version of Photoshop, but the same results can be achieved using a layer style preset loaded into the presets folder in Elements. The layer styles provided on the supporting DVD give the Elements user the option of partial transparency based on tonality.

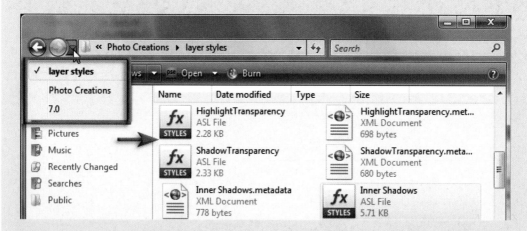

Photoshop Elements users can access the Transparency Layer style by first loading the styles and metadata available on the supporting DVD into the Layer Styles folders (<C:\Documents and Settings\All_Users\ApplicationData\Adobe\Photoshop_Elements\7.0\Photo_Creations\layer styles). The styles and metadata were created in the full version of Photoshop but can be read by Photoshop Elements. The software may have to be restarted after loading the styles and metadata into the folder before Photoshop Elements will load the new content.

Note > Vista users will find the Adobe folder in the C:\Program Data folder.

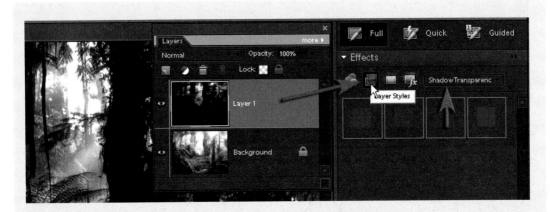

Select the top layer in the Layers palette and then click on each of the four presets in turn (now located in the Effects palette) and choose the one that renders the best tonality.

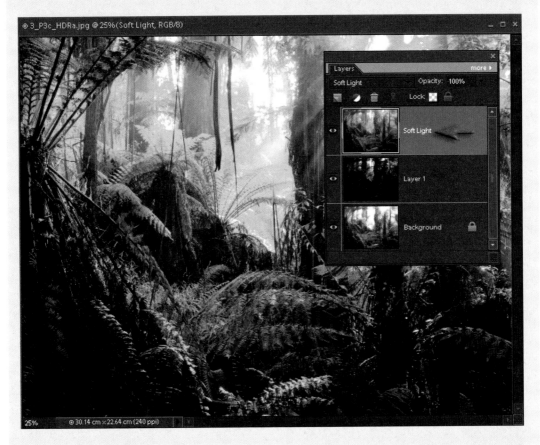

To improve the midtone contrast proceed to stamp the visible elements of both the dark and light layers into a single layer (hold down the Ctrl + Shift + Alt keys and then type the letter E). Set the blend mode of this Stamp Visible layer to Soft Light and adjust the opacity of the layer if required.

Project 4

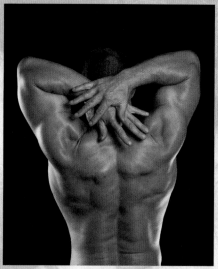

Photograph by Abhijit Chattaraj

Layer Blending

The blending technique enables the texture or pattern from one image to be merged with the form in another image. Blending two images in the computer is similar to creating a double exposure in the camera or sandwiching negatives in a traditional darkroom. Photoshop Elements, however, allows a greater degree of control over the final outcome. This is achieved by controlling the specific blend mode, position and opacity of each layer. The use of 'adjustment layer masks' can help to shield any area of the image that needs to be protected from the blend mode.

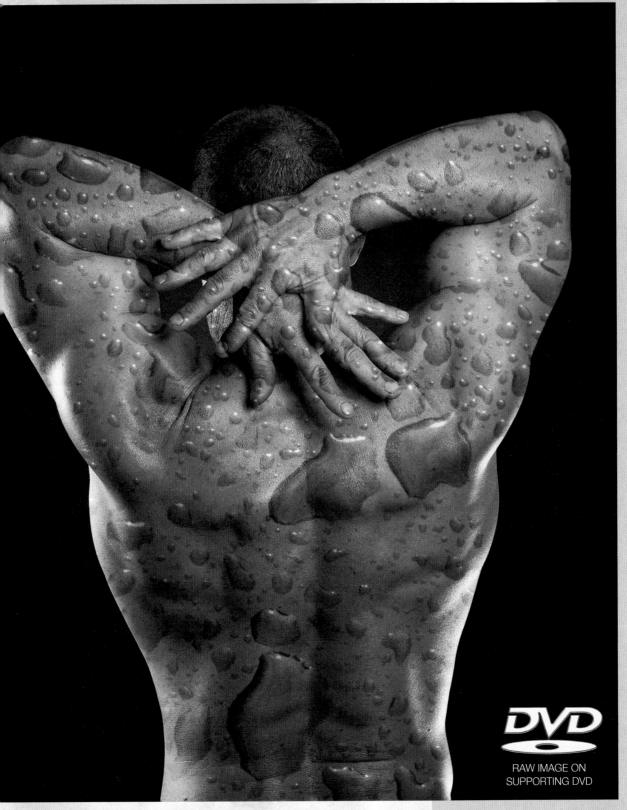

DVD

RAW IMAGE ON
SUPPORTING DVD

Body art – Blend a texture or pattern with your subject to create a dramatic or surreal effect

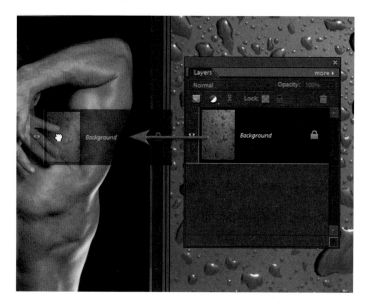

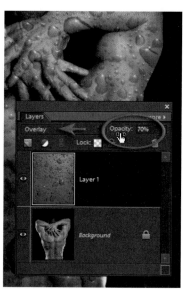

1. Click and drag the layer thumbnail of the raindrops image into the body image window. Hold down the Shift key as you let go of the drops thumbnail to center the image in the new window. Use the Move Tool to reposition the texture if required. Use the Free Transform command (Image > Transform > Free Transform) if required to resize the texture image so that it covers the figure in the image. Set the blend mode of the drops layer (Layer 1) to Soft Light or Overlay. Experiment with adjusting the opacity of the layer using the Opacity slider in the Layers panel.

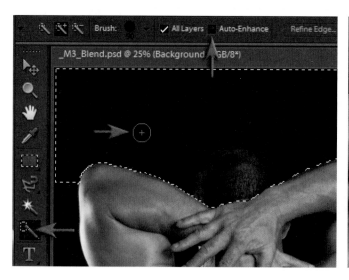

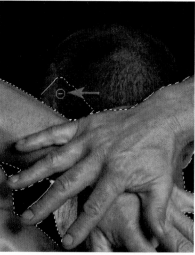

2. Select the Quick Selection Tool in the Tools panel. Deselect the 'Auto-Enhance' option in the Options bar. Make an initial selection by dragging the tool over an area of the background. Click and drag over the islands of black background between the subject's fingers to add these areas to the selection (reduce the size of the brush if necessary). Hold down the Alt key and drag over any areas that need to be removed from the selection, e.g. the head.

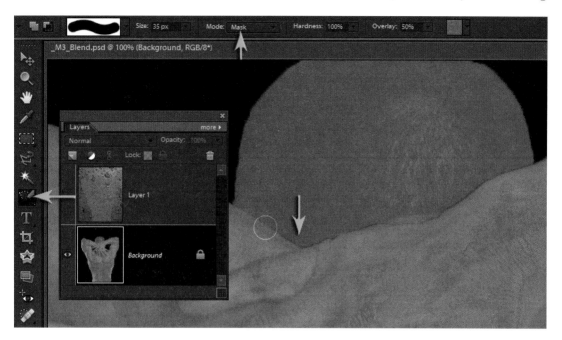

3. Select the Selection Brush Tool in the Tools panel and select the Mask option in the Options bar. Paint over any gaps in the mask (using a brush at 100% Opacity) to perfect the resulting selection. Zoom in and move around the edge of the body to ensure all of the body is fully masked. Switch back to selection mode in the Options bar when this step is complete.

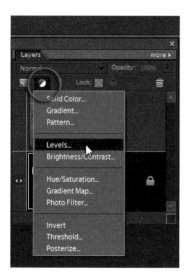

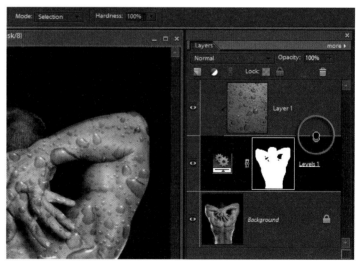

4. From the Create adjustment layer menu in the Layers panel select a Levels adjustment layer. The active selection will be converted into a layer mask. Select OK in the Levels dialog without making any adjustment. Switch on the visibility of the raindrops layer and group the raindrops layer with the adjustment layer below (hold down the Alt key and click on the dividing line between the two layers).

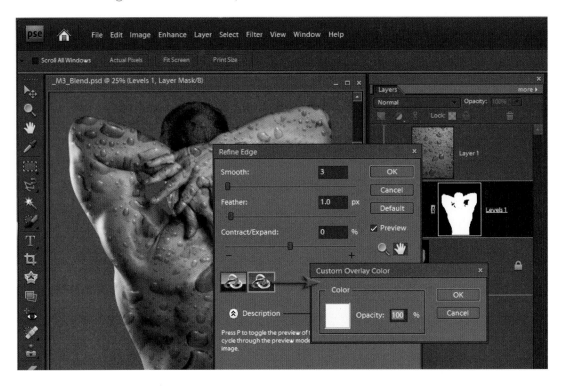

5. Click on the layer mask thumbnail in the Layers panel and then from the Select menu choose the Refine Edge command. Double-click the Custom Overlay Color option to access the overlay options. To get an accurate view of how appropriate the edge of the mask is for our final result we will create a white matte in the Refine Edge dialog to help us choose the optimum settings. Click on the color swatch in the Custom Overlay Color dialog and set the color to white. Set the Opacity to 100% and select OK to close and apply the Custom Overlay Color options.

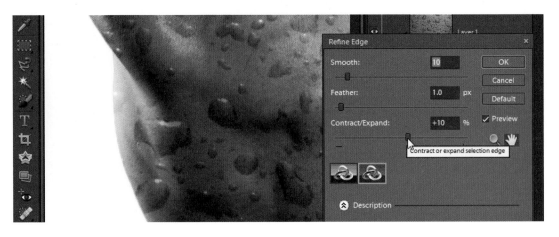

6. Adjust the Smooth slider to 3 and the Feather slider to 1.0 pixel to help refine the edge and then drag the Contract/Expand slider to the right to hide any of the dark edges from the old black background. Select OK when you have achieved a good clean edge.

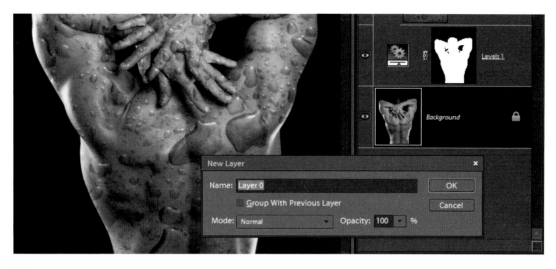

7. We need to unlock the background layer to perfect this composite image. Double-click the Background layer in the Layers panel to open the New Layer dialog and select OK to accept the 'Layer 0' name. This action will allow us to add a mask to the this layer and a new layer below (not possible when the layer is a background layer).

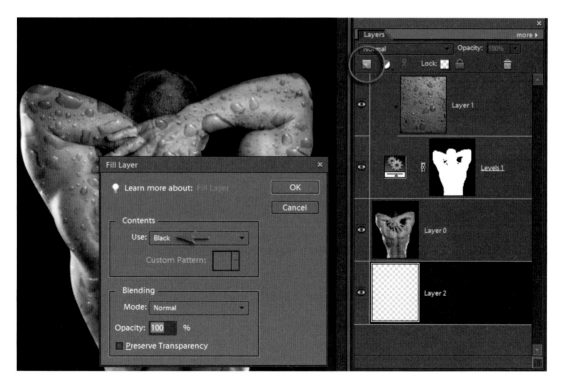

8. Hold down the Ctrl key and click on the Create a new layer icon in the Layers panel to create an empty new layer below Layer 0. Go to Edit > Fill Layer and choose black as the contents color. Select OK to create a black layer (Layer 2).

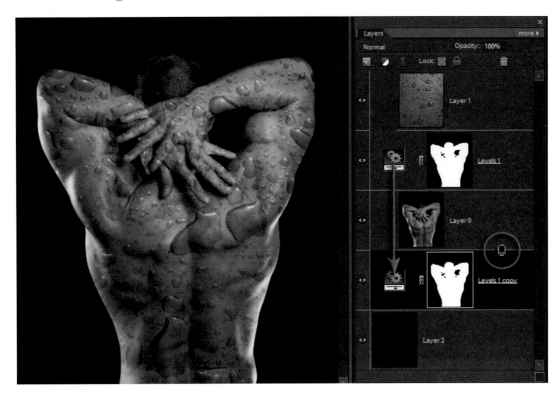

9. Hold down the Alt key and click and drag the Levels 1 adjustment layer to copy it. Drag it to a position between Layer 2 (the new black layer) and Layer 0 before releasing the mouse button. Hold down the Alt key again and click on the dividing line between the copy adjustment layer and Layer 0 to create a clipping mask or group. This new mask and the new black layer will ensure a perfect edge when we lighten the background in the final stages of the project.

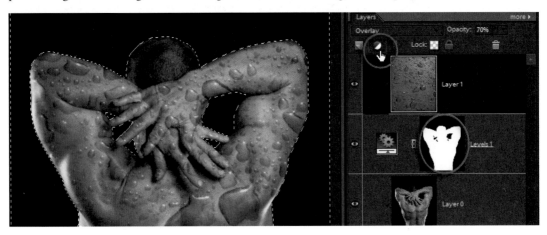

10. Hold down the Ctrl key and click on the layer mask thumbnail to load the mask as a selection. Click on the raindrops layer (Layer 1) to make this the active layer and then select a Levels adjustment layer from the Create adjustment layer menu in the Layers panel.

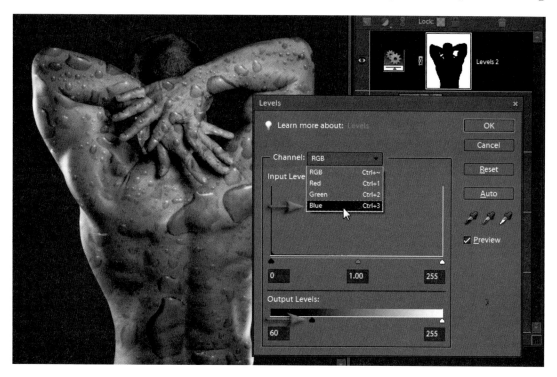

11. In the Levels dialog drag the black Output Levels slider to the right to lighten the background to a dark gray tone. From the Channel menu select the Blue channel and once again drag the black Output Levels slider to the right to introduce a blue color to the gray background. The precise shade of blue can be controlled by adjusting the black Output levels slider in either the Red or Green channel. Select OK to apply these changes.

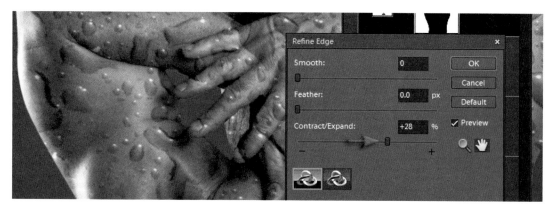

12. Now that the background has been lightened it may be necessary to expand the edge of this layer mask (Select > Refine Edge). The Smooth and Feather sliders can both be set to 0 so the edge does not get softened and smoothed a second time. Adjust the Expand/Contract slider to perfect the edge once again and then select OK.

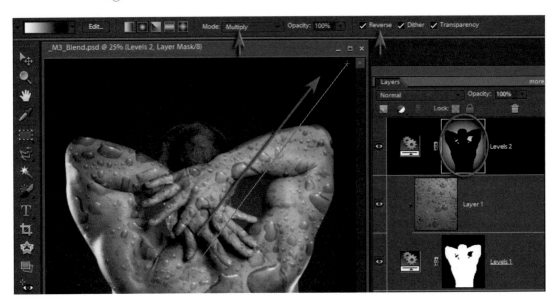

13. Select the Gradient Tool in the Tools panel. Select the Foreground to Transparent and Radial Gradient options With Black selected as the Foreground color. Set the opacity to 100% and select the Reverse, Dither and Transparency options. Click and drag from a position in the center of the man's body out past the top right-hand edge of the image window to create a backlight effect.

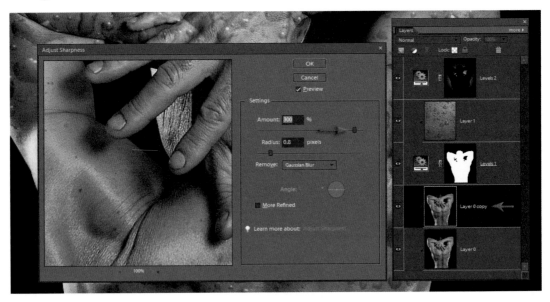

14. Select Layer 0 in the Layers panel and use the keyboard shortcut Ctrl + J to duplicate the layer. Group this copy layer with the layer below and from the Enhance menu choose Adjust Sharpness. Select a generous Amount of sharpening with a low Radius setting (300 and 0.8) and select OK. The opacity of this duplicate layer can be lowered to adjust levels of sharpening for your required output device.

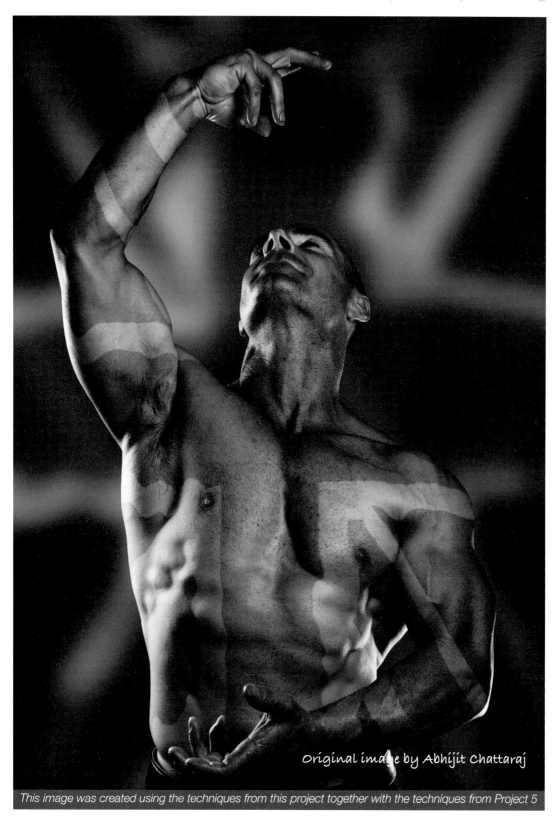

Original image by Abhijit Chattaraj

This image was created using the techniques from this project together with the techniques from Project 5

Project 5

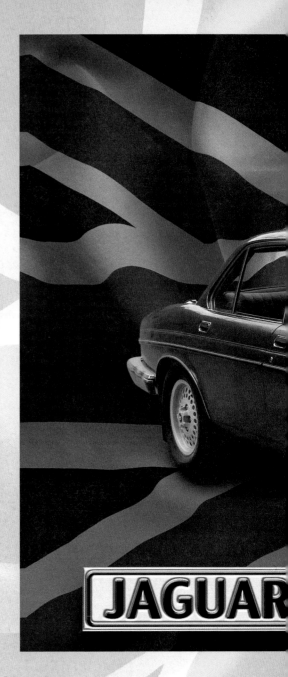

Displacement

Create a showpiece montage by elevating an old Jag into a classic motor with a little spit and polish and some delectable digital deeds. Wickedly good stuff! The car's paintwork was enhanced before starting the project by increasing the overall saturation of the image and the scratches were removed using the Healing Brush. The tires were made to look like new by using the Burn tool set to 20%. If only it was this easy in real life!

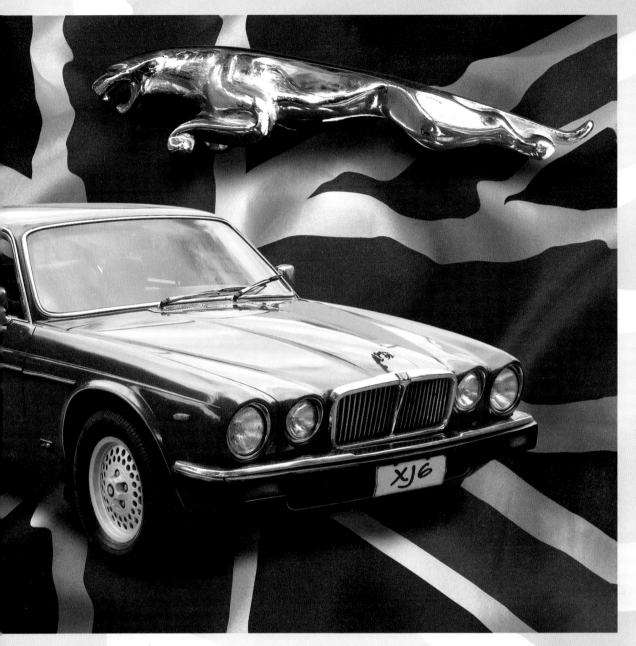

Liquid pixels – a displacement, masking and layer style 'combo'

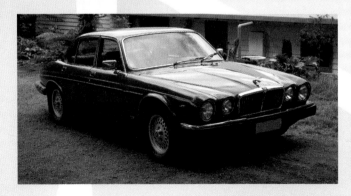

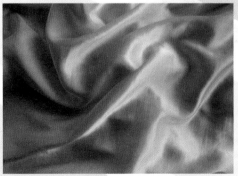

Stage 1 - Creating a backdrop using the Displacement filter

The layer blend modes are an effective way of merging or blending a pattern or graphic with a three-dimensional form. By using the blend modes the flag in this project can be modified to respect the color and tonality of the undulating silk beneath it. The highlights and shadows that give the silk its shape can, however, be further utilized to wrap or bend the flag so that it obeys the material's shape and sense of volume. This can be achieved by using the Displace filter in conjunction with a 'displacement map'. The 'map' defines the contours to which the flag must conform. The final effect can be likened to 'shrink-wrapping' the flag to the 3-D form of the undulating silk.

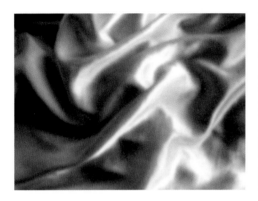 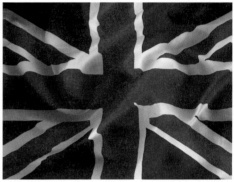

How it works: The brightness level of each pixel in the map directs the filter to shift the corresponding pixel of the selected layer in a horizontal or vertical plane. The principle on which this technique works is that of 'mountains and valleys'. Dark pixels in the map shift the graphic pixels down into the shaded valleys of the 3-D form while the light pixels of the map raise the graphic pixels onto the illuminated peaks of the 3-D form.

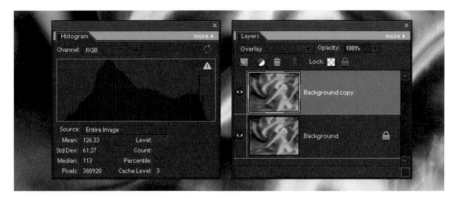

1. A silk dressing gown was photographed using the available light. For this image to act as an effective displacement map the contrast must, however, be expanded. An effective way of expanding contrast in Photoshop Elements is to duplicate the layer and set the top layer to 'Overlay' blend mode. Note the changes to the histogram by viewing the histogram in the Histogram palette.

Note > Duplicate the silk image resource file to ensure the original file is retained as a master and not lost by this manipulation. Either copy the image file before you start the project or go to 'File > Duplicate' before you proceed to step 2.

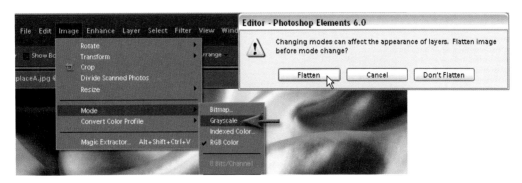

2. Go to the Image menu and from the Mode submenu select 'Grayscale'. Choose the option 'Flatten' when the Warning dialog box appears.

Note > The displacement map must be in Grayscale otherwise the color channels will upset the appropriate displacement effect.

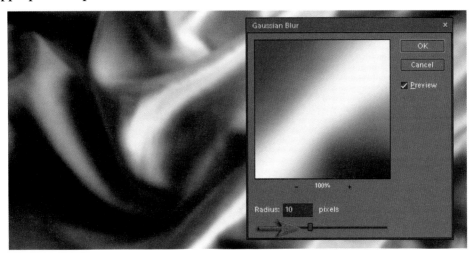

3. To further improve the effectiveness of the displacement map we must blur the image slightly. This effect of blurring the map will smooth out the lines of the flag as it wraps around the contours of the silk. Too much blur and the undulations will be lost, too little and the lines of the flag will appear jagged as it is upset by any minor differences in tone. Go to 'Filter > Blur > Gaussian Blur' and start by selecting a Radius of around 10 pixels. Increase or decrease this radius when working with images of a different resolution.

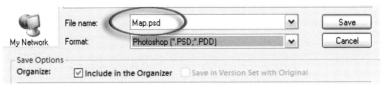

4. Save the image (displacement map) as a Photoshop (PSD) file. Close the blurred Grayscale file as the map is now complete. You will need to choose this file when the Displacement filter asks for the location of your map, so make a note of where it has been saved to on your computer.

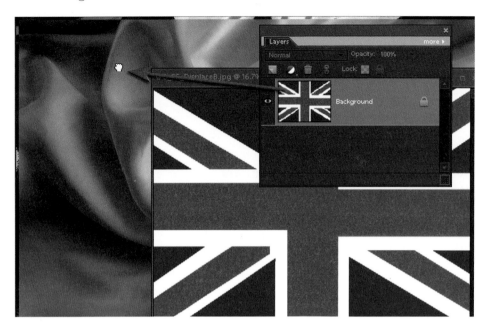

5. Open or select the RGB silk file that has not been blurred. Also open the flag image. With the flag image as the active window, choose 'All' from the Select menu and then choose 'Copy' from the File menu. Now make the silk image the active window and choose 'Paste' from the File menu. Alternatively you can just drag the thumbnail of the flag image in the Layers palette into the image window of the silk image if you can see both image windows on your desktop.

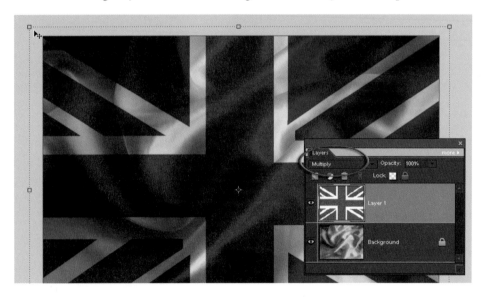

Set the blend mode of the flag layer to 'Multiply'. If you are intending to displace a graphic or a texture it is worth ensuring that you have some elbow room (when we displace the flag it will come away from, and reveal, the edges of the background layer if they are the same size). Use the Free Transform command to enlarge the flag layer so that it is a little larger than the background layer.

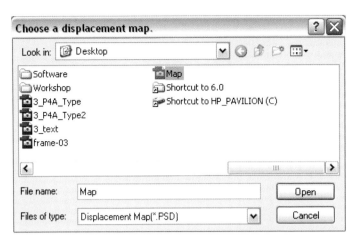

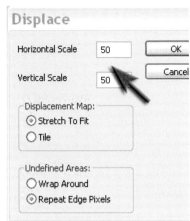

6. Go to 'Filter > Distort > Displace'. Enter in the amount of displacement in the Horizontal and Vertical fields of the Displace dialog box. The size of the displacement is dependent on the resolution of the image you are working on. Choose amounts of 40 for both fields for the Flag.jpg used in this project. Increasing the amount greater than 60 for either the Horizontal or Vertical scale will increase the amount of distortion in this project image, but will also start to break off islands of color from the design of the flag, indicating that the limit of the effect has been exceeded. Select OK in the Displace dialog box and in the 'Choose a displacement map' dialog box browse to the displacement map you saved. Select Open and your flag should now miraculously conform to the contours of the silk. If you are not entirely happy with the results go to the Edit menu and choose 'Undo'. Repeat the process choosing smaller or greater amounts in the Displace dialog box.

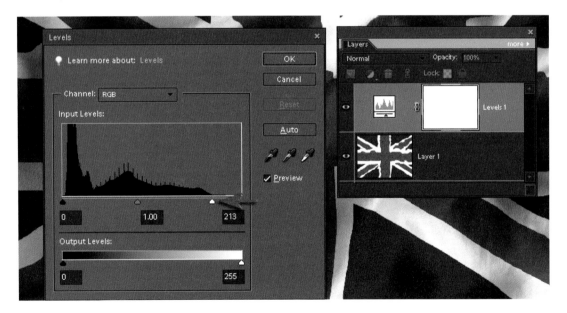

7. Add an adjustment layer and drag the Highlight slider to the start of the histogram to extend the dynamic range and make the highlights and midtones appear brighter. Your dramatic and colorful background is now complete.

Stage 2 - Creating a montage using masks

The following montage techniques are used for professional results. The techniques covered allow precise control over the alignment and quality of the edge (soft/hard) to ensure that no haloes from the old background are visible (even when using crude selection tools such as the Magic Wand).

Note > Download the completed flag file from the supporting DVD if you would like to start the project at this point.

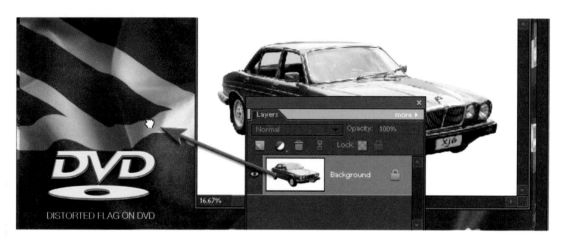

8. Open the image of the Jaguar car and add this as a layer above the adjustment layer and flag in the master project file (see step 5 for a guide on combining two images). I have made the background behind the car white in order to make it easier for you to remove it from view in this project.

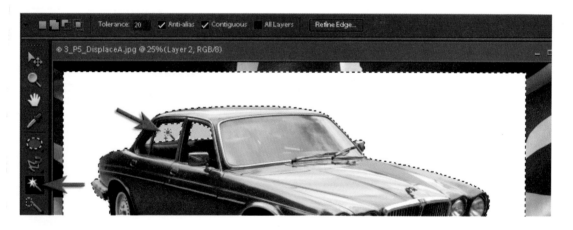

Select the 'Magic Wand tool' in the Tools palette. Select the Add To icon in the Options bar and set the tolerance in the Options bar to 20. Click on the white background surrounding the car and then click on the rear window behind the back seat to add these sections to the selection. You do not need to delete the white background in order to conceal it (deleting pixels is considered destructive editing and can restrict the control over the edge quality later).

Note > The TIFF image on the supporting DVD has a saved selection of the car.

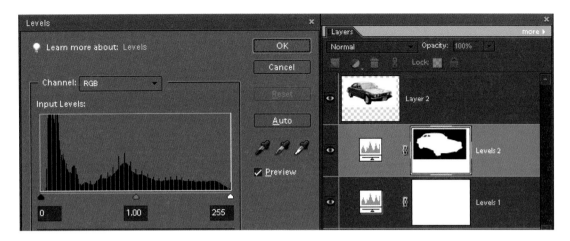

9. Go to the Select menu and choose 'Inverse Selection'. Then proceed to select an adjustment layer from the Layers palette. It does not matter which adjustment layer you choose as we will only be borrowing its layer mask and not using it to make any adjustments to the layers beneath. Just select OK without making any adjustment. Click on the car layer above the adjustment layer and choose 'Group' from the Layer menu.

Note > The background will now have been removed but the edge still needs to be refined to improve its appearance.

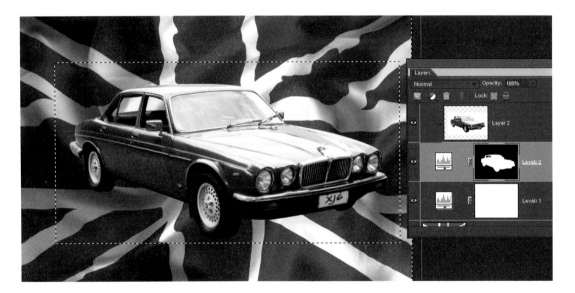

10. The resulting mask is likely to have a 1-pixel white line visible around the edge of the old background. To remove this thin white line paint with black directly into the layer mask of the adjustment layer. Alternatively a quicker option (if you know your shortcuts) is to make a rectangular selection around the car using the Marquee tool (M), invert the selection (Ctrl + Shift + I) and fill this selection with black (Alt + Backspace if black is in the foreground swatch).

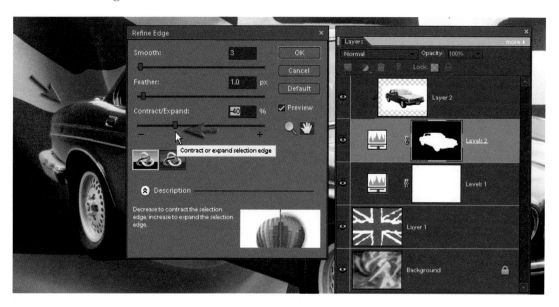

11. The edge of the mask needs to be softened and moved to conceal the remnants of the old white background. From the Select menu choose 'Refine Edge'. Use a Smooth value of 3 and a feather value of 1.0 pixel to smooth and soften the edge of the outline of the car. Slide the Contract/Expand slider to the left to hide any white edges from around the car. Select OK to apply the changes to the mask.

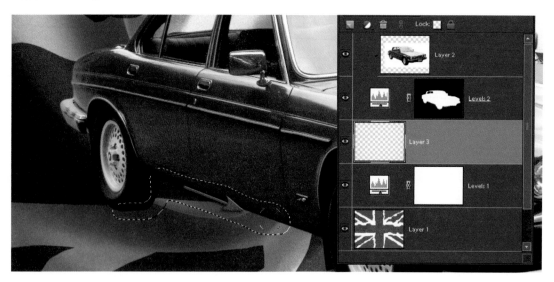

12. Now we're going to create a shadow. Select the adjustment layer below the mask layer and then click on the New Layer icon in the Layers palette. Select the 'Selection Brush tool' in the Tools palette and then paint a selection that extends just in front of the tires and underneath the car. Extend some way over the edge of the car as this will be needed later (blurring the shadow will reduce its opacity at the edges). From the Edit menu choose the Fill command, select 'Black' as the color and click OK.

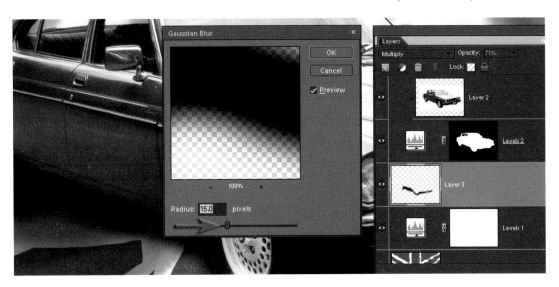

13. Apply a Gaussian Blur filter to this layer and then refine the shadow by setting the blend mode to 'Multiply' and lowering the opacity to around 70%.

Note > A second shadow layer could be added to create some smaller shadows just underneath the wheels and further underneath the car. This refinement will help create the illusion that the car is in contact with the flag.

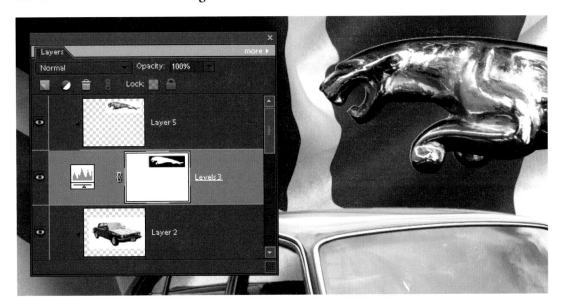

14. The image just needs a few finishing touches to complete the project. Add the leaping Jaguar and make a selection of the white background surrounding the Jaguar using the Magic Wand tool. Click on the layer below and then add an adjustment layer. Select OK without making any adjustments. Group the two layers (Layer > Group with Previous) and then use the Refine Edge command (Select > Refine Edge) to perfect the new addition.

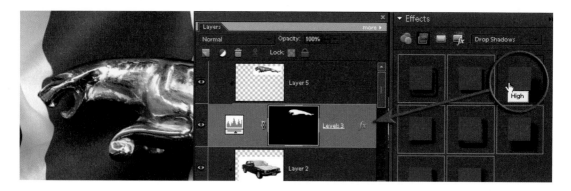

15. As the Jaguar does not need to appear to be in contact with the flag we can simply add a drop shadow to this layer rather than create a shadow by hand. Go to the Effects palette and click on a Drop Shadow style. This can be modified or perfected by going to the Layers menu and choosing 'Style Settings'. The angle and distance of the shadow from the object can be controlled from this dialog box or the user can simply click inside the image window and drag the shadow to a different position to obtain the best effect.

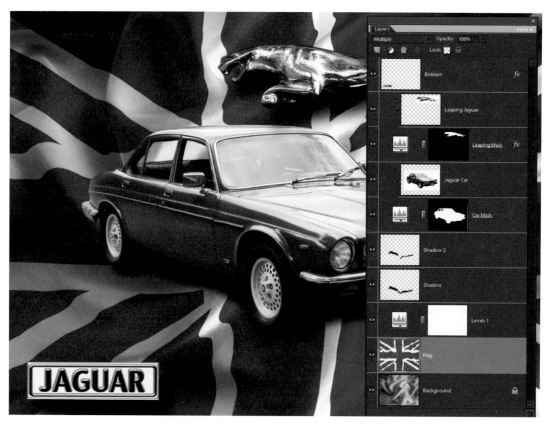

16. Complete the image by adding the image of the badge in the lower left-hand corner. Add a drop shadow to this layer and the project is complete.

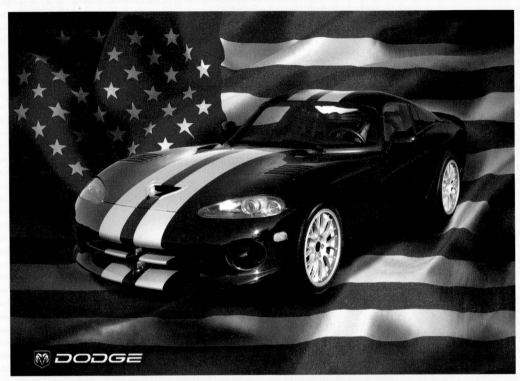

Car photograph courtesy of www.iStockphoto.com

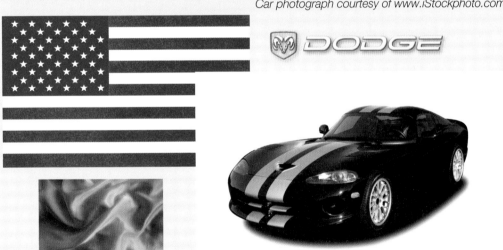

iStock_0000002I3548 (Dodge Viper GTS ACR - 2000 by Stan Rohrer)

PERFORMANCE TIP

An American flag is available on the DVD. The steps to creating a USA classic car and flag are pretty much the same as for the British car. A non-destructive dodge and burn layer was, however, grouped with the car layer to darken the tires and edge of windshield. Select the color of the car using the Eyedropper tool and paint in Darken mode at 20% in a new layer grouped with the car layer to darken the paint further.

Project 6

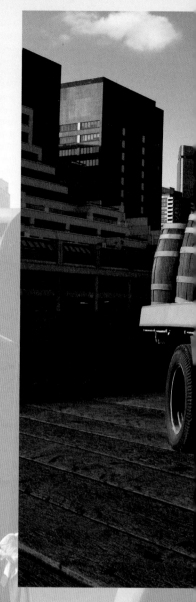

Preserving Shadows

The truck used in this project was photographed in the hills of southern Queensland, Australia, while the river dock hails from more than a thousand miles south on the banks of the Yarra river in Melbourne, Victoria. Unlikely bedfellows, but with a little craft the two can lie together comfortably within the same frame - but only if the shadow is transplanted with all of its subtlety and delicately transplanted to its new home on the wooden dock.

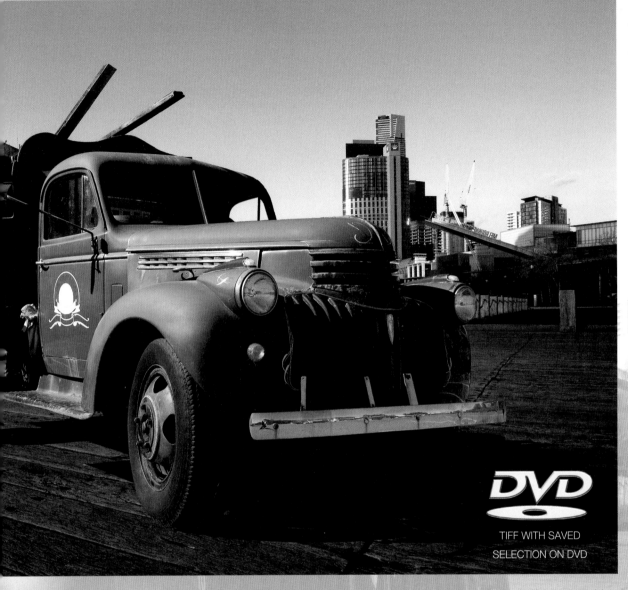

DVD

TIFF WITH SAVED
SELECTION ON DVD

The 'shadow catcher' technique – designed to preserve the natural shadows of a subject

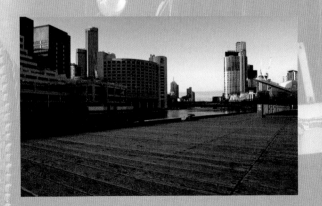

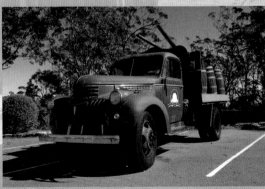

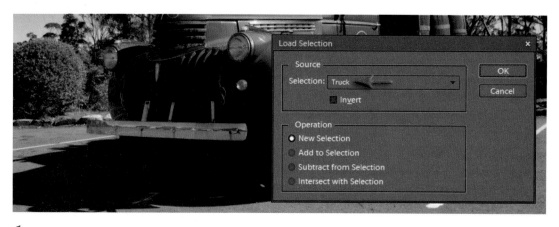

1. Open the Truck TIFF image from the supporting DVD and go to Select > Load Selection. From the Selection menu choose Truck and select OK to load this selection.

Note > This selection has already been refined (see project 1 in this module) so no further action needs to be taken to optimize the edge quality at this point in time. Raw and JPEG files are also available on the DVD but these do not contain saved selections that can fast-track this project.

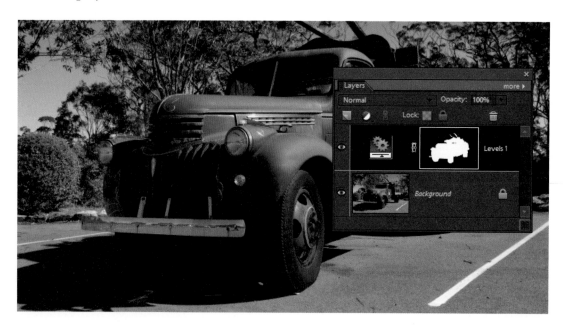

2. In the Layers panel choose a Levels adjustment layer from the Create adjustment layer menu. Make no adjustment in the Levels dialog and select OK. Go to Filter > Adjustments > Invert to invert the mask so that the truck is masked rather than the background.

Note > We could have inverted the selection prior to creating the Levels adjustment layer but this leads to problems around the edges of the mask when we move and scale the truck later in the project. All subsequent layer masks in this project will be created the same way to avoid problems later on, i.e. creating a mask that then has to be inverted.

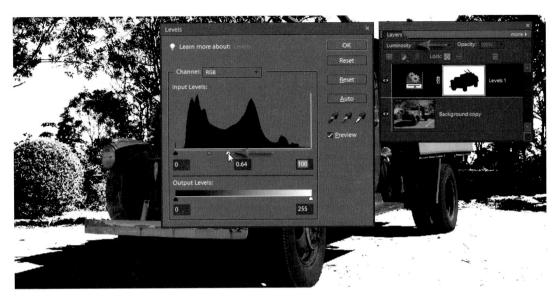

3. Hold down the Alt key and click and drag the white input Levels slider to the left. The Alt key will give you a Threshold view and as you drag the slider to the left you will see increasing areas of tone being clipped to white. Continue to drag the slider to the left until the shadow appears as an island of black tone surrounded by white clipped tone. Select OK to apply this levels adjustment. Set the mode of the levels adjustment layer to Luminosity to preserve the original Hue and Saturation values of the shadow tones.

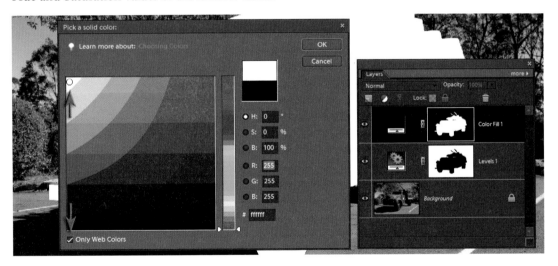

4. Hold down the Ctrl key and click on the adjustment layer mask from the Levels 1 layer to load it as a selection. Invert the selection using the keyboard shortcut Ctrl+Shift+I. From the Create adjustment layer menu in the Layers panel choose a Solid Color adjustment layer. Select White as the foreground color and then select OK to create a Color Fill layer.

Note > Make sure the white you pick from the Pick a solid color dialog is 255 in all three channels. A quick way of doing this is to select Only Web Colors option and then click in the top left-hand corner to select white.

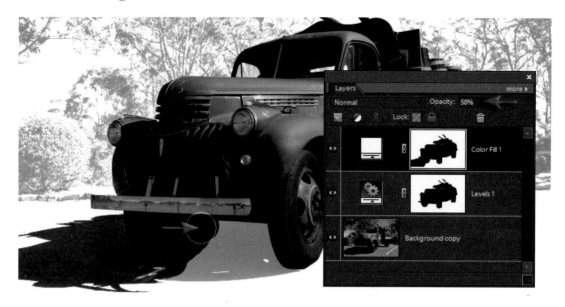

5. Invert the layer mask of the Color Fill adjustment layer using the keyboard shortcut Ctrl+I. Lower the opacity of the Color Fill (Solid Color) layer. Select the Brush Tool from the Tools panel and choose a hard-edged brush set to 100% Opacity in the Options bar. Paint over the shadow to mask this area on the Color Fill adjustment layer mask (no accuracy is required). When the masking is complete set the opacity of the Color Fill layer back to 100%.

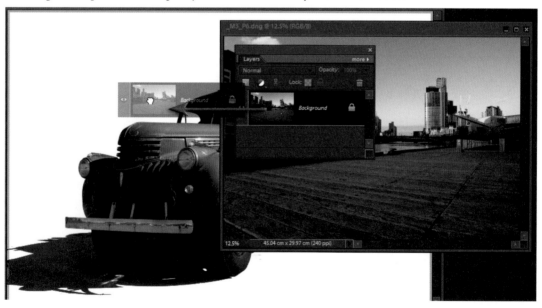

6. Open the river dock image from the supporting DVD and drag the Background layer thumbnail into the image window of the truck. Hold down the Shift key as you release the mouse button to center the image. Go to Image > Transform > Free Transform and resize the image to fit the canvas size of the truck image (use the keyboard shortcut Ctrl+0 to see the bounding box).

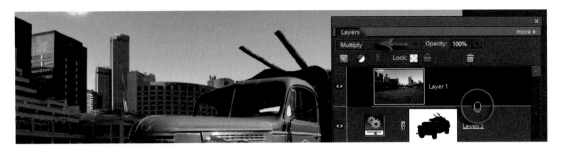

7. Hold down the Ctrl key and click on the Levels 1 adjustment layer mask to load it as a selection. Inverse the selection (Ctrl+Shift+I) and then click on the Color Fill adjustment layer to make it the active layer. From the Create adjustment layer menu in the Layers panel choose another Levels adjustment layer. Make no adjustment in the dialog and select OK . Invert the layer mask using the keyboard shortcut (Ctrl+I). Hold down the Alt key and click on the dividing line between the Levels 2 adjustment layer and the river dock layer to group them. Set the mode of the river dock layer to Multiply. You should now see the truck and its shadow against its new background.

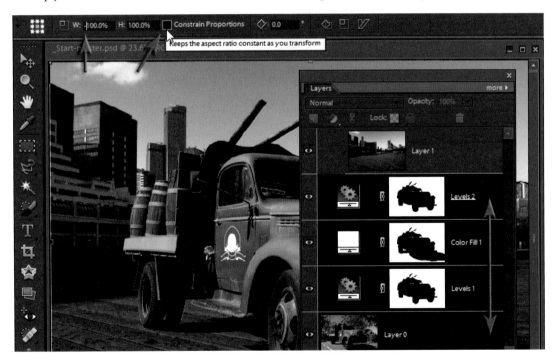

8. To resolve the lighting direction problem (the shadows are being cast in different directions in the two images) we must flip either the truck or the background. Double-click the background layer and select OK in the New Layer dialog to unlock the Background layer. To select multiple layers hold down the Shift key and select the truck layer (Layer 0) and all of the adjustment layers. Go to Image > Transform > Free Transform. In the Options bar deselect the Constrain Proportions checkbox and then enter a minus before the 100% width to flip the image and all of the supporting adjustment layers. Rotate the image anti-clockwise slightly and drag the truck into the best position. Click the commit current operation to complete the process.

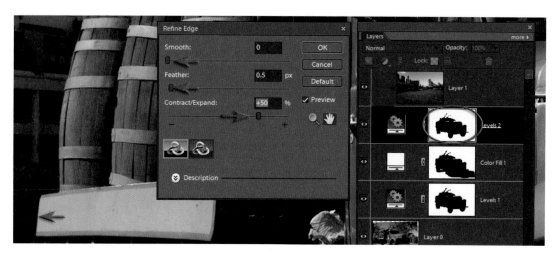

9. Go to View > Actual Pixels and examine the edge of the truck. Now that the background has changed it may be necessary to expand the edge of this layer mask. Select the Levels 2 adjustment layer and go to Select > Refine Edge. From the View menu choose Selection to hide the selection edges. The Smooth slider can be set to 0 and the Feather sliders may need only a 0.5 px adjustment (the edge has already been feathered and smoothed before). Adjust the Expand/Contract slider to remove any white halo from around the edge and then select OK.

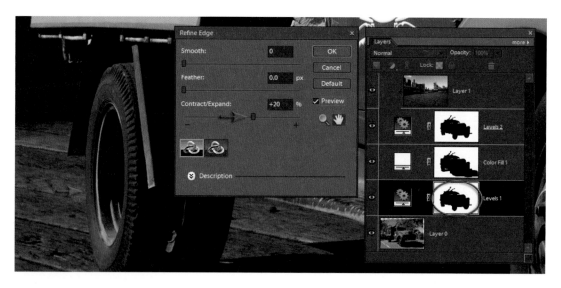

10. If you are left with a thin dark line on the inside edge of the truck select the Levels 1 adjustment layer mask and then go to Select > Refine Edge once again. Set the Smooth and Feather sliders to 0 and move the Contract/Expand slider to the right to reduce any dark line that may be visible. Select OK to apply the changes.

Note > If any black edges are present in any of the layer masks this will lead to white edges or transparency around the edges of the canvas. Paint with white around the edge of any mask creating a problem.

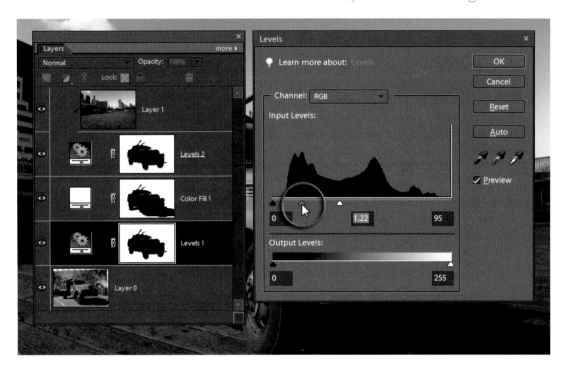

11. To adjust the density of the shadow double-click the Levels 1 Adjustment layer thumbnail to open the dialog. Drag the central gamma slider beneath the histogram to the left or right to lighten or darken the shadows under the truck.

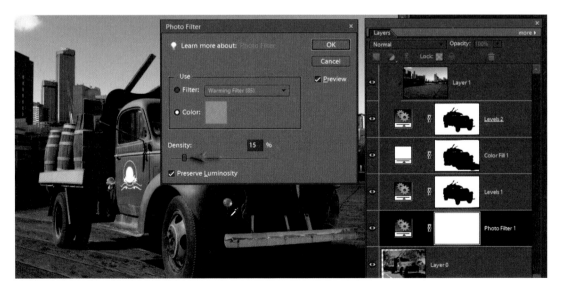

12. The color temperature (white balance) of the two images is slightly different. To correct this difference add a Photo filter adjustment layer menu above the truck layer. From the Photo Filter dialog choose a Warming Filter (85) and adjust the opacity until the white balance between the two images appears consistent.

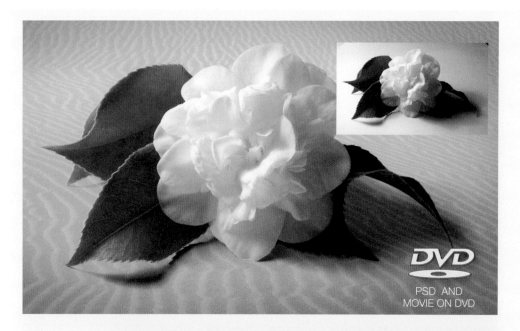

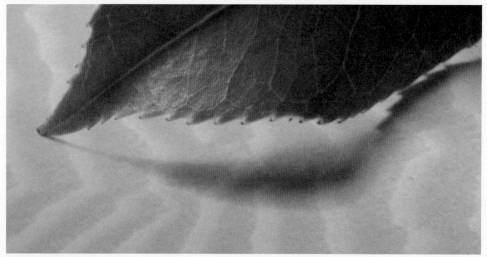

THE BEST TECHNIQUE FOR SUBTLE SHADOWS

The technique to preserve shadows provides those photographers burdened with a meticulous eye a useful way of retaining and transplanting subtle and complex shadows. Observe the subtle shadow cast by the leaf above that would be virtually impossible to re-create using any other technique. The primary reasons for not being able to use this technique are when the shadow falls over a surface with a different texture to the one in the new location, or the surface over which the shadow falls is particularly uneven or moves from a horizontal to a vertical plane over the length of the shadow.

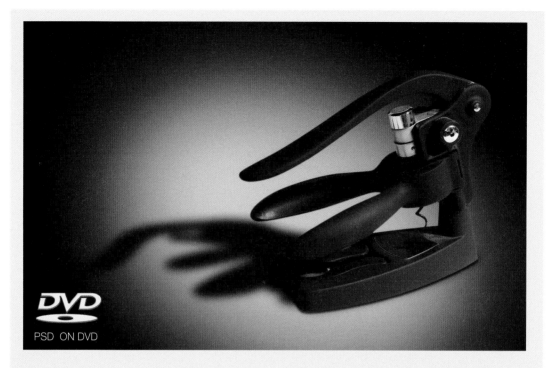

PSD ON DVD

PERFORMANCE TIP

If it is not possible to preserve the original shadow, try to capture a second image from the direction of the light source. This second image will allow you to create a more accurate shadow than simply using the outline of the subject as seen from the camera angle instead of the direction of the light source.

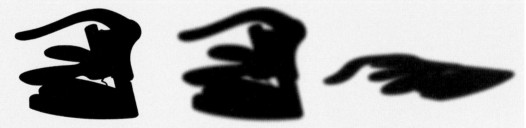

This process would include the following steps:

- Make a mask of your subject and place it on a layer above a background.
- Import the second image captured from the direction of the light source and position it between the subject layer and the background layer.
- Make a selection of the subject in this second image (your shadow resource).
- Create a new empty layer that sits below the actual subject and above the background layer, and then fill this selection with black.
- Hide or delete the layer that the selection was made from.
- Place your new shadow layer in Multiply mode.
- Lower the opacity of your shadow layer and apply the Gaussian Blur filter.
- Use the Free Transform command to distort and move the shadow into position.

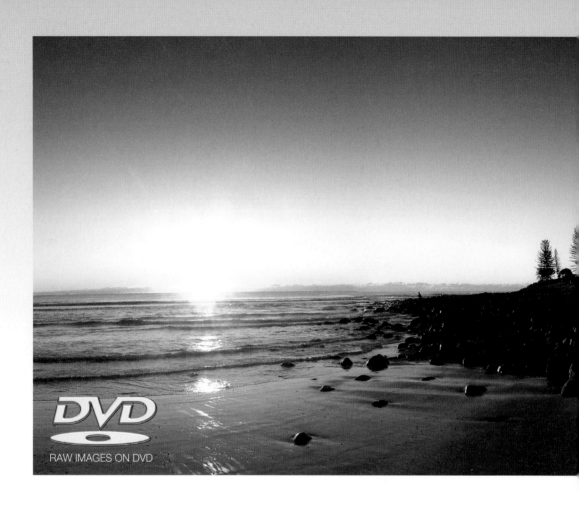

RAW IMAGES ON DVD

Project 7

Photomerge

Photomerge is capable of aligning and blending images without any signs of banding in smooth areas of transition. The new and improved Photomerge first made its appearance in Photoshop CS3 but the maths got even better when it appeared in Photoshop Elements 6, and the stitching is now so clever it will really have you amazed at the quality that can be achieved.

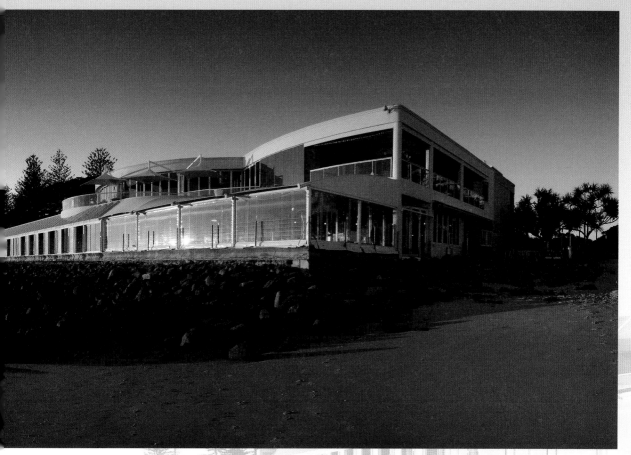

Spot the joins – upgrade from 10 to 30 megapixels with seamless stitching

The quality will be even better if you capture the component images with a 50% overlap, use manual exposure, focus and white balance setting (or processed the images identically in Camera Raw). The results are now truly seamless – an excellent way of widening your horizons or turning your humble compact camera into a 30 megapixel blockbuster.

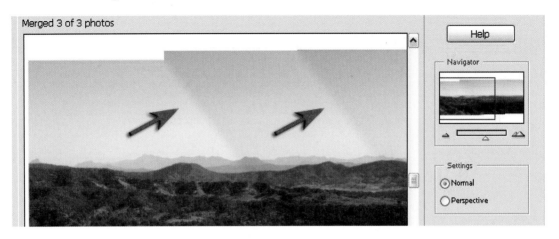

The Photomerge feature in version 5 of Photoshop Elements and the full version of Photoshop CS2 left a lot to be desired. All of the flaws and weaknesses of this feature were removed with the release of Photoshop Elements 6.

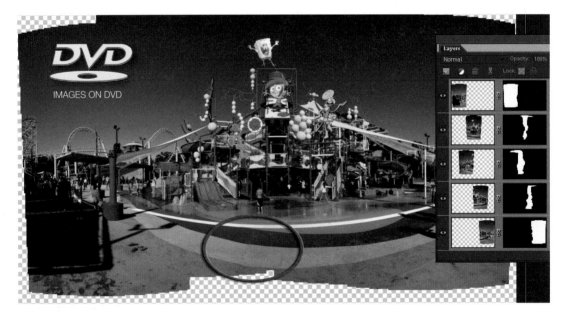

Now the only limitation you may run up against is Photoshop Elements's ability to align and blend strong geometric lines that come close to the camera lens. If the camera is hand-held to capture the component images (you have not used a specialized tripod head designed for professional panoramic stitching work) then the problem of aligning both foreground and distant subject matter is a big problem for any software (Photoshop Elements handles it better than the rest). The camera should ideally be rotated around the nodal point of the lens to avoid something called parallax error. You will probably not encounter any problems with the new Photomerge feature unless you are working with strong lines in the immediate foreground. Notice how the curved lines in the image above are slightly crooked due to the fact that these images were shot with an 18 mm focal length and these lines are very close to the lens. Still pretty good – but not perfect.

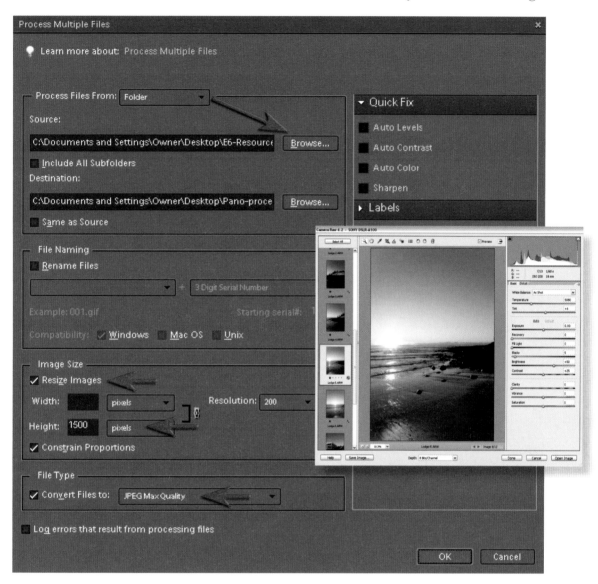

1. The images for this project are available as Camera Raw files but it is strongly recommended when using an older computer or a computer with less than 1 GB of RAM to downsample the images before attempting this project. To efficiently downsample multiple images go to 'File > Process Multiple Files'. Select the 'Source' folder of raw images (hit the Browse button) and then select a destination folder of where you would like your processed files to be saved. Check 'Resize Images' and select a height of 1500 pixels. Check 'Convert Files to:' and choose the JPEG Max Quality option. Select OK to process the images.

Note > If you wish to make a monster panorama (there are 12 X 10 megapixel images used in this project) select all of the Camera Raw files and open them in Adobe Camera Raw. Choose the Select All option in the top left-hand corner of the dialog box and select OK. The default settings in Adobe Camera Raw are OK for the images used in this project.

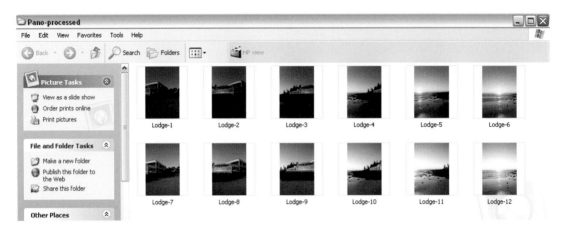

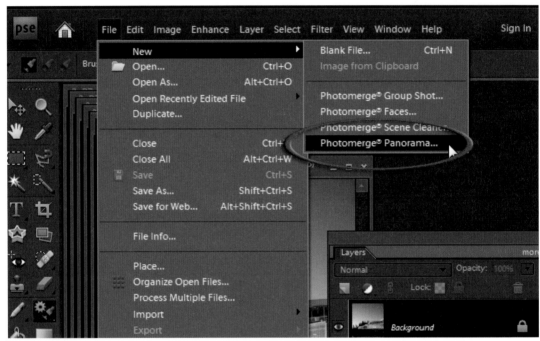

2. Select all of the images from the destination folder you created in the Process Multiple Files dialog box. Open the processed images in Photoshop Elements. From the File > New menu choose Photomerge Panorama.

Note > The observant amongst you will notice there are two images for every section of the panorama. There are twelve images in total using two different exposure settings. The camera first captured a set of images with an exposure that was perfect for the rising sun in this scene (the brighter side of the panorama). A second set of six images was then created with an exposure that was optimized for the right side of the panorama (the dark side). Having the extra exposures helps in the creation of a higher quality result. Photomerge will choose the best exposure for each aspect of the scene and blend them all seamlessly.

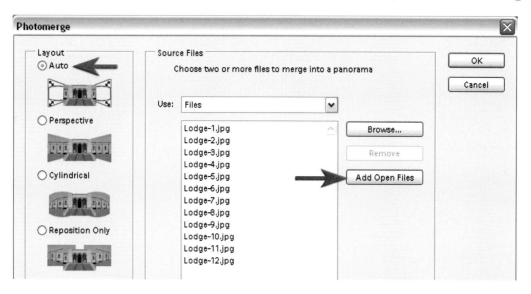

3. In the Photomerge dialog box click on the Add Open Files button and select the 'Auto' radio button in the Layout options. Select OK and let Photoshop Elements do all of the work – and what a lot of work it has to do, aligning and blending all of these images and even juggling which is the best exposure to use for any given location.

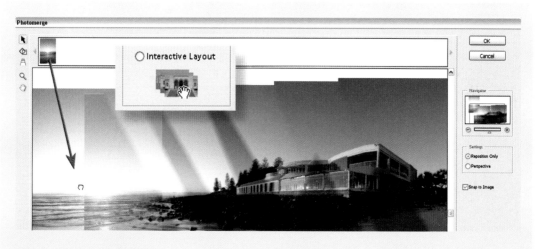

PERFORMANCE TIP

The 'Auto' layout setting gets it right pretty much most of the time. Occasionally you may need to select either the 'Perspective' or 'Cylindrical' options for very wide panoramas. The Interactive Layout can be selected when Photoshop Elements is having trouble deciding where one or two of the component images should be placed. This can occur when there is little detail in the image to align, e.g. a panorama of a beach scene where the only obvious line in the image is the horizon line. When this occurs you will need to drag the problem file into the best location in the Interactive Layout dialog box.

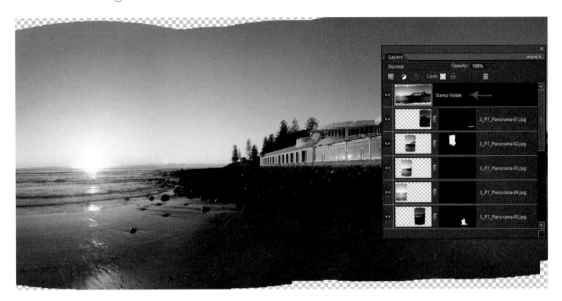

4. In previous articles I have written I would have been rattling on for another six steps of manual techniques to circumnavigate the shortcomings of Photomerge – but as you can see from the results in this project we just about have perfection handed to us on a plate. Fantabulous (I know that's not in the dictionary but neither is Photomerge – yet)! If you have used the full resolution images you probably had to go and make a cup of coffee while Photoshop Elements put this one together (all 120 megapixels) and will now be considering downsampling your file – but wait, we have one small glitch.

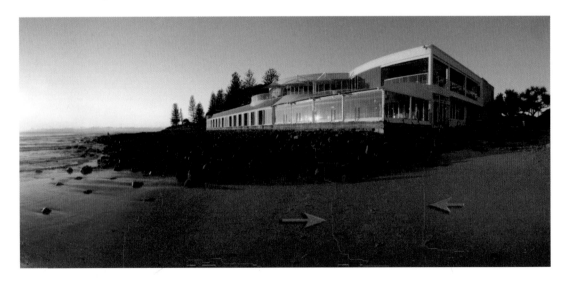

If you downsample before you flatten your file you will probably encounter hairline cracks appearing in your image after reducing the image size. The solution to this problem is to either flatten the file or stamp the visible content to a new layer (Ctrl + Shift + Alt and then type the letter E) before you reduce the size of the image.

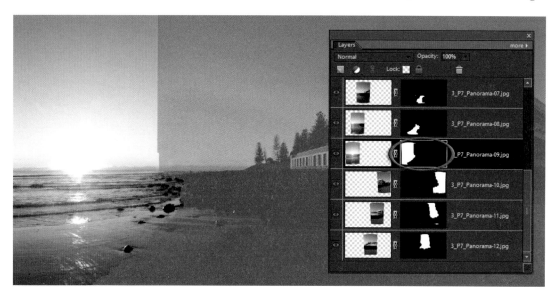

5. This is not really a step, more of an observation (you can see I am struggling to find things for you to do so you feel you have earned your medal on this project); if you hold down the Alt key and click on each layer mask in turn you will notice that Elements has done a great job of working out the optimum exposure for each part of this panorama. Photomerge in Photoshop Elements does an even better job than Photomerge in Photoshop CS3 on this particular project.

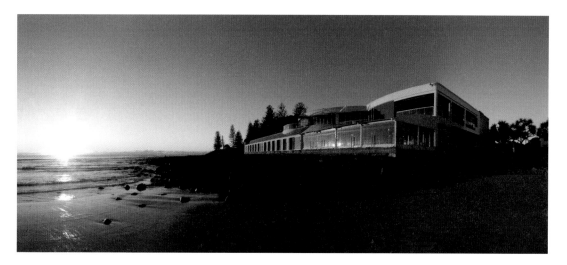

If you don't believe that the humble Photoshop Elements can do a better job than Photoshop CS3 – take a look at the same files aligned and blended in the premium software package. It's chosen good exposures for the sunrise and the right side of the building but has chosen to include darker sections of the component images for the sky over the building and the building itself. When I completed this project in Photoshop CS3 I had to montage the two sets of panoramas manually to overcome this problem.

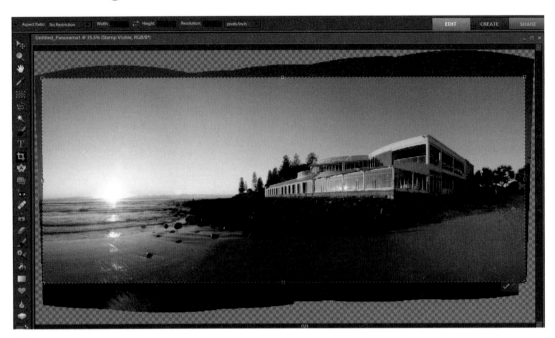

6. If you crop away 'that which is surplus to requirements' before flattening the file, be sure to select the 'No Restriction' option in the Options bar and leave the width and height fields blank. This is a big image (especially if you used the full resolution files), so don't be surprised if things are a little slower in computer land right now.

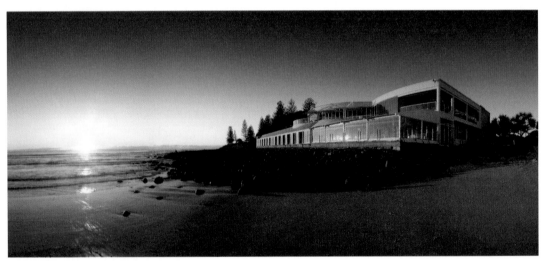

7. Sharpen the image and apply a linear gradient to darken the sky and the project is complete. It is important to note that the view of this particular building could not be captured any other way to achieve the same result. If I had moved back to encompass the entire view and then cropped down I would be left with less than 5 megapixels of data and the skyline above the building would be very busy as the buildings behind this beach house came into view. The dramatic sense of perspective would also be lost the further I moved away from the building.

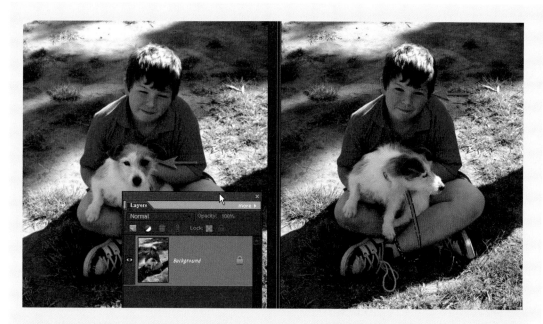

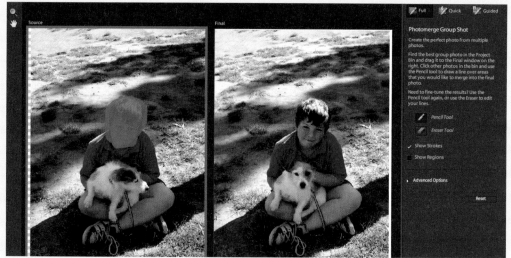

PHOTOMERGE GROUP SHOT

Photomerge also has a 'Group Shot' option. This allows you to merge the best aspects of several images into the same image - especially useful when someone in a group has blinked or looked away. In this group shot (if you can call one boy and his dog a group) it has been decided to combine two images (captured hand-held) so both the boy and his dog are looking at the camera. In the Group Shot dialog box you just scribble over the part of the 'source' image you would like to merge with the 'final' image. Although Photomerge will align and blend the component images with the same skill as the Panorama option the user will be presented with an additional flattened file when Group Shot has finished weaving its magic.

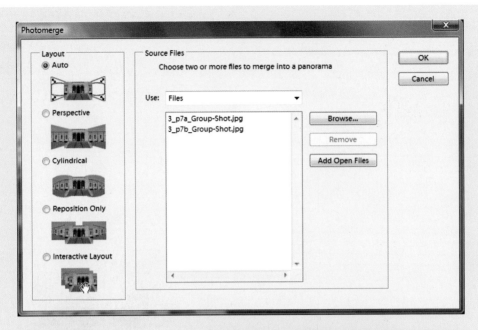

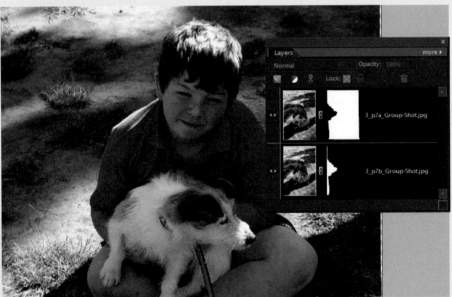

For those users who are still amazed at the results that can be achieved using Photomerge, but who mourn the loss of layers when using Group Shot, they can continue to use the Panorama option – even for group images. This is, however, only recommended for those photographers who use manual white balance rather than auto white balance in camera. When the Panorama option has finished aligning the images it will have no idea of the 'best bits' it should include in the final result. In the image above it has decided that neither the boy nor the dog need to be looking at the camera. Note how the layer masks, yes layer masks, are concealing the best bits of each image. Fear not, for we can modify these layer masks so we do get the bits that we want.

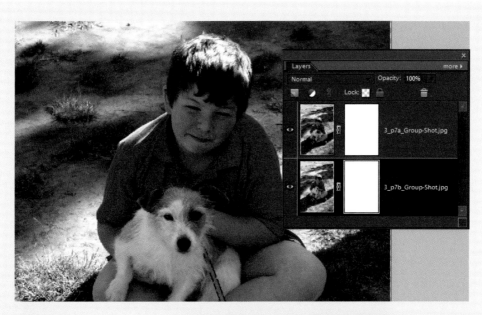

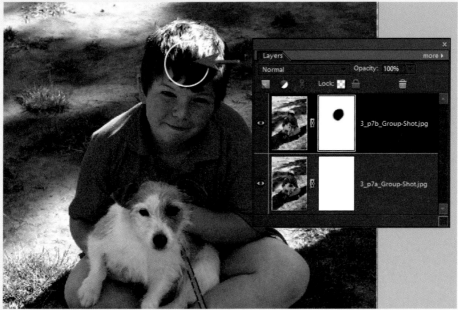

Clear both of the layer masks by clicking on each one in turn and then filling them with white. If white is the foreground color hold down the Alt key while pressing the Backspace key. Then choose the Brush tool and paint with black into the mask to shield any of the pixels you do not want to see on this layer. This may seem like a novel approach to montage as we are now enjoying layer masks without having to hijack one on an adjustment layer. You will need to crop the image to finish your project. If you can see the value of this technique then you will quickly realize that taking multiple shots the next time you are presented with a group (or even just one man and his best friend) ensures the decisive moment is history (sorry Henri).

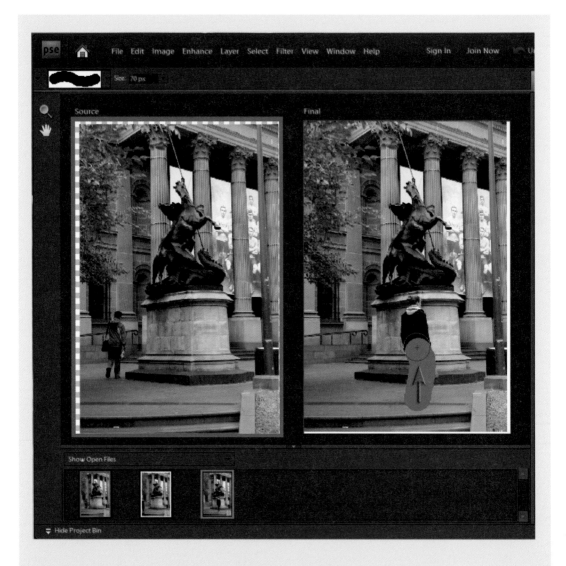

PHOTOMERGE SCENE CLEANER

The newest Photomerge feature (introduced with Photoshop Elements 7) is the Scene Cleaner. The Scene Cleaner is designed to rid your scenic shots of tourists. You no longer have to wait for the scene to be empty before capturing your shot. Just take multiple shots (no tripod required) as the people move around and you can then clean the scene using the new Photomerge Scene Cleaner. The process is remarkably simple, just drag one of your images into the Final window and then click on any of the other images in the Project Bin to set it as the source image. Then paint over any tourist in the Final window or any part of the source file on the left that does not have a tourist (no accuracy is required in the painting action) and the scene in the final window on the right is cleaned automatically. Move your mouse off the image and the strokes will disappear. The auto align component of the Photomerge dialog means that the patch is seamless.

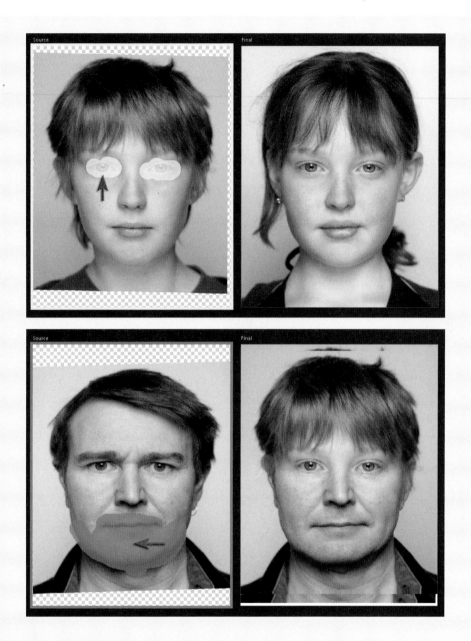

PHOTOMERGE FACES

The strangest of the automated features in the Photomerge bag of tricks called Photomerge Faces. The results are often delightfully random, even though you are supposed to define the bits you want merged. You must first use the Alignment Tool to indicate where the eyes and mouth are in each image and then click the Align Photos button. In the top part of the example above, the boy's eyes have been merged seamlessly into the girl's face, while in the lower examples Photomerge has happily lifted the nose and lower portion of the ears in the source image in order to achieve a seamless stitch. Great fun (if slightly disturbing) – absolutely no commercial value – but will keep the kids amused for hours!

Project 8

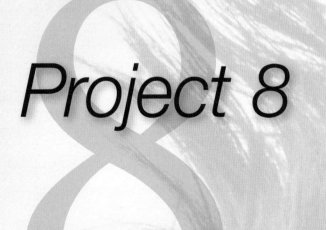

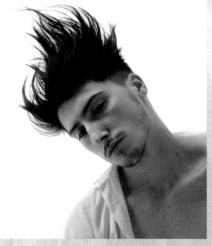

Photograph by Daniel Stainsby

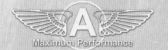

Maximum Performance

Use the Mask Hair Against White
action to fast-track this technique

Hair Transplant

One of the most challenging montage or masking jobs in the profession of post-production editing is the hair lift. When the model has long flowing hair and the subject needs to change location many post-production artists call in sick. Get it wrong and, just like a bad wig, it shows. Extract filters, Magic Erasers and Tragic Extractors don't even get us close. The first secret step must be completed before you even press the shutter on the camera. Your number one essential step for success is to first shoot your model against a white backdrop, sufficiently illuminated so that it is captured as white rather than gray. This important aspect of the initial image capture ensures that the resulting hair transplant is seamless and undetectable. The post-production is the easy bit – simply apply the correct sequence of editing steps and the magic is all yours. This is not brain surgery but follow these simple steps and you will join the elite ranks of image editing gurus around the world. Celebrity status is just a few clicks away.

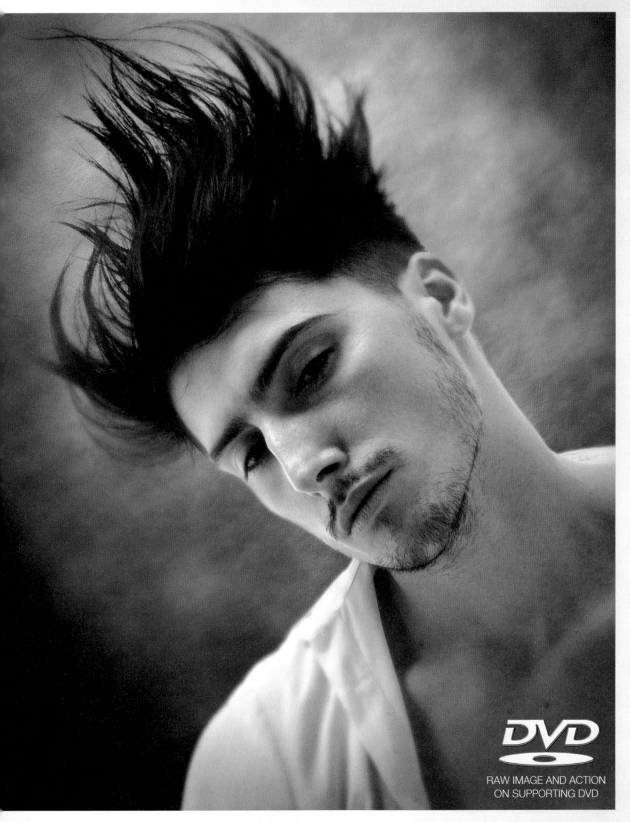

DVD

Hair extraction – not as painful as pulling teeth

Stage 1: Masking hair - tips for tremendous transplants

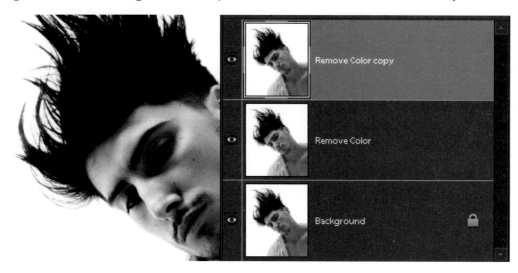

1. The initial steps of this tutorial are concerned with creating a mask that can be used in the final montage. Start by dragging the background layer to the New Layer icon to duplicate it. Choose 'Remove Color' from the Adjust Color submenu found in the Enhance menu (Enhance > Adjust Color > Remove Color). Drag this desaturated/monochrome layer to the New Layer icon in the Layers palette to duplicate it. Set the blend mode of this new layer (now on top of the layers stack) to 'Overlay' mode.

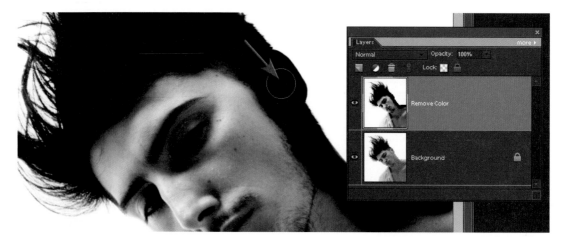

2. From the Layer menu choose 'Merge Down' to create a single high-contrast monochrome layer. Select 'Black' as the foreground color and the 'Brush tool' from the Tools palette. Choose a large hard-edged brush and 100% opacity from the Options bar and set the mode to 'Overlay' (also in the Options bar). Painting in Overlay mode will preserve the white background and darken the rest of the pixels. Accuracy while painting in Overlay mode is not a concern when the background is white or is significantly lighter than the subject. Avoid going anywhere near the tips of the hair at this stage.

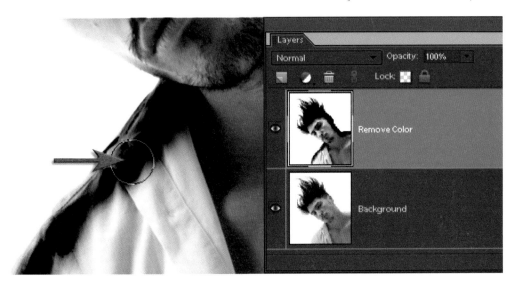

3. Even the bright tones of the white shirt can be rendered black by repeatedly clicking the mouse while using a large brush in Overlay mode. Again it is important to avoid going anywhere near the hair.

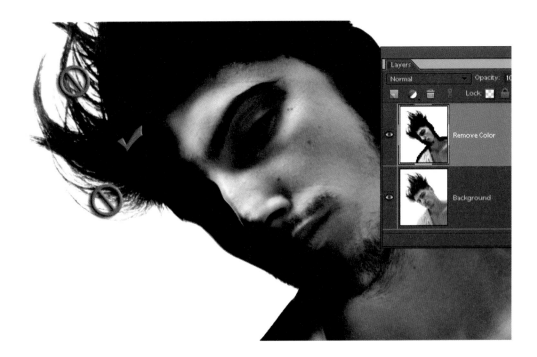

4. Darken the body of the hair near the scalp but avoid the locks of hair that have white background showing through. Painting these individual strands of hair will thicken the hair and may lead to subsequent haloes appearing later in the montage process.

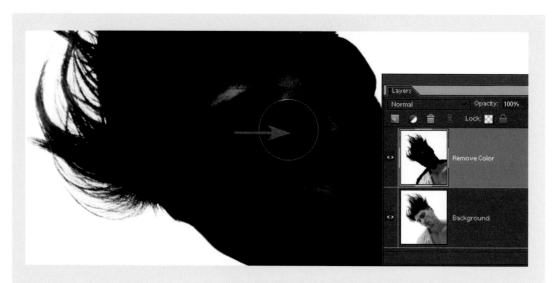

PERFORMANCE TIP

Switch the blend mode of the brush in the Options bar to 'Normal' mode when painting away from the edge of the subject. This will ensure a speedy conclusion to the mask-making process. The mask is now ready to use in the montage.

Note > If any of the background has been darkened in the process of creating a black and white mask switch the foreground color to 'White' and choose 'Overlay' in the Options bar. Paint to render any areas of gray background white. It is again important to avoid painting near the edges containing delicate hair detail.

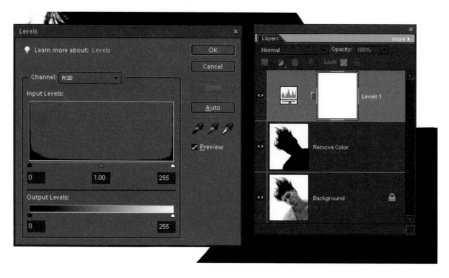

5. With the Remove Color layer selected add a Levels adjustment layer. Without making any adjustment simply select OK. This Levels adjustment layer has a layer mask that we can use to house the mask that we have created in the previous step.

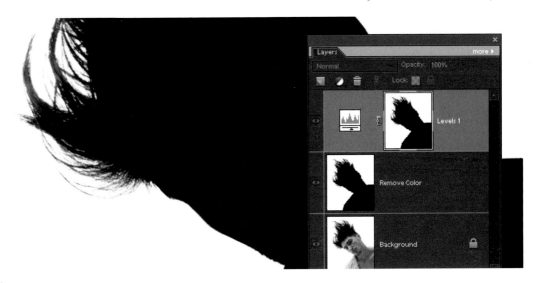

6. The next step relocates the mask you have just created into the layer mask of the adjustment layer. From the Select menu choose 'All' and from the Edit menu choose 'Copy Merged'. Hold down the Alt key and click on the layer mask thumbnail in the Layers palette. The image window will momentarily appear white as you view the empty contents of the layer mask. From the Edit menu choose 'Paste' to transfer the contents of the clipboard to this layer mask. Click on the layer below to select it and then click on the Visibility icon of this layer to switch it off. This mask layer serves no purpose now that it has been successfully transferred to the adjustment layer mask.

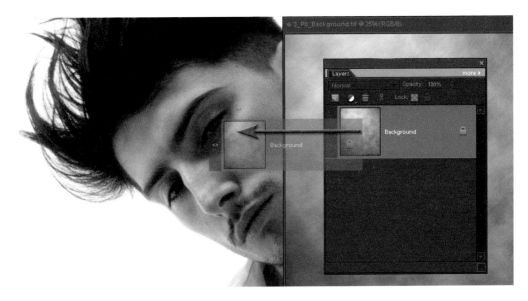

7. The new background is placed on its own layer above the figure and mask layers. Open the background image and drag the thumbnail of this new file into the image window of your project file from the layer thumbnail in the Layers palette. Group this new background layer with the adjustment layer beneath (Layer > Group with Previous). Alternatively you can hold down the Alt key and click on the dividing line between the two layers to group them.

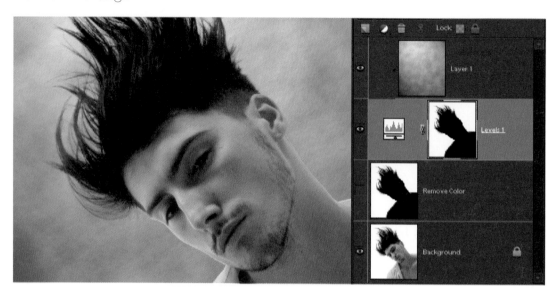

8. Grouping the new background with the adjustment layer will mask the background in the region of the figure but the quality will not yet be acceptable. Setting the blend mode of the adjustment layer to 'Multiply' will bring back all of the fine detail in the hair. The background will not be darkened by applying the 'Multiply' blend mode as white is a neutral color. The subtle details in the fine strands of hair will, however, be preserved in all their glory.

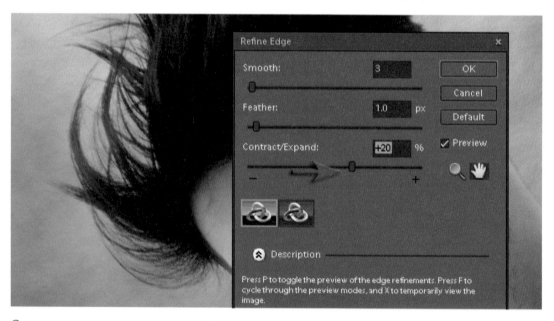

9. The accuracy and quality of the edge of the mask will usually require some attention in order for the subject to achieve a seamless quality with the new background. Go to the Select menu and choose 'Refine Edge'. Choose the default values for the Smooth and Feather sliders (3 and 1.0) and then move the Contract/Expand slider to the right to hide any white edges from around the body and shirt.

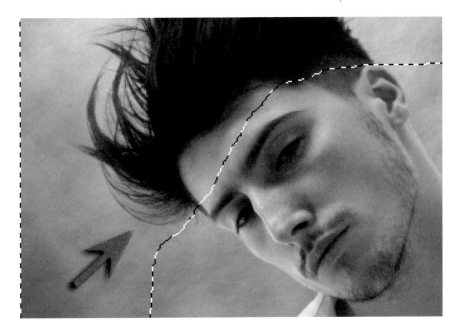

10. In most instances the hair is already looking pretty fabulous but to modify and perfect the hair even further you will need to make a selection of just the hair with the Lasso tool. Choose 'Levels' once again and move the central Gamma slider to the left to increase the density of the hair and eliminate any white haloes that may be present. Moving the White slider to the left a little may help the process of achieving a perfect blend between subject and background. Select OK and choose 'Deselect' from the Select menu.

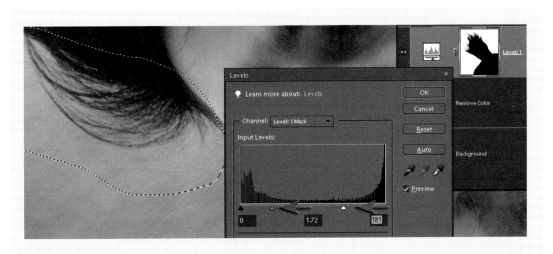

PERFORMANCE TIP

Make a selection of any portion of the edge that requires a localized adjustment with the Lasso tool with a small amount of feather entered in the Options bar. Use a Levels adjustment (Enhance > Adjust Lighting > Levels) to optimize this portion of the edge.

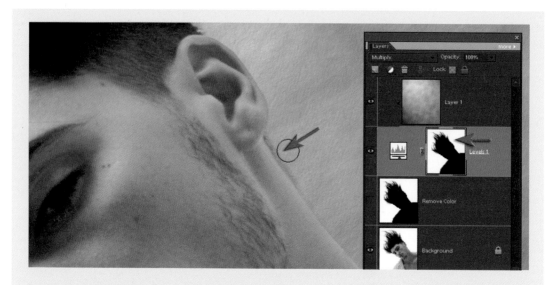

PERFORMANCE TIP

Any localized refinement of the mask can also be achieved manually by painting with a small soft-edged brush directly into the layer mask. Paint with white at a reduced opacity (10–20%) to remove any fine haloes present in localized areas. Several brush strokes will slowly erase the halo from the image.

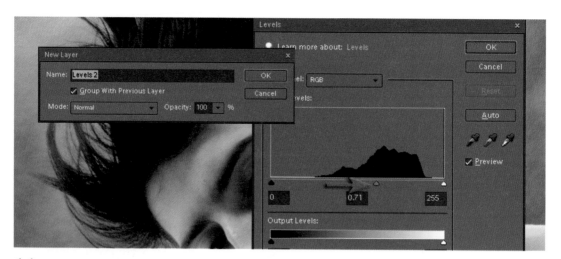

11. The true test of an accurate mask for a subject that was photographed against a white background is when you place the subject against a very dark background. Grouping a Levels adjustment layer with the new background layer can darken the background image used in this project. Hold down the Alt key when you select a Levels adjustment layer from the Layers palette. Click on the Group with Previous box in the New Layer dialog box and then select OK to open the Levels dialog box. Move the Gamma slider to the right in order to preview your subject against a darker background in the image window.

Stage 2: Split tone styling and depth of field tweaking

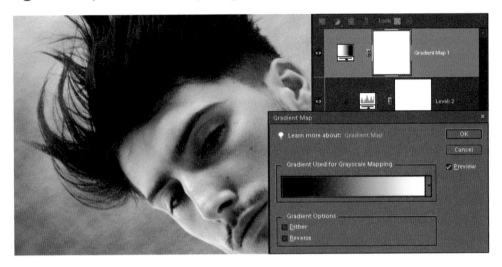

12. Now that the hair transplant is complete the styling can commence. Select the top layer in the Layers palette and then click on the Create Adjustment Layer icon and choose 'Gradient Map'. I have applied one of the split tone presets that are available on the supporting DVD. See the Toning project in Part 2. A split tone that has a cool shadow tone and warm highlight tone has been used to achieve the split tone effect for this project. The opacity of the Gradient Map layer is then lowered.

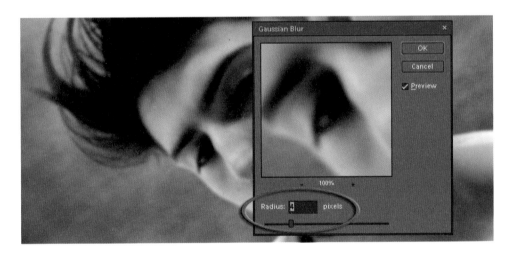

13. A shallow depth of field can be achieved by first merging the contents of all of the layers to a new layer. With the top layer in the Layers palette selected choose 'All' from the Select menu and then choose 'Copy Merged' from the Edit menu. Click on the New Layer icon in the Layers palette and then choose 'Paste' from the Edit menu. The keyboard shortcut for the last sequence of commands is to hold down the Ctrl, Shift and Alt keys while pressing the letter E on the keyboard (users of Elements 3.0 must type the letter N followed by the letter E). Apply a 4-pixel Gaussian Blur to this layer (Filter > Blur > Gaussian Blur).

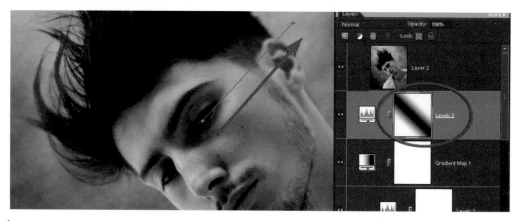

14. Click on the layer beneath the merged layer (the one you have just blurred) and then create a Levels adjustment layer. Select OK without making any adjustment. Group the layer above with this adjustment layer and then click on the adjustment layer mask to select it. Select the 'Gradient tool' from the Tools palette and choose 'Reflected Gradient' and the 'Black, White' options from the Options bar. Click in the central part of the model's face and drag outwards to a position just beyond the ear. The sharp focus should now be restored to the central portion of the face only.

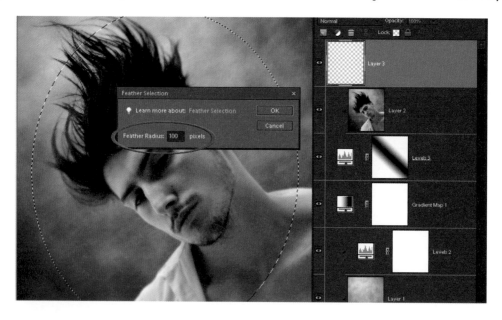

15. Create a vignette for this image. Hold down the Alt key and click on the Create a New Layer icon. In the New Layer dialog box set the mode to Multiply and choose the 'Fill with Multiply-neutral color (white)' option. A selection is then made using the Elliptical Marquee tool, feathered by 100 pixels (Select > Feather) and then in the Fill Layer dialog box, in the Contents section, choose 'Use Black' (Edit > Fill Selection). The vignette is then subdued by lowering the opacity of the layer.

Note > A small amount of noise must be added if you are creating a vignette in a very smooth-toned background in order to prevent any tonal banding (Filter > Noise > Add Noise).

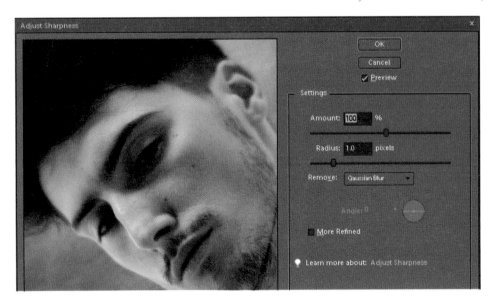

16. Create a merged copy of all of the layers (hold down the Ctrl + Shift + Alt keys and type the letter E as in step 13) and apply the Unsharp Mask (Enhance > Unsharp Mask) to complete the project.

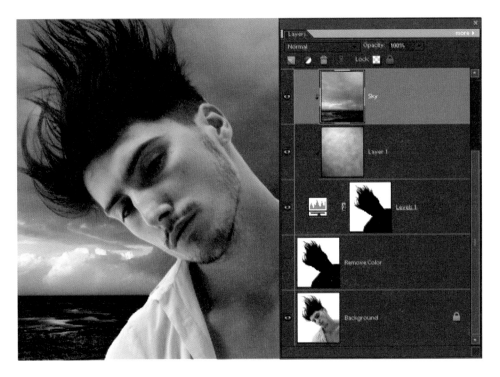

To change the scenery (background) simply trash the sharpened and blurred layers and cut and paste a new image into the layer that was clipped with your adjustment layer mask. One face, lots of hair – a million locations. Now you don't have to put a hat on to go traveling.

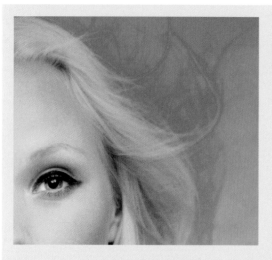
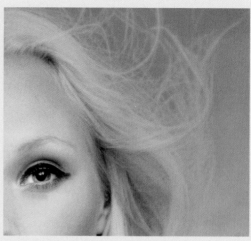

MAXIMUM PERFORMANCE

When masking hair that was shot against a black background, setting the Levels adjustment layer (the one holding the mask) to the Screen Blend mode is the secret to success. Note the difference between Normal mode and Screen Blend mode in the illustrations above.

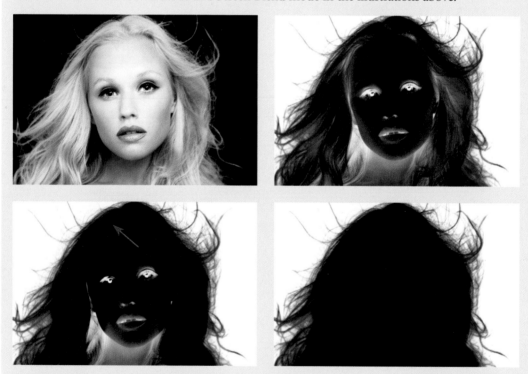

You will need to invert the layer mask when using a model shot against a black background (Filter > Adjustments > Invert). Paint in Overlay mode as in steps 2 to 4 of the Hair Transplant project. Apply a Levels adjustment to the layer mask and fine-tune the brightness of the hair against the background by moving the Gamma slider.

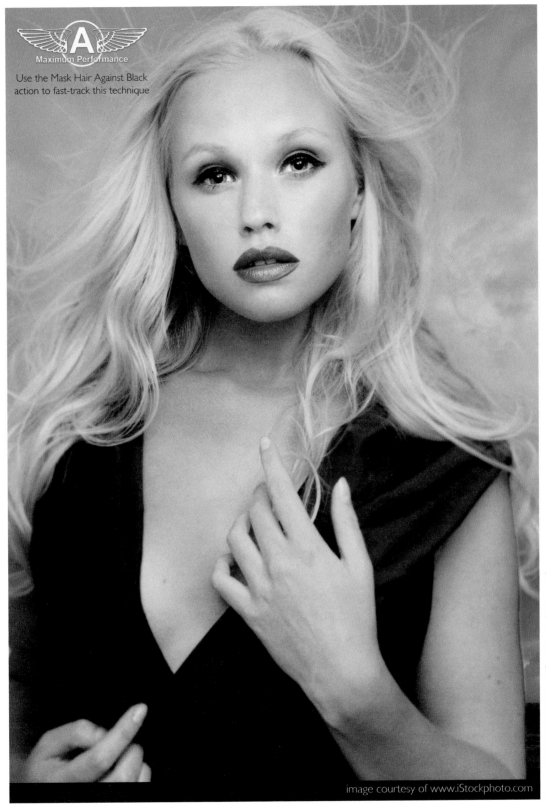

image courtesy of www.iStockphoto.com

iStock_00000803940 (Blond Goddess by Iconogenic)

Jargon Buster

A

ACR: *Adobe Camera Raw. Raw processing utility supplied with Photoshop Elements.*

Adjustment layers: *Non-destructive (always editable) image adjustment placed on a layer.*

Aliasing: *The display of a digital image where a diagonal or curved line appears jagged due to the square pixels.*

Anti-aliasing: *The process of smoothing the appearance of lines in a digital image.*

Artifacts: *Pixels that are significantly incorrect in their brightness or color values.*

B

Bit: *Short for binary digit, the basic unit of the binary language.*

Bit depth: *Number of bits (memory) assigned to recording color or tonal information.*

Blend mode: *The formula used for defining the mixing of a layer with those beneath it.*

Brightness: *The value assigned to a pixel in the HSB model to define the relative lightness of a pixel.*

Byte: *Eight bits. Standard unit of data storage containing a value between 0 and 255.*

C

CCD: *Charge-coupled device. A solid-state sensor used in digital image capture.*

Channel: *A division of color or luminance data.*

Clipboard: *The temporary storage of something that has been cut or copied.*

Clipping group: *Two or more layers that have been linked. The base layer acts as a mask limiting the effect or visibility of those layers grouped with it.*

Cloning tool: *A tool used for replicating pixels.*

Color fringing: *Bands of color on the edges of lines within an image.*

Color gamut: *The range of colors provided by a hardware device, or a set of pigments.*

Color management: *A system to ensure uniformity of color between the subject, monitor display and final print.*

Color Picker: *Dialog box used for the selection of colors.*

Compression: *A method for reducing the file size of a digital image.*

Constrain proportions: *Retains the proportional dimensions of an image when changing the image size.*

Continuous tone: *An image containing the illusion of smooth gradations between highlights and shadows.*

Contrast: *The difference in brightness between the darkest and lightest areas of the image or subject.*

Crash: *The sudden operational failure of a computer.*

Crop: *Reduce image size to enhance composition or limit information.*

Curves: *A control in the full version of Adobe Photoshop only for adjusting tonality and color.*

D

Default: A 'normal' or 'start' setting as chosen by the manufacturer or user.

Depth of field: The zone of sharpness variable by aperture, focal length or subject distance.

DNG: Digital Negative (Adobe's Raw file format).

Dpi: Dots per inch. A measurement of resolution.

E

Editable text: Text that has not been rendered into pixels.

Exposure: Combined effect of intensity and duration of light on a light-sensitive material or image sensor.

Exposure compensation: To increase or decrease the exposure from a meter-indicated exposure to obtain an appropriate exposure.

F

Feather: The action of softening the edge of a digital selection.

File format: The code used to store digital data, e.g. TIFF or JPEG.

File size: The memory required to store digital data in a file.

Format: The orientation or shape of the image or the erasure of a memory device.

Freeze: Software that fails to interact with new information.

G

Galleries: A managed collection of images displayed in a conveniently accessible form.

Gaussian Blur: A filter used for defocusing a digital image.

Gigabyte: A unit of measurement for digital files, 1024 megabytes.

Grayscale: An 8-bit image used to describe monochrome (black and white) images.

H

High Dynamic Range (HDR): A subject brightness range that exceeds the ability of the capture medium (film or sensor) to record both the highlight and shadow information simultaneously.

Highlight: Area of subject receiving highest exposure value.

Histogram: A graphical representation of a digital image indicating the pixels allocated to each level.

Hue: The name of a color, e.g. red or green.

I

Image size: The pixel dimensions, output dimensions and resolution used to define a digital image.

Interpolation: Increasing the pixel dimensions of an image by inserting new pixels between existing pixels within the image.

ISO: International Standards Organization. A numerical system for rating the speed or relative light sensitivity of a film or sensor.

J

JPEG (.jpg): Joint Photographic Experts Group. Popular but lossy (i.e. destructive) image compression file format.

K

Kilobyte: 1024 bytes.

L

Lasso tool: Selection tool used in digital editing.

Latitude: Ability of the film or device to record the brightness range of the subject.

Layer mask: A mask attached to an adjustment layer that is used to define the visibility of the adjustment. It can also be used to limit the visibility of pixels on the layer above.

Layers: A feature in digital editing software that allows a composite digital image where each element is on a separate layer or level.

Levels: Shades of lightness or brightness assigned to pixels.

Luminance adjustment: The ability to adjust the brightness of a color without affecting either the Hue or Saturation.

M

Magic Wand tool: Selection tool used in digital editing.

Marching ants: A moving broken line indicating a digital selection of pixels.

Marquee tool: Selection tool used in digital editing.

Megabyte

Megabyte: A unit of measurement for digital files, 1024 kilobytes.

Megapixels: More than a million pixels.

Memory card: A removable storage device about the size of a small card.

Minimum aperture: Smallest lens opening.

Mode (digital image): The tonal and color space of the captured or scanned image.

N

Noise: Electronic interference producing speckles in the image.

O

Opacity: The degree of non-transparency.

Opaque: Not transmitting light.

Optimize: The process of fine-tuning the file size and display quality of an image.

Out of gamut: Beyond the scope of colors that a particular device can create, reproduce or display.

P

Pixel: The smallest square picture element in a digital image.

Pixellated: An image where the pixels are visible to the human eye and curved or diagonal lines appear jagged or stepped.

Primary colors: The three colors of light (red, green and blue).

R

RAM: Random access memory. The computer's short-term or working memory.

Reflector: A surface used to reflect light in order to fill shadows.

Resample: To alter the total number of pixels describing a digital image.

Resolution: This term can be applied to optical resolution (how sharp the image was captured), screen resolution (the number of pixels being displayed by your monitor, e.g. 1024 x 768) printer resolution (dots per inch or dpi) or image resolution (pixels per inch or ppi).

RGB: Red, green and blue. The three primary colors used to display images on a color monitor.

Rubber Stamp: Another name for the Clone Stamp tool used for replicating pixels.

S

Sample: To select a color value for analysis or use.

Saturation (color): Intensity or richness of color hue.

Save As: An option that allows the user to create a duplicate of a digital file with an alternative name or in a different location.

Scale: A ratio of size.

Scratch disk: Portion of hard disk allocated to software such as Elements to be used as a working space.

Screen redraws: Time taken to render information being depicted on the monitor as changes are being made through the application software.

Sharp: In focus. Not blurred.

Sliders: A sliding control to adjust settings such as color, tone, opacity, etc.

Stamp Visible: The action of copying the visible elements from a number of layers and pasting them on to a new layer.

System software: Computer operating program, e.g. Windows or Mac OS.

T

TIFF: Tagged Image File Format. Popular image file format for desktop publishing applications.

Tone: A tint of color or shade of gray.

Transparent: Allowing light to pass through.

U

Unsharp Mask: See USM.

USM: Unsharp Mask. A filter used to sharpen images.

W

Workflow: Series of repeatable steps required to achieve a particular result within a digital imaging environment.

Z

Zoom tool: A tool used for magnifying a digital image on the monitor.

Shortcuts

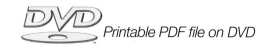 *Printable PDF file on DVD*

Action

Keyboard Shortcut

Navigate and view

Fit image on screen	Ctrl + 0
View image at 100% (actual pixels)	Alt + Ctrl + 0
Zoom tool (magnify)	Ctrl + Spacebar + click image or Ctrl + +
Zoom tool (reduce)	Alt + Spacebar + click image or Ctrl + -
Show/hide rulers	Shift + Ctrl + R
Hide palettes	Tab key

File commands

Open	Ctrl + O
Close	Ctrl + W
Save	Ctrl + S
Save As	Ctrl + Shift + S
Undo	Ctrl + Z
Redo	Ctrl + Y

Selections

Add to selection	Hold Shift key and select again
Subtract from selection	Hold Alt key and select again
Copy	Ctrl + C
Cut	Ctrl + X
Paste	Ctrl + V
Paste into selection	Ctrl + Shift + V
Free Transform	Ctrl + T
Distort image in Free Transform	Hold Ctrl key+move handle
Feather	Alt + Ctrl + D
Select All	Ctrl + A
Deselect	Ctrl + D
Reselect	Shift + Ctrl + D
Inverse selection	Shift + Ctrl + I

Painting

Set default foreground and background colors	D
Switch between foreground and background colors	X
Enlarge brush size (with Paint tool selected)	]
Reduce brush size (with Paint tool selected)	[
Make brush softer	[+ Shift
Make brush harder	] + Shift
Change opacity of brush in 10% increments (with Paint tool selected)	Press number keys 0–9
Fill with foreground color	Alt + Backspace
Fill with background color	Ctrl + Backspace

Image adjustments

Levels	Ctrl + L
Hue/Saturation	Ctrl + U
Group layer	Ctrl + G

Layers and masks

Add new layer	Shift + Ctrl + N
Load selection from layer mask	Ctrl + click thumbnail
Change opacity of active layer in 10% increments	Press number keys 0–9
Add layer mask - Hide All	Alt + click Add Layer Mask icon
Move layer down/up	Ctrl+[or]
Stamp Visible	Ctrl + Alt + Shift then type E
Disable/enable layer mask	Shift + click layer mask thumbnail
View layer mask only	Alt + click layer mask thumbnail
View layer mask and image	Alt + Shift + click layer mask thumbnail
Blend modes	Alt + Shift + (F, N, S, M, O, Y) Soft Light, Normal, Screen, Multiply, Overlay, Luminosity

Crop

Commit crop	Enter key
Cancel crop	Esc key
Constrain proportions of crop marquee	Hold Shift key
Turn off magnetic guides when cropping	Hold Alt + Shift keys + drag handle

Index